When Nations Can't Default

War reparations have been large and small, repaid and defaulted on, but the consequences have almost always been significant. Ever since Keynes made his case against German reparations in *The Economic Consequences of the Peace*, the effects of transfer payments have been hotly debated. *When Nations Can't Default* tells the history of war reparations and their consequences by combining history, political economy, and open economy macroeconomics. It visits often forgotten episodes and tells the story of how reparations were mostly repaid – and when they were not. Analysing fifteen episodes of war reparations, this book argues that reparations are unlike other sovereign debt because repayment is enforced by military and political force, making it a senior liability of the state.

Simon Hinrichsen runs investments in emerging market sovereign bonds for a pension fund and has published in journals on history and economics. He is an external associate professor at the University of Copenhagen where he teaches a course on sovereign debt. He has advised governments and was previously a visiting fellow at the London School of Economics.

STUDIES IN MACROECONOMIC HISTORY

Series Editor: Michael D. Bordo, *Rutgers University*

Editors:

Owen F. Humpage, *Federal Reserve Bank of Cleveland*
Christopher M. Meissner, *University of California, Davis*
Kris James Mitchener, *Santa Clara University*
David C. Wheelock, *Federal Reserve Bank of St. Louis*

The titles in this series investigate themes of interest to economists and economic historians in the rapidly developing field of macroeconomic history. The four areas covered include the application of monetary and finance theory, international economics, and quantitative methods to historical problems; the historical application of growth and development theory and theories of business fluctuations; the history of domestic and international monetary, financial, and other macroeconomic institutions; and the history of international monetary and financial systems. The series amalgamates the former Cambridge University Press series Studies in Monetary and Financial History and Studies in Quantitative Economic History.

Other Books in the Series:

Barry Eichengreen and Andreas Kakridis, *The Spread of the Modern Central Bank and Global Cooperation: 1919–1939* (2023)

Alain Naef, *An Exchange Rate History of the United Kingdom: 1945–1992* (2021)

Barrie A. Wigmore, *The Financial Crisis of 2008: A History of US Financial Markets 2000–2012* (2021)

Max Harris, *Monetary War and Peace: London, Washington, Paris, and the Tripartite Agreement of 1936* (2021)

Kenneth D. Garbade, *After the Accord: A History of Federal Reserve Open Market Operations, the US Government Securities Market, and Treasury Debt Management from 1951 to 1979* (2020)

Harold James, *Making a Modern Central Bank: The Bank of England 1979–2003* (2020)

Claudio Borio, Stijn Claessens, Piet Clement, Robert N. McCauley, and Hyun Song Shin, Editors, *Promoting Global Monetary and Financial Stability: The Bank for International Settlements after Bretton Woods, 1973–2020* (2020)

Patrick Honohan, *Currency, Credit and Crisis: Central Banking in Ireland and Europe* (2019)

William A. Allen, *The Bank of England and the Government Debt: Operations in the Gilt-Edged Market, 1928–1972* (2019)

Eric Monnet, *Controlling Credit: Central Banking and the Planned Economy in Postwar France, 1948–1973* (2018)

Laurence M. Ball, *The Fed and Lehman Brothers: Setting the Record Straight on a Financial Disaster* (2018)

Rodney Edvinsson, Tor Jacobson, and Daniel Waldenström, Editors, *Sveriges Riksbank and the History of Central Banking* (2018)

Peter L. Rousseau and Paul Wachtel, Editors, *Financial Systems and Economic Growth: Credit, Crises, and the Regulation from the 19th Century to the Present* (2017)

Ernst Baltensperger and Peter Kugler, *Swiss Monetary History since the Early 19th Century* (2017)

Øyvind Eitrheim, Jan Tore Klovland, and Lars Fredrik Øksendal, *A Monetary History of Norway, 1816–2016* (2016)

Jan Fredrik Qvigstad, *On Central Banking* (2016)

Michael D. Bordo, Øyvind Eitrheim, Marc Flandreau, and Jan F. Qvigstad, Editors, *Central Banks at a Crossroads: What Can We Learn from History?* (2016)

Michael D. Bordo and Mark A. Wynne, Editors, *The Federal Reserve's Role in the Global Economy: A Historical Perspective* (2016)

Owen F. Humpage, Editor, *Current Federal Reserve Policy Under the Lens of Economic History: Essays to Commemorate the Federal Reserve System's Centennial* (2015)

Michael D. Bordo and William Roberds, Editors, *The Origins, History, and Future of the Federal Reserve: A Return to Jekyll Island* (2013)

Michael D. Bordo and Ronald MacDonald, Editors, *Credibility and the International Monetary Regime: A Historical Perspective* (2012)

Robert L. Hetzel, *The Great Recession: Market Failure or Policy Failure?* (2012)

Tobias Straumann, *Fixed Ideas of Money: Small States and Exchange Rate Regimes in Twentieth-Century Europe* (2010)

Forrest Capie, *The Bank of England: 1950s to 1979* (2010)

Aldo Musacchio, *Experiments in Financial Democracy: Corporate Governance and Financial Development in Brazil, 1882–1950* (2009)

Claudio Borio, Gianni Toniolo, and Piet Clement, Editors, *The Past and Future of Central Bank Cooperation* (2008)

Robert L. Hetzel, *The Monetary Policy of the Federal Reserve: A History* (2008)

Caroline Fohlin, *Finance Capitalism and Germany's Rise to Industrial Power* (2007)

John H. Wood, *A History of Central Banking in Great Britain and the United States* (2005)

Gianni Toniolo (with the assistance of Piet Clement), *Central Bank Cooperation at the Bank for International Settlements, 1930–1973* (2005)

Richard Burdekin and Pierre Siklos, Editors, *Deflation: Current and Historical Perspectives* (2004)

Pierre Siklos, *The Changing Face of Central Banking: Evolutionary Trends since World War II* (2002)

Michael D. Bordo and Roberto Cortés-Conde, Editors, *Transferring Wealth and Power from the Old to the New World: Monetary and Fiscal Institutions in the 17th through the 19th Centuries* (2001)

Howard Bodenhorn, *A History of Banking in Antebellum America: Financial Markets and Economic Development in an Era of Nation-Building* (2000)

Mark Harrison, Editor, *The Economics of World War II: Six Great Powers in International Comparison* (2000)

Angela Redish, *Bimetallism: An Economic and Historical Analysis* (2000)

Elmus Wicker, *Banking Panics of the Gilded Age* (2000)

Michael D. Bordo, *The Gold Standard and Related Regimes: Collected Essays* (1999)

Michele Fratianni and Franco Spinelli, *A Monetary History of Italy* (1997)

Mark Toma, *Competition and Monopoly in the Federal Reserve System, 1914–1951* (1997)

Barry Eichengreen, Editor, *Europe's Postwar Recovery* (1996)

Lawrence H. Officer, *Between the Dollar-Sterling Gold Points: Exchange Rates, Parity and Market Behavior* (1996)

Elmus Wicker, *The Banking Panics of the Great Depression* (1996)

Norio Tamaki, *Japanese Banking: A History, 1859–1959* (1995)

Barry Eichengreen, *Elusive Stability: Essays in the History of International Finance, 1919–1939* (1993)

Michael D. Bordo and Forrest Capie, Editors, *Monetary Regimes in Transition* (1993)

Larry Neal, *The Rise of Financial Capitalism: International Capital Markets in the Age of Reason* (1993)

S. N. Broadberry and N. F. R. Crafts, Editors, *Britain in the International Economy, 1870–1939* (1992)

Aurel Schubert, *The Credit-Anstalt Crisis of 1931* (1992)

Trevor J. O. Dick and John E. Floyd, *Canada and the Gold Standard: Balance of Payments Adjustment under Fixed Exchange Rates, 1871–1913* (1992)

Kenneth Mouré, *Managing the Franc Poincaré: Economic Understanding and Political Constraint in French Monetary Policy, 1928–1936* (1991)

David C. Wheelock, *The Strategy and Consistency of Federal Reserve Monetary Policy, 1924–1933* (1991)

When Nations Can't Default

*A History of War Reparations and
Sovereign Debt*

SIMON HINRICHSEN
University of Copenhagen

CAMBRIDGE
UNIVERSITY PRESS

Shaftesbury Road, Cambridge CB2 8EA, United Kingdom

One Liberty Plaza, 20th Floor, New York, NY 10006, USA

477 Williamstown Road, Port Melbourne, VIC 3207, Australia

314–321, 3rd Floor, Plot 3, Splendor Forum, Jasola District Centre, New Delhi – 110025, India

103 Penang Road, #05–06/07, Visioncrest Commercial, Singapore 238467

Cambridge University Press is part of Cambridge University Press & Assessment, a department of the University of Cambridge.

We share the University's mission to contribute to society through the pursuit of education, learning and research at the highest international levels of excellence.

www.cambridge.org
Information on this title: www.cambridge.org/9781009343923

DOI: 10.1017/9781009343978

First published 2024

A catalogue record for this publication is available from the British Library

A Cataloging-in-Publication data record for this book is available from the Library of Congress

ISBN 978-1-009-34392-3 Hardback

To Mathilda

Contents

List of Figures   *page* xv

List of Tables   xvii

Acknowledgements   xix

Data and Replication   xxi

1   Introduction   1
    1.1   Defining War Reparations and Indemnities   2
    1.2   War Finance and Sovereign Debt   6
    1.3   Summary   10

2   A Framework for War Reparations   17
    2.1   How to Finance Reparations   19
    2.2   Balance of Payments   22
    2.3   Terms of Trade   25
    2.4   A Terms of Trade Model   26
          2.4.1   Growth after Wars   28
          2.4.2   The Model   32
          2.4.3   Equilibrium   35
          2.4.4   Calibration   36
          2.4.5   Results   38

3   Sovereign Debt   41
    3.1   Sovereign Debt Defaults   45
          3.1.1   When to Default   46
          3.1.2   Frequency of Defaults   48
          3.1.3   How to Default on Sovereign Debt   50
          3.1.4   Costs of Sovereign Debt Default   53
    3.2   Sovereign Debt Restructurings   56
    3.3   Odious Debts   60

3.4 A Practical Guide for Restructuring Sovereign Debt 61
   3.4.1 The Fundamental Problem 62
   3.4.2 The Restructuring Process 63
   3.4.3 The Players 64
   3.4.4 The Legal Aspects 65
3.5 A Sovereign Debt Model 65
   3.5.1 Government 68
   3.5.2 Firms 69
   3.5.3 Households 69
   3.5.4 Equilibrium 70
   3.5.5 Default 71
   3.5.6 Calibration 73
   3.5.7 Sensitivity 78
3.6 Stylised Macroeconomic Facts about Sovereign Debt Defaults 79
3.7 The Sovereign Debt Default Set 83

4 Napoleonic Wars Reparations 86
4.1 Terms of Trade 94
4.2 How France Paid Reparations 96

5 Haiti Indemnity and Sovereign Debt 100

6 Franco-Prussian War Indemnities 104

7 Smaller Nineteenth-Century War Reparations 112
7.1 Mexican–American War Reparations 112
7.2 Cretan War Reparations 113
7.3 Chinese Reparations to Japan and Britain 113

8 German World War I Reparations 115
8.1 Germany after the War 116
8.2 The Dawes Plan 120
8.3 The Young Plan 122
8.4 Enforcement of Reparations 124
8.5 Germany's Sovereign Debt Default 126

9 Russian and Bulgarian World War I Reparations 130

10 World War II Reparations to the Soviet Bloc 133
10.1 Finnish Reparations to the Soviet Union 134

11 World War II Reparations to the Allies 139
11.1 German Reparations to Denmark 142

12 Iraq Gulf War Reparations 144
12.1 Historical Background 147
12.2 The Iran–Iraq War (1980–1988) 149
12.3 The Gulf War and Reparations (1988–1991) 157
12.4 Sanctions (1991–2003) 160
12.5 Terms of Iraqi Borrowing 163
12.6 The Iraq Sovereign Debt Restructuring 167
   12.6.1 Iraqi Debts 169

12.6.2	Immunising Iraqi Assets and Reconciling Debts	170
12.6.3	Paris Club Negotiations	174
12.6.4	Non-Paris Club Bilateral Debt Negotiations	177
12.6.5	Commercial Debt Claims and Restructuring	179
12.7	Haircuts and Odious Debts	184
13	When Nations Can't Default	188
Appendix: Letter to Creditor Committees		191
References		193
Index		215

Figures

2.1   Smoothing of reparations liabilities.   *page* 21
2.2   Long-run secular and cyclical real GDP (1870–1960).   29
2.3   Change in detrended real GDP per capita
      (after first transfer).   31
2.4   Trade balance impulse response for different values of ρ.   38
2.5   Response to a terms of trade shock for $\rho = 0.25$.   39
3.1   Countries in default (1800–2020).   49
3.2   Global sovereign debt in default since 1960.   50
3.3   Paris Club restructurings (1956–2020).   58
3.4   Secular and cyclical components of real GDP (1860–1960).   74
3.5   Log-linear detrending and HP-filter of real GDP
      (1860–1960).   75
3.6   Distribution of external debt.   77
3.7   German model output for different values of β.   80
3.8   Stylised sovereign debt defaults.   81
3.9   Estimate of capital controls.   83
3.10 Default sets.   84
4.1   French trade balance and fiscal balance (1815–20).   90
4.2   French government debt stock (1800–30).   91
4.3   French long-term bond yields (1799–1830).   93
4.4   French terms of trade (1805–20).   95
4.5   French government expenditures (1815–20).   98
6.1   French savings, investments, and current account
      (1868–80).   106
6.2   French default set, debt stock, and detrended output.   107
6.3   Model estimate and French historical data (1870–73).   108

8.1	German savings, investments, and current account (1925–33).	117
8.2	German secular and cyclical real output per capita (1860–1940).	118
8.3	German default set, debt stock, and detrended output.	121
8.4	Model estimate and German historical data (1930–33).	127
8.5	Yields on German external bonds (1931–35).	129
9.1	Bulgaria net debt-to-GNP (1921–39).	131
10.1	Finnish savings, investments, and net goods exports (1945–52).	135
10.2	Finnish default set, debt stock, and detrended output.	136
10.3	Model estimate and Finnish historical data (1945–48).	138
12.1	Iraq government debt-to-GDP (1979–2020).	149
12.2	Iraqi expenditures and revenues (1980–89).	153
12.3	Iraqi trade balance and total trade in percentage of GDP (1980–95).	156
12.4	Iraqi debt and GDP.	161
12.5	Iraqi dual-currency values (1998–2003).	163
12.6	IMF oil price assumption and actual term structure.	175
12.7	BNL mark-to-market of Iraq loans (per cent of nominal and accrued).	183
12.8	Comparison of NPV haircuts in debt restructurings (1980–2009).	185

Tables

1.1	War reparations and indemnities since 1800.	*page* 5
2.1	Iraq balance of payments (US dollar billion).	23
2.2	Model parameters.	37
3.1	Model parameters.	78
3.2	Model statistics.	79
4.1	French reparations (million francs).	88
8.1	German economic phases between 1921 and 1933.	119
11.1	Recipients of reparations from Germany.	140
12.1	Iraqi debt by creditor, 1979.	148
12.2	Iraqi growth rates, 1970–89 (yearly average in percentage).	150
12.3	Iraqi debt by creditor, 1988.	155
12.4	Iraqi debt by creditor, 1991.	159
12.5	Iraqi debt by creditor, 2003.	162
12.6	Iraqi borrowing costs in US dollars and risk premium (1985–90).	165
12.7	Iraqi debt by creditor, 2019.	186

Acknowledgements

This book is the product of many years of work. It started because I thought there were not sufficiently good answers to questions I had about war reparations. Those questions led me more and more to focus on sovereign debt, my knowledge of which was only better because my day job for many years has been to invest in sovereign debt instruments. The book is therefore a good mix of academic, professional, and personal interests, and hopefully brings together a lot of the thoughts I have spent the better part of a decade formulating.

It is difficult to thank everyone who has been involved in the journey, because you always risk forgetting someone. If I do, I apologise, but I would like to thank everyone who helped with thoughts, discussions, and encouragement at the London School of Economics and Political Science, in particular Albrecht Ritschl, who spent many hours reading the manuscript and suggesting edits. Giancarlo Corsetti and Harold James both provided invaluable feedback on an early draft of the, at the time, thesis, which helped in expanding it into a book. Michael Bordo supported the idea of turning it into a book. Alain Naef read many drafts and I really thank him. Lots of people have been very helpful on the individual chapters that form the book. I would like to thank you all: Alan Beattie, Andrew Kilpatrick, Anna Gelpern, Anthony Marcus, Brad Setser, Clay Lowery, Daniel Zelikow, Eugene White, Francesco Saverio Leopardi, Gregor Smith, Jeremiah Pam, Lee Buchheit, Maanik Nath, Massimiliano Trentin, Mitu Gulati, Nazareth Festekjian, Olin Wethington, Patricia Adams, Patrick O'Brien, Sam Foxall, and Yasmin Shearmur. Finally, I want to thank the editors, who have been immensely helpful in making it into a final and much better read.

Above all else, I'd like to thank all my friends and family for support. I hope you enjoy the book.

Data and Replication

The data and code used in the book is available at the following link: https://sites.google.com/view/shinrichsen/research.

The replication files run in MATLAB and are available alongside the underlying data. The names of the replication files used are specified under each figure or model, alongside the data source.

I

Introduction

In many ways, 1907 was a watershed year for the worlds of sovereign debt and war reparations. It was the year the Hague Convention agreed to a set of treaties that govern how we think about sovereign debt and war reparations in international law. In Article 2, the Drago Doctrine was introduced, which established the idea that countries should not use the military to enforce sovereign debt repayment. In Article 3, countries were given the right to claim war reparations for damages from an unjust war. The themes of this book are, in some ways, found within those pages and articles. In other ways, the treaties changed nothing. Just because something is written down in a treaty does not make it so when it is a matter of international politics. There were legal and illegal war reparations and sovereign debt enforcements before and after 1907.

The core thesis of this book is that nations cannot really default on war reparations, no matter what international law says. That is what makes reparations a special kind of sovereign debt. War reparations are enforced by military power and only when the geopolitical situation changes is it possible to renegotiate the debt. States do not default on war reparations, because doing so would put the survival of the state in question. War reparations are paid under duress, at risk of crippling sanctions or an invasion, and the debtor is always in a position of having just lost a war. How do you manage an economy coming out of a war if you then have to pay reparations? Is it possible? The answers can teach us a lot about the effects of debt repayment in an economy and the functioning of a state. They can tell us how devastating debt spirals can be if there is no choice to default. They can tell us what happens in other cases where governments continue to repay their debt to the detriment of the economy, just to maintain a reputation of good credit.

Sovereign debt management is at the core of almost all nation states and has been for hundreds of years. The choice on how to finance government expenditures is a political decision but sovereign assets and liabilities do not change because the government does. The choice is always either taxes, printing money, or borrowing. After a war there is usually not much of a choice. Fighting a war is expensive and the economy is typically not in a good state afterwards. Infrastructure investments are needed, money is lacking, war debts have historically been high, and assets have been sold to finance a war. States do not have the resources to come up with 5 or 10 per cent of the economy every year in reparations transfers, especially not historically, when the government was a smaller part of the economy. That leaves borrowing to come up with the money.

No sovereign debt is more political than war reparations. That is why the topic is interesting. Reparations played a significant part in stoking political unrest in Germany in the interwar years, which ultimately led to World War II. The subject warrants a book, not only because of reparations' economic effects but because of their political effects. Reparations can stoke anger and resentment. How a country reacts to reparations can teach us about the political economy.

In this book, I use a range of different methods to analyse reparations. Common to them all is that they have sovereign debt at their core. In the following chapters, I will give an overview of a framework for reparations and sovereign debt. Almost all the parts can be read by non-specialists. The two sections that specify models can be skipped without losing the context of the book, as they are described in words. Following Chapters 2 and 3, I lay out the episodes of war reparations since 1800 that form the core of the book. It is not enough to simply look at economics, because each case is complex and interesting. I have had to make choices on what to include and what to leave out. I am sure that somewhere, there will be a case study that would have been worthwhile, but I had to draw a line somewhere. What you will read are stories about how countries were forced to pay damages for war, how those transfers were financed, and what consequences they had. Those consequences have broader implications for sovereign debt as we know it.

1.1 DEFINING WAR REPARATIONS AND INDEMNITIES

The legal basis for demanding war reparations lies in the articles governing war that were agreed at the Hague Convention in 1907. Article 3 of the Hague Convention of 1907 stipulates that '[a] belligerent party which violates the provisions of the said Regulations shall, if the case demands, be liable to pay compensation'. If the war is unjust, countries can ask for compensation and know that it is based in international humanitarian law. That is the current legal basis for reparations, but it is not as if reparations did not occur before 1907. It is just that they did not have a basis in international law. Now, as before, reparations are negotiated on an ad hoc basis as part of peace settlements.

This is usually a complex process where countries and their citizens can claim to be compensated for war damages. The debt can take many forms, such as commercial or bilateral loans, war bonds, or fiscal arrears, and damages can be everything from farmland to factories. Wars represent large fiscal outlays and often result in large war debts and much destroyed property (Shea and Poast 2018). Victors have historically asked for restitution based on an account of actual damages, either in the form of reparations or indemnities. Stevenson (2010, p. 1505) defines reparations as '[t]he compensation for war damage paid by a defeated state', and indemnities as '[a] sum of money paid as compensation, especially one paid by a country defeated in war as a condition of peace' (p. 888). Reparations and indemnities are much alike, in that the outcome for states is the same, but the difference lies in what sort of compensation they are. It is the study of reparations and indemnities, and how they relate to sovereign debt and defaults, that is the driving topic of the book.

War reparations can take many forms. Most common are monetary transfers in hard currency, where hard currency is either the global dominant currency or the creditors' currencies. But reparations have included precious metals such as gold and silver, natural resources such as oil, the transfer of industrial assets, intellectual properties, or compensation for specific damages. These sorts of transfers are often governed by treaties, which are negotiated as part of a peace settlement. The repayment of reparations is often a condition for the removal of occupying troops, or they are paid under the threat of reoccupation. Military or political force incentivises the debtor to pay because they are paid for a reason – a lost war.[1] The agreement of monetary reparations is easy to track historically because they are written down in treaties or agreements. It is harder to understand illicit money flows, theft, or confiscations. It is also often difficult to track actual payments made because they span a much larger time frame. An example is the transfer of intellectual property and scientific know-how, which might be seized as a spoil of war but without

[1] An exception is Haitian reparations to France, which are discussed in Chapter 5.

direct attribution. The transfer of intellectual property does not require borrowing, as the patents are owned already, but can affect trade flows and future income streams. Another thing that can have both economic and political consequences is the loss of territory. This is common in post-war settlements but has not been thought of as reparations. It only features in the analysis as it relates to loss of economic output or changes to trade patterns.

War reparations go back thousands of years, and it would not be possible to cover all episodes in one book. At least as far back as 241 BC, Rome imposed an indemnity of 3,200 talents of silver on Carthage following the First Punic War, to be paid over ten years (Treaty of Lutatius, 241 BC). The monetary indemnity was later accompanied by Rome's seizure of Corsica and Sardinia (237 BC). The number of armed conflicts since the first Punic War is high and unknown, and a full history of war reparations since, and how sovereign debt has been used to pay reparations, would likely miss some important episodes. Cirillo and Taleb (2016) find at least 565 armed conflicts involving governments since 1 AD, using a threshold of 3,000 deaths to qualify. Even assuming the dataset is complete, there would be too many episodes to investigate. The focus of the book is instead on recent reparations where it is known that sovereign debt played a role. This book investigates fifteen war reparations since 1800. The episodes are listed in Table 1.1.[2] The episodes have been chosen because they represent monetary reparations for major conflicts, where reliable macroeconomic data and historical accounts are available, and there is a treaty that governs the transfers. Some reparations values have been so small as to be meaningless in national income terms, while others have represented significant transfers of wealth in terms of gross domestic product (GDP).

---

[2] Not included are US reparations made in 1988 to Japanese Americans who had been interned during World War II (Civil Liberties Act of 1988); and US reparations to Cuba in exchange for prisoners captured during the Bay of Pigs. The latter is one of only two cases of the United States paying reparations to a country (the other being to Mexico in 1848). Also left out are all non-war reparations, such as reparations awarded by the International Center for Transitional Justice in Tunisia for human rights violations, because they occurred within a country rather than between countries (www.ictj.org/about, accessed 18 February 2020). Reparations currently being negotiated, such as German reparations to Namibia for the colonial-era massacres from 1904 to 1908, are also left out.

TABLE 1.1 *War reparations and indemnities since 1800*

Reparations related to	Per cent of output	Who paid?	Repaid in full?
1815–1819: Napoleonic Wars	22	France	Yes
1825–1947: Haiti independence	300	Haiti	Yes
1848–1881: Mexican–American War	<1	US	Yes
1871–1873: Franco- Prussian War	25	France	Yes
1895–1901: Sino- Japanese War	–	China	Yes
1897–1898: Greco- Turkish War	–	Greece	Yes
1901–1939: Boxer Rebellion	–	China	Yes
1919–1964: WWI (Bulgaria)	>150	Bulgaria	Yes
1923–1933: WWI (Germany)	100	Germany	No
1945–1952: WWII (Finland)	20	Finland	Yes
1947–1965: WWII (Italy)	1	Italy	Yes
1953–1965: WWII (Germany)	3	Germany	No
1955–1965: WWII (Japan)	4	Japan	Yes
1994–2022: Gulf War	>400	Iraq	Yes

Source: Sources are provided in chapters covering each case.

Each episode in Table 1.1 is described in detail in later chapters. As can be seen from the table, some reparations were big and some were small when compared to one year's national output. This is a crude way of comparing reparations because there are several data issues. First, GDP data is increasingly unreliable the further back one goes and is unavailable for China and Greece in the late twentieth century. The year chosen to estimate the percentage of GDP is, to my best effort, the year of the first payment. However, post-war output sometimes differs significantly from pre-war output. The value of the reparation in terms of GDP is therefore the best datapoint chosen for ease of comparison. The comparison also does not consider over what time frame reparations are paid nor discount rates. The early French reparations were repaid in less than five years, while it took China thirty-eight years to pay for the Boxer Rebellion. Only two reparations are listed as not repaid. Again, this is a bit of an oversimplification. Both Germany's and Russia's reparations were negotiated away, while other episodes saw some leniency on behalf of creditors. Chapters 4–12 dive into each of these cases to understand how and why countries paid large sums to their former belligerents.

I.2 WAR FINANCE AND SOVEREIGN DEBT

The main topics of the book, war reparations and sovereign debt, address major questions of political economy. What is the impact of external debt on a country's economy? At what point should countries stop repaying their debts and default instead? The two questions will be addressed in this book.

Even before Keynes (1919) made his famous case against German war reparations after World War I, indemnities and war reparations had been hotly debated throughout history. One issue has always been the reason for imposing reparations. Is the point to punish a country for an unjust war or to prevent it from regaining military or political power, or are reparations meant to incentivise re-entrance into a future political alliance? The answers are usually found in the structure and size of reparations. Because the other issue is a question of economics. What is the size of reparations transfers that a country can possibly extract without inflicting disastrous economic consequences on the debtor? Sometimes economic ruin might be part of the point the creditor wants to make. Because reparations are paid as part of peace settlements, the incentives of the debtor and creditor are very different. The creditor's incentives and wishes can differ. The debtor's incentives are almost always to repay reparations quickly to regain full sovereignty. Because reparations carry more penalties and limitations than sovereign debt, the debtor often issues sovereign debt to repay reparations. The two might be identical in economic value but, as this book argues, they are different in seniority and enforceability.

Mantoux's (1946) analysis of Keynes suggested studying reparations as a question of willingness to pay, rather than of capacity to pay. He argued that logic would dictate that reparations violate a country's willingness-to-pay constraint by default because they are involuntary. A country's capacity to pay can therefore be much larger than its willingness to pay, especially when it can borrow all the money to smooth the cost of paying. The willingness-to-pay approach to reparations, as first pointed out by Albrecht Ritschl (1996a, 1996b, 2002), is identical to a sovereign debt approach. The capacity to pay is thus less interesting because it is not what constrains a country from paying reparations. Instead, what constrains a country from paying reparations is the possibility of political and economic crisis. It is important to understand if the level of sovereign debt, including reparations, violates a country's willingness to pay. The sovereign debt literature has recently developed frameworks to analyse this question in a new way. I use one of these off-the-shelf sovereign debt models to analyse whether reparations were paid despite being outside the participants' willingness-to-pay constraint.

Countries can meet budgetary expenditures either through taxes, by printing money, or by borrowing money (domestically or internationally). The reparations studied in this book were financed by a mix of taxes, money printing, and borrowing, but almost all reparations were primarily financed by sovereign debt. Using sovereign debt to pay reparations is practical because it allows states to smooth their consumption and extend the costs over time. Tax revenues were mostly not high enough to cover reparations transfers by themselves, so sovereign debt played an important role, just like it has in fighting recessions and depressions.[3] The willingness to pay reparations depends to a large degree on how easy it is to issue and service debts, but successfully repaid debt stocks are often much higher than suggested by Reinhart and Rogoff (2010). This raises the question of whether creditor enforcement for war reparations is fundamentally different from other sovereign debts. I argue that it is. I show that reparations were repaid in several instances in which a sovereign debt analysis would suggest a default. In fact, it is a core theme of this book that countries pay reparations because they need to do so to survive.

These political economy themes are important. They are not limited to a narrow set of technical questions but have important real-world implications for war, peace, and prosperity. This book explores what happens when countries borrow large amounts of money to pay reparations. Sometimes it ends well, sometimes it does not. Understanding the causes of success and failure is paramount.

The issue of sovereign debt is crucial for the analysis of war reparations because borrowing money is required to repay large reparations. If a country does not have the ability to borrow money on sovereign debt markets, it might be forced to sell valuable assets upfront, or undertake painful tax increases. If a country can borrow at reasonable

---

[3] Fiscal multipliers have been consistently positive during times of crisis because of the lack of demand, both in the 1930s (Gordon and Krenn 2010; Cloyne et al. 2021) and during the financial crisis in 2008 (DeLong and Summers 2012). The effects are multiplied when the buyers of sovereign debt are external investors (Zimic and Priftis 2021).

interest rates, the liability flow can be smoothed over many years. Barro (1979, 1987) showed how public debt can help smooth out changes in tax rates in the face of temporary increases in government spending. War reparations constitute a temporary increase in expenditures. Increases in taxes can introduce inefficiencies that can be overcome by increasing the level of sovereign debt, to smooth out the cost of the reparations over time. Sovereign debt levels have increased in almost all cases of war reparations for this reason. The adjustment to the macroeconomy is spread out over many years, as countries structure the cash flow of their liabilities to make them longer. While war reparations are unavoidable, the adjustment costs therefore crucially depend on how the transfers are financed. Reparations are not voluntary, and unlike most sovereign debt there is an enforcement mechanism to force repayment: often the country is still occupied. Reparations are imposed because the victor demands them, not because there is an economic rationale for the debtor. Reparations can be considered senior claims to other state liabilities.

Sovereign debt enforcement is different from the enforcement of household or corporate debt because there are no legal remedies to make a sovereign pay. Countries can be coerced to pay by military force, but unlike the bankruptcy of people and firms there is no international bankruptcy court to settle claims. Creditors cannot take control of sovereign assets through enforcement of debt contracts because foreign official assets (such as embassies, military bases, or consulates) tend to be immune from creditor attachment (Buchheit 2013). Despite the limited enforcement mechanism, most sovereign debt is still repaid. Two reasons have generally been offered to explain why. The first is that countries want to maintain a good reputation as a borrower. The reputational explanation originating with Eaton and Gersovitz (1981) explains repayment of sovereign debt as an incentive to borrow again. A default causes an exclusion from capital markets for a period, which means the country cannot borrow to smooth consumption. Defaults occur when countries find debt service to be costlier than a default, where most papers specify a time period where the country is excluded from capital markets as a result. The incentive to repay sovereign debt is thus not a legal one. Chapter 3 will provide more details on the various models and theories of sovereign debt. The second reason is that countries want to avoid financial sanctions that follow defaults. In this part of the literature, creditors have certain legal remedies to force economic sanctions on the defaulting countries, as first suggested by Bulow and Rogoff

(1989a, 1989b).[4] An example of a sovereign asset seizure was when the hedge fund Elliott seized an Argentine navy ship in Ghana in 2012 to collect on defaulted bonds from the 2001 restructuring (Cotterill 2012).

Recent sovereign defaults have carried high costs for the country in default, but countries were nevertheless able to make the decision to default on their sovereign debt (see, e.g., Kuvshinov and Zimmermann 2019). War reparations are different. They are a special case of sovereign debt because the enforcement mechanism is binding,˙often by military occupation or the threat of occupation. The case of war reparations is thus an extreme version of 'gunboat diplomacy'. Gunboat diplomacy, or imposed fiscal control, was commonly used to ensure repayment on sovereign loans if the borrower threatened to default. The practice of gunboat diplomacy was common before World War I. In the period between 1870 and 1913, more than 40 per cent of sovereign defaults resulted in some of sanctions (Mitchener and Weidenmier 2010). The enforcement of debt contracts happened either through creditor countries' legal or military power, or because international banks got involved. International banks were able to set conditions on loans because they had legal and military remedies to monitor and enforce their claims, and the banks thus acted as a lender of reputation to ensure payment (Flandreau and Flores 2012).[5] The practice of militarily enforcing sovereign debt became much less common after the Drago Doctrine was adopted by the Hague Conference in 1907. The Drago Doctrine states that military force should not be used to enforce sovereign debt payments.

Despite sovereign debt playing such a prominent role in the financing of reparations, the economics literature has mostly studied them as examples of the transfer problem. Even though one reason to enforce reparations might be to increase the stock of sovereign debt, because high debt levels would render the debtor country unable to borrow money to engage in another war. The study of sovereign debt has also been quite uninterested in reparations. Studies of sovereign debt have mainly concerned themselves with more recent defaults in emerging markets, even though reparations are a fascinating area of state liabilities that can shed light on what happens when countries cannot default. This book takes aim at these deficiencies. It links reparations to the study of sovereign

---

[4] See, e.g., Aguiar and Amador (2014) for a recent contribution.
[5] For a list of case studies during the period, see, e.g., Tunçer (2015).

debt more generally, by studying war reparations in the context of a sovereign debt analysis. The next section presents a short summary of the rest of the book.

1.3 SUMMARY

The main argument of this book is that reparations are unlike other sovereign debt because the repayment is enforced by military and political force, making it a senior liability of the state. Non-payment of reparations only occurs when the creditor allows it, either because they are not interested in collecting on the transfer or because they are not able to enforce it because their political or military power no longer allows them to. Because the collection of reparations is enforced, debtor countries end up in suboptimal economic situations that do not occur during normal sovereign debt management. The argument is made by using a sovereign debt analysis on fifteen episodes of war reparations.

I show that if we treat reparations as standard non-contingent sovereign debt instruments, in many instances there should be no willingness to pay. Yet there was. Only when the creditor agrees to a standstill can reparations be restructured or written off. Otherwise, payments of reparations impose large economic and political costs on the debtor nation. Economic and political costs that are much higher than countries are normally willing to pay to stay current on their sovereign debt. The costs can be crippling economic performance or political turmoil.

How did countries manage to pay transfers under stretched capacity to pay? Was it simply that creditors could enforce reparations, or did market access gains outweigh the cost of repaying the total debt including reparations? To answer these questions, it is necessary to understand when countries are normally willing to repay debt. One way is to look at sovereign debt models where the government is in control of both the decision to default and conducts optimal monetary policy. The latter ensures the government can devalue its currency, to lower real wages, while the decision to default is taken when the benefits from continued borrowing no longer outweighs the costs of default. Such a model allows me to characterise a default set, which can be compared to the historical episodes of reparations. The combination of default and devaluation is empirically founded as it has been observed in many emerging markets during defaults (Reinhart 2002). The goal is to figure out if reparations are considered payable in terms of a standard sovereign debt analysis. If the macroeconomic conditions lie outside what is normal willingness to pay, the reason for repayment is likely to be found in the political economy.

The book shows how episodes of war reparations exhibit many of the same characteristics of sovereign defaults yet were repaid. The literature on sovereign debt defaults has shown that defaults typically occur after a sharp contraction in output, are followed by a devaluation of the currency, and are costly. The devaluation of the currency lowers the relative price level and real wages. Governments choose to default when it is economically beneficial not to pay interest and principal and instead incur the loss associated with a default and financial autarky. The costs of default are both the inability to smooth consumption, by not being able to borrow again, as well as an explicit output loss that occurs because of the default. To account for these stylised facts, I apply a sovereign debt model by Na, Schmitt-Grohé, Uribe, and Yue (2018) to the Franco-Prussian War indemnity, to German interwar reparations, and to Finnish World War II reparations. This narrow set of reparations cases are the largest transfers studied (over 20 per cent of GDP) where there was agreement to pay in a relatively short time span (less than ten years). I collected data for the output, interest rates, debt stocks, wages, and exchange rates (nominal and real) for each episode. Common for them was that reparations were paid because they were enforced by military or political power, even if the country was situation in the default set of the model. The cases are studied in Chapters 6, 8, and 10. In Chapters 4, 5, 7, 9, 11, and 12, I study other war reparations that do not lend themselves to such economic modelling because the payment occurs over decades or is insignificant. Each is discussed because the repayment is closely linked to the enforcement of the treaties. The next paragraphs summarise the rest of the books.

Chapter 2 introduces a framework for how to think about war reparations. It discusses how a reparation transfer can be smoothed out over time by borrowing the money. I then discuss other ways a transfer can be paid, by taxes or printing money, and the effects it has on the balance of payments and the terms of trade. Finally, in a technical appendix that can be skipped, I show how changed terms of trade affect the current account and national income.

Chapter 3 discusses sovereign debt theory and practice. It goes through the history of sovereign debt and how the current theories of borrowing and lending developed in the 1980s. I argue that countries want to be part of global society, and that means they sometimes repay unsustainable debt. The chapter dives into why countries might default, when they might default, how often countries have defaulted, and what the economic and political costs are. I then describe what happens when countries need to restructure their sovereign debt, both in theory and with a practical guide for the process. Finally, in another technical appendix that can be skipped by the lay reader, I describe a sovereign debt model. The model explains when countries should have no willingness to repay their debt. It allows me to characterise a set of stylised macroeconomic facts that usually accompany sovereign debt defaults. The default set that comes out of the model states when countries should default. These facts and default set (not part of the technical section) is used in Chapters 6, 8, and 10. Chapter 3 is the last overview chapter. The rest of the chapters in the book are case studies.

Chapter 4 studies the Napoleonic War reparations. France lost the Napoleonic Wars in 1815, which ended decades of revolution and counterrevolution. After Napoleon's final defeat at Waterloo, France was forced to pay just under two billion francs in reparations, around a quarter of output in 1815, over the following five years. With French government revenues of around 700 million francs in 1816, the transfer represented almost three times the annual budget. That is a big transfer, even more so as France faced significant credit constraints because earlier defaults prevented it from tapping sovereign debt markets.[6] Not until 1817 did France manage to borrow large amounts of money, paying back reparations with two years to spare. How did France manage to pay the large reparations transfer? I argue that France benefited economically from a positive shock to its terms of trade as the war wound down. The French peacetime economy was structurally different in terms of its imports and exports, which had been changed during many years of war and blockades. Using the terms of trade framework from Chapter 2, I show how the improved terms of trade created an economic windfall similar in size to the transfer.

Chapter 5 is a brief history of Haitian indemnities to France. The chapter gives an overview of the how France used gunboat diplomacy to 'negotiate' a large indemnity in exchange for recognition of the Haitian state. Even though Haiti won their independence in 1804, they had to pay transfer to France until 1947. Haiti had to borrow from French banks to finance the transfers, which settled them with a crippling stock of sovereign debt for more than a century. I discuss how the debt can be considered odious.

---

[6] Bordo and White (1991) show how French war financing was affected by its poor fiscal reputation.

Chapter 6 studies the case of Franco-Prussian War indemnities of 1871. France paid the indemnity of 25 per cent of output in three years to Prussia. The years following the end of the war features several default-like characteristics (output contraction and high debt levels) but sees no devaluation of its currency nor a fall in real wages. France had easy access to loans at reasonable interest rates, with high investor participation from both foreign and domestic sources. The most important factor was that France had accumulated a high stock of foreign assets, meaning its net debt was essentially 0, which incentivised a settlement that did not include sanctions or confiscations. It is a case in which enforcement of sovereign debt played a positive role, in that a default would have been more costly than repayment. It is also likely that military enforcement was not needed, because France was incentivised to repay because of its easy access to debt and stock of foreign assets. The macroeconomic situation was, crucially, one in which the current account was positive, meaning that while France repaid the indemnity it did not do so by indebting itself.

Chapter 7 is a brief overview of Mexican–American War reparations (1848 to 1881), Cretan War reparations (from 1897), and Chinese reparations following the Sino-Japanese War (1895–1901) and the Boxer Rebellion (1901 and 1939). The chapter is a tale of how reparations can be so small as to be meaningless for the economy (in the American case) to be long, painful, and enforced by political and military power (Greek and Chinese cases).

Chapter 8 looks at the famous case of German World War I reparations. When estimating Germany's capacity to pay after World War I, diplomats and politicians looked to what amounts France paid after the Franco-Prussian War. German headline reparations were bigger in terms of GDP, but not in terms of the government's capacity to levy taxes. German real output contracted by over 20 per cent during the hyperinflation of the Weimar Republic (1921–23), as Germany refused to pay reparations in 1922. It was forced to resume negotiations by military force after the Allied occupation of the Ruhr. Reparations were rescheduled in 1924 and were subsequent paid throughout the 1920s with disastrous long-term consequences. Germany had limited access to borrowing until 1925, from which point it managed to escape output losses by borrowing abroad. Economic growth from 1925 to 1929 was built on a debt spiral and real wages that were too high, given Germany's external position.[7]

---

[7] For an overview of this debate, see, For example, James (1986), Borchardt (1990), Holt-frerich (1990), or Ritschl (2002).

A continuously negative current account helped keep real wages and the real exchange rate high, but it could only last if debt could be rolled over into new loans. Once capital flows reversed by the 1930s, austerity replaced debt, which translated into output losses and a downward adjustment to real wages. I use the sovereign debt model described in Chapter 3 to analyse when Germany entered the default set and should have no willingness to pay. The model suggests that Germany was in the default set in 1920, in 1924 (using the present value of the Dawes annuity), in 1931 and in 1932. The model suggests Germany should repay in 1929, but we know that it was folly – the debt stock could not be rolled over. Austerity by the Brüning cabinet was implemented to maintain market access, but it relied on two crucial facts. First, that the market would acknowledge debt sustainability and keep lending, and second, that domestically the policies could be implemented without political chaos. Both proved unsustainable. Based on the net foreign asset position, the current account, the high level of real wages and the real exchange rate, only a small shock to output would put Germany into the default set. Two years of costly austerity only yielded further ground for the Nazi takeover, rather than regaining market access as was the goal. Had Germany defaulted already in 1929, it would have saved two years' worth of interest payments and entered autarky at the same time, as market access was by then de facto gone. At this point, the European nations did not have the ability to enforce debt contracts and the United States agreed to a de facto cancellation of reparations. The German sovereign default in the 1930s was on debt issued to pay reparations, but it also had several effects on other state liabilities, with loans offering different kinds of creditor-protection. Germany in the 1920s had high levels of reparations but was able to borrow, because it offered de-facto seniority to new loans. Creditors were willing to lend into a large debt stock because they thought they would rank senior to reparations. The German default on its sovereign debt was special because it was allowed by its politically weak creditors, who were unable to enforce debt contracts in the 1930s.

Chapter 9 is the brief story of the lesser-known World War I reparations of Bulgaria and Russia. Both reparations were large in terms of each country's output but were subsequently negotiated away in political treaties. In the Soviet Union case, it is one of the examples of how you can repudiate debt completely but under the cost of exiting the global trading system.

Chapter 10 is the story of World War II reparations to the Soviet Bloc. While Italy, Romania, Hungary, Bulgaria, and Finland were meant to pay reparations, only Italy and Finland did outright because the other countries fell under the Soviet Bloc and instead paid indirectly. The chapter focuses on Finnish reparations in the 1940s, which were repaid under great economic strain. The economy exhibited all the characteristics normally associated with a sovereign debt default. Unable to default because of geopolitical considerations, it took Finland years to grow its economy following the war because large parts of its domestic resources went to produce reparations. Finland did not have the option of defaulting because of political pressure in the new geopolitical landscape that emerged from World War II. Finland managed to eventually grow its way out of debt trouble. The trajectory was suboptimal, however. It involved three devaluations, a fall in real wages of more than 50 per cent, and large inflationary problems. I argue a sovereign debt default would have allowed foreign exchange to be used for domestic purposes, but because it was not possible the macroeconomic adjustment had to come from elsewhere. Finnish state survival and its geographically location meant that it chose to repay reparations rather than attempt a default.

Chapter 11 look at the much smaller World War II reparations to the Allies. The Allies had learnt from previous reparations disasters and focused on the de-industrialisation of Germany and Japan. Only small reparations were actually paid, and the transfers were offset by US loans from the Marshall Plan. I show how even though reparations were agreed, they were not necessarily paid through a case study of German reparations to Denmark.

Chapter 12 is the story of Iraqi reparations that were imposed after the Gulf War. Because the debt history of Iraq is less documented, I first reconstruct the build-up of debt through the 1980s and 1990s from primary and secondary sources. The rise in Iraqi indebtedness was a consequence of global geopolitical trends in the 1980s where political lending trumped solvency concerns. It allowed Iraq to obtain financing on terms more favourable than the US government, without conditionality of reform. Reparations were a consequence of the end of the Iran–Iraq War when Iraq invaded Kuwait. Reparations were imposed by a United Nations (UN) Resolution with a direct enforcement mechanism to take money from oil revenues. I then use oral history to trace how Iraqi debt was restructured after the US invasion in 2003. The restructuring was permeated by politics to inflict harsh terms on creditors at the Paris Club, at a time when creditor-friendly restructurings were the norm. Despite its apparent success however, in going for a politically expedient deal at the Paris Club, I argue the restructuring missed an opportunity to enshrine a doctrine of odious debt in international law. All debt was written off, except war reparations, which were paid in full through sanctions and war. They proved to be senior to all other debt and did not enter the sovereign debt restructuring. The restructuring talks are documented in detail, so that readers can understand how the process works both in theory (in Chapter 3) and in practice.

Chapter 13 makes an argument that militarily enforcing sovereign debt is akin to a debtors' prison for states, based on the cases in the book.

2

A Framework for War Reparations

Any framework for war reparations must include several things: a definition of reparations, a way of understanding why they are imposed, and a way to estimate the true costs of paying them. This chapter provides a way to analyse reparations, which is used in the rest of the book. The reasons for imposing reparations, though, are always political and differ in each case. They will therefore be explained in the later chapters on each of the cases. But because the enforcement of reparations is directly linked to the reasons why they are imposed, a pure historical account can never be isolated from an economic analysis of reparations. Some background and concepts are therefore required upfront.

The reasons for imposing war reparations have been, and are, many. They include punishment for war; the need or desire to impose restitution; a desire to increase soft power in a geopolitical setting; and the utter destruction of the defeated nation's economic and political structure. The reasons often overlap and punishment can take many forms. It can be proportional to the economic damage wrought or be much larger. If the reparations sum imposed is much higher than war damages and too high for the country to pay, it lowers the chance of repayment. The economic structure of the debtor country might not be able to sustain large-scale borrowing, which can destroy the political legitimacy of the surviving state. The creditor winner therefore faces a trade-off between extracting the maximum amount of money and increasing the likelihood of repayment – unless, that is, the desired outcome is to cause economic and political collapse. The utility of reparations for the creditor country depends on whether they want hard currency or power. The history of reparations shows that terms and reasons have varied from small, specific claims to larger damages that have destroyed the polity of the paying country.

In their most simple form, war reparations are no different from any other sovereign debt. They represent a liability of the state that the country promises to pay to a creditor. Of course, things are never as simple in practice as in theory, because while reparations are a state liability, they are a senior liability. Unlike sovereign debt, reparations are enforced by diplomatic or military power, either directly by occupying forces or indirectly by threat of invasion. War reparations are therefore repaid much more frequently than other sovereign debt. Often the sovereign borrows on the regular international loan markets to finance the repayment of reparations, but that leaves it with a higher stock of junior sovereign debt afterwards. One creditor (the receiving country) is swapped for another (the lenders of the sovereign debt), usually at a monetary cost. The choice of how to finance reparations has consequences for the economy and the total costs of repayment.

The value of a war reparation in and of itself is a stock notion. It is the present discounted value of all future transfer payments. The value of the reparation depends on the structure of future liability flows, which can either occur as an upfront payment or be spread out over many years. The structure of the cash flow is negotiated or dictated in a peace treaty, but the debtor country can unilaterally change the cash flow profile by issuing sovereign debt. Borrowing can change the cash flow profile, which affects the present value of the reparation. But the reparation itself is an actual transfer of resources from one country to another. The resource transfer occurs either through an increase in the production and subsequent exports of tradable goods or by transfers of income-generating assets. Transfers of income-generating assets (either through a sale or transfer) have second-order effects because they mean that the country gives up future income.

Countries can ask for different kinds of reparations and indemnities. Most commonly, as part of a peace process, a commission or agency is created to which claims can be filed. Either the commission has a mandate to approve or deny claims, or it can provide the input for further negotiations. These types of claims are typically composed of many small claims (e.g., a farmer who had lands destroyed or a factory owner who wants compensation for property damage), but countries can also ask for bigger reparations. In addition, countries often ask for compensation for military equipment or wages for soldiers (during the enforcement period), or simply ask for money for 'war damages'. The total size can be considerable because wars cause large-scale damage. The specific types of claims differ, as will be evident in later chapters. Regardless of what the reparations are directed towards, what matters for the debtor country is the overall size of the transfer and how it can pay the reparations – which is what I turn to first.

2.1 HOW TO FINANCE REPARATIONS

One of the most important questions concerning reparations is how they are financed. A government can raise money in one of four ways, and each of these has different economic consequences. The first way is for a government to tax its citizens and companies in some form. The second option is for the country to print money, thereby increasing the money supply, which it can then use to pay its debt. The third option is to borrow the money by issuing sovereign debt in some form. The fourth category is to sell assets. It is not always possible for a country to freely choose how to finance a large-scale payment. War reparations occur after wars, which, as will be shown in later chapters, leave countries with few or no assets left, as war financing is expensive. If the political structure of the country is in ruins, it might also be difficult to collect taxes efficiently, and historical reparations before World War I occurred under states that had much lower power of taxation as the fiscal state was smaller. Money printing can have unwanted secondary consequences. If core institutions are not well established or reparations are due in foreign currency, a likely outcome of money printing is inflation or a weaker currency, or both. Reparations are almost always payable in foreign currency, so increasing the money supply might increase the risk of a currency crisis. Raising taxes, on the other hand, takes domestic resources directly out of the economy, instantly affecting households and corporations. That leaves sovereign debt as the most likely option for a country wishing to repay reparations quickly. Using borrowed money to pay allows a country to smooth costs, which is why sovereign debt has played a major role in almost all war reparations.

The issue of sovereign debt is crucial for the analysis of war reparations because the total cost depends on whether a country can issue debt and at what price. If a country does not have the ability to borrow money on the sovereign debt markets, it might be forced to sell valuable assets upfront or undertake painful tax increases. If a country can borrow money at reasonable interest rates, the liability flow can be smoothed over many years. Barro (1979, 1987) showed how public debt can help smooth out changes in tax rates in the face of temporary increases in government spending. War reparations constitute a classic instance of a temporary increase in expenditures. Increases in taxes can introduce inefficiencies, which can be overcome by increasing the level of sovereign debt instead, to smooth out the cost of the reparations over time. Sovereign debt levels have increased in almost all cases of war reparations for this reason. The adjustment to the macroeconomy is spread out over many years, as countries have structured the cash flow of their liabilities to make it longer. While war reparations are unavoidable for the debtor country (at least initially), the adjustment costs therefore crucially depend on how the transfers are financed.

A stylised example of how sovereign debt can change the liability flow is shown in Figure 2.1. The figure depicts the annual cash flows for hypothetical reparations of 25 per cent of GDP in year 0, with four different financing options. For simplicity, it is assumed that the entire transfer is due in year 0. The first line shows a total upfront payment of 25 per cent of GDP. In this scenario the country would pay the reparations out of a combination of tax increases, cuts to other government spending, asset sales, or sales of its foreign reserves. The adjustment cost to the economy is very high upfront, but low after the shock (assuming that this shock does not create a political crisis). It is an extreme case in which the government has no ability or willingness to borrow but can raise the money domestically. In the second line, it is assumed that half of the reparations is paid upfront, while the rest financed by borrowing. The upfront transfer is transformed into a sovereign liability, which is partly paid back upfront and partly paid back in equal instalments over five years, this time to a sovereign creditor. The third line shows a scenario in which the reparations are split into an upfront payment of 2.5 per cent and then a ten-year loan with instalments of equal size. Finally, the fourth line shows the liability stream if the entire reparation is repaid with a loan, which is then paid back over twenty years.

Changing the liability flow means that the macroeconomic adjustment cost is smoothed, but borrowing money has other long-term costs because interest costs must be factored into the total costs. In the theoretical exercise shown in Figure 2.1 it is assumed that the country can borrow at a fixed interest rate of 4 per cent, regardless of the maturity of the loan. In that case, the total cost of the reparations increases from 25 per cent of year-zero GDP in the first scenario (no borrowing) to 26.5 per cent in the second scenario (half upfront), 32 per cent in the third scenario (ten-year borrowing), and 61 per cent in the fourth scenario (if the entire amount is borrowed and paid back over twenty years), although the net present value will be lower depending on the discount rate. The cost, and when those costs are incurred, thus depends crucially on the

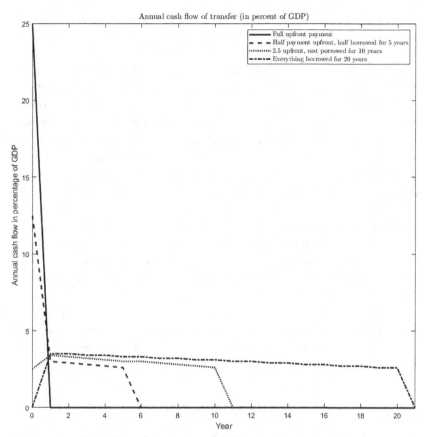

FIGURE 2.1 Smoothing of reparations liabilities.
Note: Theoretical depiction of annual cash flows of an assumed reparations transfer of 25 per cent of GDP. It is assumed the country can borrow at a fixed rate of 4 per cent, with repayment in equal instalments. Replication file: *plot_smooth.m*.

country's ability to access financing via the sovereign debt markets and subsequent output growth

Some benefits of using sovereign debt are direct, such as not having to come up with all the money at once, while others are indirect. If a country needs to rebuild infrastructure after a damaging war, there are many types of productive investments with a high return on capital, of which the country can undertake more if it borrows more money. If there is a lack of capital domestically, external capital can finance productive investments and will have high benefits. The cost of borrowing is the interest rate paid, but the cost must be thought of in the aggregate: does the inflow of capital help or hurt the country, compared to a state of autarky, defined here as spending being financed entirely by taxes? If the answer is yes, borrowing the money makes sense.

One risk the country faces is that sudden large-scale borrowing can cause default risk to go up. If borrowing lowers the creditworthiness of the debtor, it affects their ability to repay reparations, because it affects the interest rate paid on loans. Higher default risks can be felt throughout the economy in other ways, too. Gu (2019) showed that a country's terms of trade are affected negatively by increases in default risk. The reason is that higher default risk lowers the demand for a country's intermediate export goods, creating a pro-cyclical effect on income and consumption. A negative terms of trade shock can have negative consequences for the economy, as will be shown in Section 2.4. Because it is in the interest of the debtor country not to shock the economy when they want to borrow, they often show a willingness to pay sovereign debt. War reparations have mostly been dealt with in the literature as a problem of capacity to pay, but capacity is often secondary because war reparations are not a policy choice. The choice is how to finance war reparations, not whether to repay, because a default on reparations has political ramifications that lead to questions of state survival. In fact, a core thesis of this book is that defaults or renegotiations of war reparations happen only when the geopolitical situation changes.

2.2 BALANCE OF PAYMENTS

Reparations transfers are capital flows from one country to another and are often financed by borrowing on the international capital markets. The borrowing and lending of sovereign debt occurs through the financial account in the balance of payments. One cannot understand reparations without understanding the balance of payments, which shows if a country is a net borrower or a net lender. The balance of payments is an accounting identity that consists of the current account, the capital account, and the financial account (IMF 2013, pp. 9–10):

$$\text{current account} + \text{capital account} + \text{financial account} + \text{net errors} = 0. \tag{2.1}$$

The current account is made up of the trade balance (goods and services), primary income (e.g., investment income), and transfers. The capital account represents capital transfers (e.g., debt forgiveness). The flipside is the financial account, which represents net purchases of financial assets

TABLE 2.1 *Iraq balance of payments (US dollar billion)*

	Net borrower (Iraq, 2004)			Net lender (Iraq, 2018)		
	Credits (exports)	Debits (imports)	Balance	Credits (exports)	Debits (imports)	Balance
Current account						
Trade balance	17	22	–5	93	57	36
Primary income	0	0	0	1	3	–2
Transfers	3	1	2	2	1	1
Capital account	0	0	0	0	0	0
Net lending (+) or borrowing (–)			–3			35
Financial account						
Direct investments	0	0	0	0	–5	5
Portfolio investments	0	0	0	3	0	3
Other investments	10	1	9	9	2	7
Reserve assets	–6	0	–6	7	0	7
Deferred accrued interest	6	0	–6			
Net lending (+) or borrowing (–)			–3			22
Net errors and omissions			0			–13

Note: Deferred accrued interest was a special line item because Iraq was in default.
Source: IMF (2004, p. 25) for 2004 accounts and IMF online database for 2018 accounts.

and new debt. The final category is net errors and omissions, but, as the name implies, is hard to define. The total sums to 0. Table 2.1 is a standard simplified version of the balance of payments (for full details, see IMF 2013). If a country spends more on goods and services than it receives in income (e.g., from exports), it will need to pay by selling assets or borrowing. The two states (net borrower or net lender) are shown in Table 2.1, which is a stylised balance of payments for Iraq. The table shows Iraq's balance of payments in 2014, when it was a net borrower (to the left), and in 2018, when it was a net lender (to the right). In 2014, Iraq spent more money than it received, which was paid for by selling assets (or by taking on debt), as most emerging markets did before 1998. By 2018 Iraq was a net lender, accumulating net foreign assets through a current account surplus, largely because of oil exports.

War reparations show up in the balance of payments when the transfers occur. To finance the transfers, a country must either increase exports, lower imports, sell off reserve assets, or borrow the money. For example, if the country increases taxes significantly, the most likely outcome is a reduction in imports because households and corporations have less money for consumption. The stylised balance of payments does not say anything about the structure of the economy (e.g., how big the export sector is) but shows that the economic impact is different depending on how reparations are paid.

The conventional wisdom now for balance of payments is that the net flow of money runs from advanced economies to emerging market economies in search of higher yields and productive investments. In economic textbooks, emerging economies should benefit from access to capital not available domestically. But as Ikeda and Phan (2019) show, recent boom and bust cycles of capital inflows and asset bubbles have not behaved as the old textbooks would have suggested. Both the global financial crisis of 2008 and the Eurozone sovereign debt crisis that started in 2009 saw money flowing from emerging markets *to* developed markets. The money flows were a contributing factor in furthering ensuing asset bubbles in developed markets, which cannot be explained by changes to economic fundamentals (especially housing prices). Output volatility increased globally because of these money flows.

The emerging-to-developed direction of money flows is a relatively new phenomenon. In the 1980s and 1990s, capital generally flowed from developed to emerging markets (Carstens and Schwartz 1998). After the Asian financial crisis in 1997–98, however, emerging market governments began to hoard foreign reserves. They accumulated reserves through large current account surpluses, which amount to capital outflows (Lee and Luk 2018). The change in policy aimed to increase resilience in the face of sudden stops to capital inflows and to lower reliance on foreign debt financing. Central banks and governments, especially in Asia, now hold large stocks of foreign securities (Fatum and Yetman 2020, p. 4). The change in policy was a consequence of misguided advice from the International Monetary Fund (IMF) during the 1990s: incorrect economic diagnoses led to advice that exacerbated the Asian financial crisis (Bullard et al. 1998).[1] As a result, the global flow of money switched direction. Before 1998, the

---

[1] Devereux et al. (2019) show how one policy option would have been to introduce capital controls.

current account for the average emerging market economy was negative. Afterwards, it was positive.

The effects on the global economy were large because capital flows can lead to global imbalances. Capital flows played a key role in both the 2008 financial crisis and the Eurozone crisis. European and US capital markets are the most liquid and the deepest financial markets in the world, which means they act as a residual to global savings. The accumulation of savings in the form of reserves from Asian foreign reserves therefore appears on American balance sheets as capital flows into the United States. In the early 2000s, this forced down interest rates and led to a search for yields (see, e.g., Tooze 2018). Ultimately, as Bernanke (2005) argued, the global savings glut ended up fuelling money flows into the US subprime mortgage market. In this respect, recent crises are akin to the Great Depression of the 1930s, where Ho and Yeh (2019) found that capital flows were the main culprit for the German interwar default. The comparison with reparations is straightforward: transfers represent an export of capital to the country receiving reparations, something that can shock economies on both side of the transfer. For the debtor, it means a transfer of resources, which will have to be financed in some way with an allocation of economic cost to someone. For the creditor, it means a large capital inflow, which can, but does not have to, stoke financial instability in the medium term.

2.3 TERMS OF TRADE

Reparations are a transfer of resources, which means that the debtor gives up net wealth, either by exporting more and using the proceeds to pay the creditor, or by importing less. This means that the relationship between imports and exports is important for measuring the true economic costs of reparations.[2] In the international finance literature, reparations have therefore mostly been studied as a transfer problem. This problem originates with Mill (1844) and seeks to understand what, if any, consequences unilateral fiscal transfers have on savings and the current account (Obstfeld and Rogoff 1995, pp. 1755–59). Reparations are one such transfer. The transmission mechanism in much writing on the topic is the level of interest rates and the terms of trade, where the latter is defined as the price of exports in terms of imports. If the terms of

---

[2] I go into more detail on this topic in Hinrichsen (2023), where I focus on the transfer problem rather than the sovereign debt aspect of reparations.

trade improve, a country can buy more imports for the same amounts of exports. This was the framework for much of the interwar debate on the economics of reparations.

In several papers, Keynes (1929a, 1929b, 1929c) stated that reparations would have negative second-order effects. He suggested that the debtor would experience a worsening of the terms of trade, due to low import and export elasticities. A large transfer of capital abroad puts downward pressure on the real exchange rate, as the reparations are paid. If import and export elasticities are low and not adjusting, the lower real exchange rate means that imports become relatively more expensive in terms of exports. In contrast, Ohlin (1929a, 1929b) posited that reparations would improve the terms of trade, because the debtor would have lower purchasing power, which means less money spent on imports, in turn lowering their relative price. The adjustment in the relative price of non-traded goods means the debtor's terms of trade will improve to offset the capital flow, and the cost of the reparations would be the stipulated sum. The Keynes–Ohlin debate about German reparations thus came down to discussions about how the terms of trade reacted to a fiscal transfer. Keynes' (1919) critique of Versailles ended up as the theoretical framework for much of the debate. Studies of war reparations have therefore tended to focus on a transfer's terms of trade effects; one example is Deveraux and Smith's (2007) study of the Franco-Prussian War indemnity.[3] The transfer problem suggests that reparations worsen the terms of trade, but, of course, it is difficult to isolate any one economic shock. What is possible is to create a model that explains how a terms of trade shock influences the economy and then keep that in mind as we look at historical cases and actual changes in import and export prices. The next section presents one such simple model, although the rest of the book can be understood without reading it. The first part of the section is a discussion of the academic discussion of the transfer problem since the end of World War II, which can be read even if you want to skip the model itself.

2.4 A TERMS OF TRADE MODEL

The problem of transfers in economies with high capital mobility was formalised in models as a standard part of open economy macroeconomics

---

[3] Corsetti et al. (2013) and Epifani and Gancia (2017) study the transfer problem in a contemporary setting.

by Metzler (1942), Johnson (1955, 1956), and Samuelson (1952, 1954). Samuelson (1952, 1954) showed how Keynes' insights held in theory in a competitive two-good, two-country model. He showed that the terms of trade would deteriorate if the debtor's marginal propensity to consume its export goods was larger than the recipient's. In other words, if the debtor's consumption basket, which is no longer purchased, is the same as that which the creditor chooses to purchase, there is no transfer problem. But in any instance when preferences differ, the terms of trade of the debtor will deteriorate. As Keynes' views were formalised, the assumption underlying Samuelson's original analysis was that the current account balance would remain unchanged – that the trade balance would match the capital flow. Machlup (1964) and Gavin (1992) noted that this did not fit the evidence from French reparations after the Napoleonic Wars or the Franco-Prussian War indemnity; nor did it fit German World War I reparations.

The problem was that the prevalent static models did not incorporate the importance of the political economy in explaining economic performance, with full employment simply assumed to occur (Brakman and van Marrewijk 1998). Balogh and Graham (1979) first noted that if there was no active aggregate demand policy in the creditor country, the debtor country would have to incur unemployment. Similarly, by changing preferences of substitution, the sign on the terms of trade adjustment could change (Djajic et al. 1998). The literature evolved towards more dynamic models of small open economies, with Obstfeld and Rogoff (1995, 1996) using an intertemporal approach to the current account to show that a wealth transfer causes a deterioration in the terms of trade. This happens because households in the recipient country choose to spend some of the financial gains on leisure, which lowers total output and raises prices. Brock (1996) viewed the transfer problem as fundamentally one of adjustments in the relative price of non-traded goods, allowing for borrowing in a small open economy setting. Building on the resource discovery literature (the 'Dutch disease'), he considered the transfer a permanent increase in income in an economy facing fixed terms of trade. Cremers and Sen (2009) showed how impacts from an increase in world net wealth affect the terms of trade, but also raise welfare in both countries. Corsetti et al. (2013) accounted for product varieties in their study of the transfer in the context of the US current account deficit. Most dynamic models of the terms of trade, such as Uribe and Schmitt-Grohé (2017), emphasise the difference between a permanent and a temporary shock, with no long-run effect from the latter.

2.4.1 Growth after Wars

Growth rates in the aftermath of wars should be high because investments in infrastructure have a high return on capital and in most postwar economies there is abundance of infrastructure projects that need to be implemented. But if the projects cannot be financed because a lot of capital goes towards paying reparations, then growth might be lacking. A first, simple step is therefore to compare growth rates across reparations episodes to see if detrended growth rates are abnormally low. I start by looking at long-term real (inflation-adjusted) growth rates, as measured by Bolt et al. (2018). GDP growth needs to be detrended because it is the cyclical component of such growth that is of interest. This is not to neglect structural changes from paying reparations, which can occur, but not in the few years following the war. If there is a structural break, that is of interest in the longer term. The cyclical component of GDP growth is found by log-quadratic detrending, but the choice of detrending method does not alter the results. It is chosen for the general fit across the different countries studied. An ordinary least squares regression is estimated for the secular parameters a, b, and c,

$$y_t = a + bt + ct^2 + \epsilon_t, \tag{2.2}$$

where y_t is real GDP per capita, the secular trend is y_t^{secular}, and the cyclical component, y_t^{cyclical}, is defined as

$$y_t^{\text{secular}} = a + bt + ct^2,$$

$$y_t^{\text{cyclical}} = \epsilon_t.$$

Data across France, Finland, Germany, Greece, Bulgaria, Italy, and Japan, which all paid war reparations, is available from 1870, although data for Bulgaria is less frequent before 1924 and has been interpolated for the period before that. The result is plotted in Figure 2.2. On the left-hand side is the level of real GDP per capita y_t, while the right-hand side shows the cyclical component y_t^{cyclical}. The cyclical component is shown as a percentage deviation from the secular trend.

Real GDP growth is volatile and trends upwards over time. The cyclical component of GDP is correlated across the countries, with large swings especially around the two world wars. The long-run trends have the same direction for each country, but at different income levels it is hard to conclude anything. What would be interesting is if growth rates were much lower as countries paid reparations, but then included the

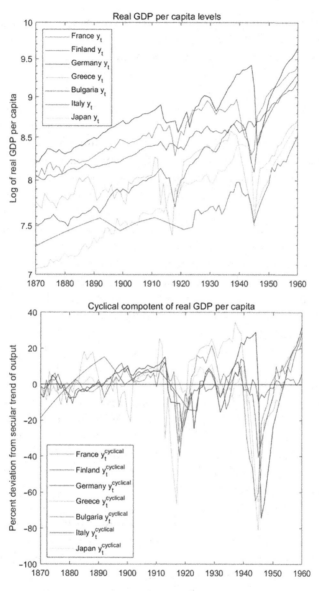

FIGURE 2.2 Long-run secular and cyclical real GDP (1870–1960).
Source: Bolt et al. (2018). Replication file: *lqtrend.m.*

same characteristics afterwards. One way to look at this is if we focus
growth rates in the years following the first transfer payment. Figure 2.3
shows the cumulative change in detrended GDP after the first payment

at t_0 to the left, and the year-on-year growth change to the right, for the countries studied in this book.

The two German output collapses in the interwar period stand out and are shown twice, starting in 1922 and 1930, because of the magnitudes. The two contractions of German real GDP are comparable in size to the average sovereign debt default of the last fifty years (see Chapter 3), but outside Germany there seems to be no distinct trend for large output collapses following wars. Countries do often experience large structural changes to their economies during the reparations period, but it is difficult to identify cause and effect because of the low number of cases and the differing size of war reparations. Some structural changes can show up as terms of trade shocks, for a variety of reasons: commodity prices might permanently change; certain export sectors might experience lower or higher demand; and new domestic industries might make imports redundant. Growth rates by themselves might therefore not tell us a lot about the true economic costs of reparations, but such rates are an important input when undertaking a debt sustainability analysis. The debt-to-GDP ratio is an important metric for debt sustainability because it is one measure of creditworthiness. Countries borrow to smooth consumption at a rate that reflects the world risk-free rate, plus a country premium, which depends primarily on the riskiness of the borrower. If a country has lost a war, it is possible that the country has no net foreign assets, making the financing more likely to be done by debt or taxes. Without any foreign assets, gross debt becomes net assets, and a higher level of net debt has been shown to empirically affect the real exchange rate (Lane and Milesi-Ferretti 2004), with the adjustment coming through changes in the relative price of non-traded goods.

So how do growth shocks affect a countries' ability to pay? One answer is directly, with the size of the transfer being the cost. But it depends on the structure of the economy, if it causes the country to lose sovereign debt market access, and if there are second-order effects. Such effects are harder to measure as we move into counterfactual analysis. The answer to the question of how large a terms of trade shock is needed to affect the economy, in most economic models, is 'pretty large and permanent'. It is worth trying to formalise one such model, which is presented in this section. As I have shown in Hinrichsen (2023), most countries did not see large and permanent terms of trade changes, but there are exceptions (mainly France following the Napoleonic Wars). It

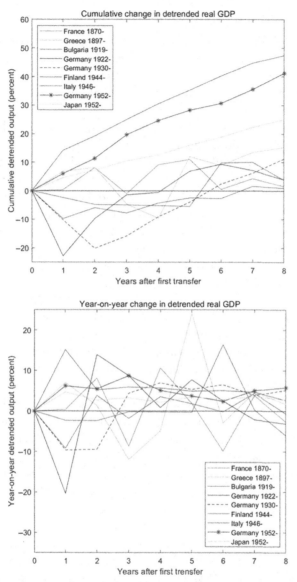

FIGURE 2.3 Change in detrended real GDP per capita (after first transfer).
Note: Year in legend denotes t_0. Replication file: *lqtrend_reps.m*.
Source: Bolt et al. (2018).

is worth trying to think through why those second-order effects occur. The non-technical reader can at this point, without loss of understanding, skip to the next chapter.

2.4.2 The Model

The model follows the one outlined in Uribe and Schmitt-Grohé (2017, pp. 73–140) of a small open economy, but with a terms of trade shock taking the place of the standard productivity shock. I use a dynamic stochastic general equilibrium model of a small open economy to imply an impulse response from the terms of trade shock. The economy is assumed to be centralised, with production happening at the household level. The model could be extended to include firms and a marketplace, but the equilibrium would be the same (Uribe and Schmitt-Grohé 2017, pp. 77–80). A decentralised economy with real wages, firm profits, and a stock market is closer to reality, but the predictions of the model cannot be tested against earlier economies that paid reparations, such as the French economy in the early nineteenth century. The model instead aims to capture the movement in the trade balance. The point of a stylised model is to help us think through the economic reaction from a shock to the economy, which I can then test against the limited economic time series available.

Any choice of model does leave some things wanting. In this model, there is an implicit assumption that output is exported, and that consumption and investment are imported. The model thus does not include non-tradable goods. But introducing such goods means further data predictions, such as their relative price. Another thing is the lack of financial frictions or nominal rigidities. Therefore, a model in which terms of trade is the sole fluctuation is chosen, and this can be calibrated to the trade balance. In that sense, the simple model presented here is like that of earlier real business cycle studies. Certain predictions, especially that for consumption, might be absent as a result. It gives predictions for output, consumption, investments, and the trade balance that can be tested against the historical data that I have collected.

The country is considered a small open economy, which consists of identical households that provide hours of labour h_t and consume c_t goods. It is assumed that each household is infinitely lived, and at each period t receives an endowment of one good, which is exogenous and stochastic. Preferences are given by a constant relative risk aversion period utility function:

$$E_0 \sum_{t=0}^{\infty} \beta^t U(h_t, c_t). \tag{2.3}$$

The utility function is assumed to be concave, decreasing with hours worked, increasing with goods consumed, and discounted at $\beta \in (0,1)$.

E_t denotes the expectations operator. Consumption and investments are assumed to be importable goods, while output is exported. Households have access to borrow to smooth out income shocks and face a budget constraint:

$$y_t + d_t = d_{t-1}(1 + r_{t-1}) + c_t + i_t + \Phi(k_{t+1} - k_t), \qquad (2.4)$$

where y_t is domestic output, d_t is the debt position of households at the end of t, r_t is the interest rate households pay on said debt, i_t is gross investments, and k_t is physical capital; the function Φ ensures there is an adjustment cost to investments to avoid excessive volatility. It is assumed that there are no adjustment costs in the steady state, so $\Phi(0) = \Phi'(0) = 0$ and $\Phi''(0) > 0$. The stock of capital at $t + 1$ is the stock of capital at t plus gross investments minus the depreciation rate $\delta \in (0,1)$, formally:

$$k_{t+1} = k_t(1 - \delta) + i_t. \qquad (2.5)$$

The shock to the economy comes in the form of a terms of trade shock. Output is produced by labour and capital in a linearly homogenous production function:

$$y_t = tot_t \, F(h_t, k_t), \qquad (2.6)$$

where tot_t is the terms of trade, defined as

$$tot_t = \frac{P_t^x}{P_t^i}, \qquad (2.7)$$

which is assumed to be exogenous and stochastic, where P_t^x is a price index of exports (output) and P_t^i is a price index of imports (consumption and investments). The law of motion for the log deviation of the terms of trade follows an AR(1) process:

$$\widehat{tot}_t = \rho \widehat{tot}_{t-1} + v\epsilon_t^{tot}, \qquad (2.8)$$

where ρ is between negative 1 and positive 1 and denotes the persistence of the terms of trade shock (the autocorrelation). ϵ_t is an independently and identically distributed variable. with parameter v standard deviations. At the start of each period, households choose the level of consumption c_t, hours worked h_t, output y_t, investments i_t, debt d_t, and capital k_t that maximises the utility function, subject to a non-Ponzi constraint:

$$\lim_{j \to \infty} E_t \left(\frac{d_{t+j}}{\prod_{s=0}^{j}(1 + r_s)} \right) \leq 0, \qquad (2.9)$$

as well as equations (2.4) to (2.6) above. Households borrow intertemporally via an international bond, which makes them indifferent at the margin between saving and consumption. The equations that govern the capital stock (2.5) and output (2.6) can be used to write the budget constraint forward:

$$\text{tot}_t\, F(h_t, k_t) + d_t = d_{t-1}(1 + r_{t-1})$$
$$+ c_t + k_{t+1} - (1-\delta)k_t + \Phi(k_{t+1} - k_t), \qquad (2.10)$$

which together with the no-Ponzi conditions yields first-order maximisation of households:

$$\lambda_t = E_t \lambda_{t+1} \beta (1 + r_t), \qquad (2.11)$$

$$\lambda_t = U_c(h_t, c_t), \qquad (2.12)$$

$$\lambda_t \,\text{tot}_t\, F_h(h_t, k_t) = -U_h(h_t, c_t), \qquad (2.13)$$

$$\lambda_t \left[1 + \Phi'(k_{t+1} - k_t) \right]$$
$$= \beta \lambda_{t+1} E_t \left[\text{tot}_{t+1}\, F_k(h_{t+1}, k_{t+1}) + (1-\delta) + \Phi'(k_{t+2} - k_{t+1}) \right], \qquad (2.14)$$

and

$$\text{tot}_t\, F_h(h_t, k_t) = -\frac{U_h(h_t, c_t)}{U_c(h_t, c_t)}. \qquad (2.15)$$

The left-hand side of (2.15) is the marginal product of labour. If capital is constant, it is a decreasing function of additional labour. The right-hand side is the marginal substitution for workers between work and time off.

The interest rate is assumed to be an increasing function of the level of French debt. This follows Kollmann (2002) and Schmitt-Grohé and Uribe (2003) to ensure stationarity. Empirically, Lane and Milesi-Feretti (2001) found a negative relationship between net foreign assets and the real interest rate differential. The intuition is that as the level of debt increases, a higher interest rate is required to lend to households, while households start to save more as they face higher debt levels. Formally the interest rate is defined as:

$$r_t = r^* + p(\tilde{d}_t), \qquad (2.16)$$

where the function $p(\tilde{d}_t)$ increases as the level of average debt $\tilde{d}_t$ increases and r^* is the world interest rate, which is assumed to be constant. For simplicity, the discount factor is assumed to be equal to the foreign interest rate, so that $\beta(1 + r^*) = 1$. There is no term structure of interest rate in the model. Before the middle of the nineteenth century, central banks rarely changed the short-term discount rates (Homer and Sylla 2005, p. 224). The short-term interest rate is less important because it is assumed that reparations are funded in the bond market, as was true in most cases, as will be shown later, and therefore there is just one domestic interest rate in the model.

2.4.3 Equilibrium

The level of debt for each household in equilibrium must equal the average as they are identical, meaning that

$$\tilde{d}_t = d_t. \tag{2.17}$$

The equilibrium for debt, consumption, hours worked, the capital stock in the next period, and the terms of trade – given initial levels of debt, the capital shock, the terms of trade and the terms of trade shock – that satisfy (2.8) and (2.16) are:

$$d_t = d_{t-1}\left[1 + r^* + p(d_{t-1})\right] + c_t + k_{t+1} - k_t(1 - \delta)$$

$$+ \Phi(k_{t+1} - k_t) - \text{tot}_t \, F(h_t, k_t), \tag{2.18}$$

$$U_c(h_t, c_t) = \beta\left(1 + r^* + p(d_t)\right) E_t U_c(h_{t+1}, c_{t+1}), \tag{2.19}$$

$$U_c(h_t, c_t)\left[1 + \Phi'^{(k_{t+1} - k_t)}\right] = \beta E_t U_c(h_{t+1}, c_{t+1})$$

$$\left[\text{tot}_{t+1} \, F_t(h_{t+1}, k_{t+1}) + (1 - \delta) + \Phi'(k_{t+2} - k_{t+1})\right], \tag{2.20}$$

$$\lim_{j \to \infty} E_t\left(\frac{d_{t+j}}{\prod_{s=0}^{j}(1 + r^* + p(d_s))}\right) = 0. \tag{2.21}$$

It is then possible to combine equations (2.5), (2.6), and (2.16) to get an equilibrium process for the trade balance:

$$tb_t = \text{tot}_t \, F(h_t, k_t) - \Phi(k_{t+1} - k_t) - i_t - c_t. \tag{2.22}$$

The reaction of the trade balance then depends on whether the terms of trade shock is permanent. If the shock is permanent, the trade balance deteriorates because there is an increase in investments to take advantage of higher export prices. If the shock is transitory, the trade balance improves as households will save the windfall and no new investments will be undertaken. Notice how the trade balance in the deterministic steady state, implied from the resource constraint and the trade balance, is $tb = r^* \bar{d}$. This is to ensure that the country generates enough foreign currency to repay its external debt. The current account is then the change in net foreign assets, or the income from investments and the trade balance:

$$ca_t = tb_t - r_{t-1}d_{t-1} = d_{t-1} - d_t. \qquad (2.23)$$

2.4.4 Calibration

The model now needs to be calibrated, which is done here to the French economy in the years following 1815. Because of the lack of historical time series for output, consumption, or investments to compare against, the model is calibrated to fit the level and volatility of the trade balance. The reaction of other macroeconomic variables is then inferred. It is assumed that the only shock to the model is a terms of trade shock, which is positive and of similar size as the historical shock described in Chapter 4. The time unit of the model is one year.

Production is described using a Cobb–Douglas specification, and the functional forms for capital adjustment costs (quadratic), debt, and utility are:

$$F(h,k) = h^{1-\alpha} k^{\alpha}; \alpha \in (0,1),$$

$$\Phi(x) = \frac{\phi}{2} x^2; \phi > 0,$$

$$p(d) = \psi \left(e^{d-d} - 1 \right); \psi > 0,$$

$$U(h,c) = \frac{G(h,c)^{1-\sigma} - 1}{1-\sigma}; G(h,c) = c - \left(\frac{h^{\omega}}{\omega} \right); \omega > 1; \sigma > 0.$$

Here, α is the capital elasticity in the production function, ϕ is the magnitude of capital adjustment costs, ψ is the debt sensitivity of the interest rate, σ is the relative degree of risk aversion, and ω is the wage elasticity of labour supply, which is independent of consumption; all are parameters. Combining those with δ, r^*, $\bar{d}$, v, and ρ described earlier, there are ten structural parameters needed in the model, as shown in Table 2.2.

The relative degree of risk aversion σ and the depreciation rate δ are standard in the literature and follow Uribe and Schmitt-Grohé (2017, p. 85).[4]

---

[4] See, for example, Thimme (2017) for a review of the literature.

TABLE 2.2 *Model parameters*

	Parameters	Value
σ	Degree of relative risk aversion	2
δ	Depreciation rate	0.1
r^*	World risk-free rate	0.045
α	Capital elasticity of production function	0.36
$\bar{d}$	Debt level	0.428
ω	Wage elasticity of labour supply	1.455
ψ	Debt sensitivity of interest rate	0.000742
ϕ	Capital adjustment cost	0.028
v	Volatility of terms-of-trade shock	0.0129
ρ	Persistence of terms-of-trade shock	0.25

The world risk-free rate is set at 4.5 per cent because yields on British bonds (3 per cent *consols*) were between 4 and 5 per cent at the time (Homer and Sylla 2005, p. 192). The capital elasticity of the production function follows the study of later French indemnity payments after the Franco-Prussian War (Devereux and Smith 2007) and α is set as equal to 0.36.

The level of debt $\bar{d}$ can be solved because we know the trade balance must be big enough to service the debt stock:

$$\bar{d} = \frac{tb/y}{r^*} y,$$

where

$$y = \left[(1-\alpha)\kappa^{\alpha\omega} \right]^{1/(\omega-1)} \text{ and } \kappa = \left[\alpha/\left(r^*+\delta\right) \right]^{1/(1-\alpha)}.$$

The French trade balance is assumed to be 1 per cent in the steady state, as it was approximately in the years following 1815; $\bar{d}$ is then equal to 0.4278. The wage elasticity of the labour supply ω, like that of the debt sensitivity of interest rates ψ, capital adjustment costs ϕ, and the standard deviation of the terms of trade shock v follow the literature, as set out in Uribe and Schmitt-Grohé (2017). A numerical solution for the endogenous variables can be obtained, with $h = 1.154$, $k = 4.779$, and $c = 1.428$. The persistence of the terms of trade shock is calibrated to the historical French trade balance and set to 0.25. Figure 2.4 shows the reaction of the trade balance to a positive terms of trade shock of 10 per cent, for different values of ρ. The best fit is an autocorrelation of 0.25, implying a lasting but not dominant positive terms of trade shock.

Figure 2.4 shows that the reaction of the trade balance depends on how persistent the terms of trade shock is. It would perhaps suggest a

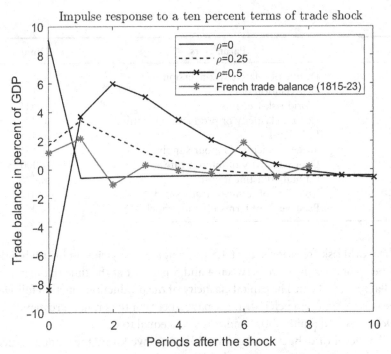

FIGURE 2.4 Trade balance impulse response for different values of ρ.
Source: Charles and Daudin (2015) Tolflit18 database. Replication file,
plot_tot_impulse.m.

higher value of ρ than 0.25, but the model in the next section is nonetheless calibrated to a value of 0.25 because the fit is better. It might be that people did not anticipate the terms of trade shock to be permanent, or that distortions from the payment meant that the actual impulse response to the trade balance was muted.

2.4.5 Results

The model is solved by a log-linear approximation of the equilibrium conditions, in their steady state. The shock to the model comes from the terms of trade shock, where $t + 1$ is assumed to be in 1815. The end of the war and the blockade, as well as the reparations shock, was not anticipated. The impulse described here is to a 10 per cent improvement in the terms of trade of a semi-persistent nature ($\rho = 0.25$). The terms of trade shock could be bigger, but given the uncertainties around the data, a 10 per cent improvement is chosen, which is the average change over a five-year period.

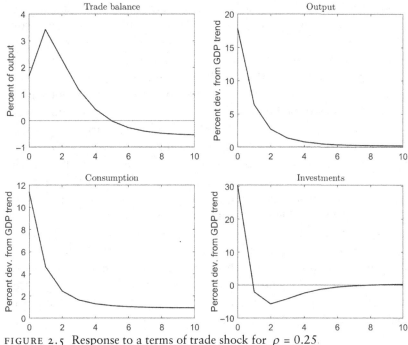

FIGURE 2.5 Response to a terms of trade shock for $\rho = 0.25$.
Note: Replication file, *plot_model.m*.

The reaction of the trade balance to a shock to the terms of trade follows Obstfeld (1982) and Svensson and Razin (1983), where only a transitory improvement in the terms of trade increases the trade balance, as shown in Figure 2.4. This is because the marginal product of capital in terms of imports for $j > 0$ is $\text{tot}_{t+j} F_k \left(h_{t+j}, k_{t+j} \right)$. This means that if the improvement in the terms of trade is permanent, there will be an increase in investments to take advantage of higher marginal product of capital, which increases imports (investments). The immediate effect on the trade balance will then be negative in the short run, as the surge in investment is larger than the gains from the terms of trade. If the shock to the terms of trade is transitory, households will save the money, which improves the trade balance, as per equation (2.20).

Figure 2.5 shows the reaction to a 10-per-cent improvement in the terms of trade for the trade balance-to-output, output, consumption, and investments, where the latter three are shown as percentage deviation from steady state.

The trade balance-to-output ratio is captured well in the model but, given that the calibration targeted the trade balance, this should come as no surprise. The rest of the macroeconomic variables are therefore of more interest. Output is predicted to increase in the first five years, converging to the steady state. As output is a factor of hours worked, capital employed, and the terms of trade shock – equation (2.6) – this is intuitive. Consumption increases as the overall impact is positive, but less than output as some of the gains are saved. Similarly, hours worked (not shown) increase because of their correlation with output. To see why, notice that the log-linear version of (2.15) describing the labour market is $\omega\hat{h}_t = \hat{y}_t$. Figure 2.5 also shows investments increasing sharply by 30 per cent as higher returns make it profitable to increase the capital stock. Because the initial increase in investments is large, the trade balance does not improve greatly, despite much higher output. The adjustment to the capital stock (2.5) is short-lived, which pushes up the trade balance at $t + 1$.

The point of this model is to show some proportion of the macroeconomic reaction to a sizeable terms of trade shock. It gives some economic intuition of the direction in which output, investments, consumption, and the trade balance move as reparations are paid and influence the economy. The model and framework will be used as a foundation to analyse French reparations in 1815 in Chapter 4.

3

Sovereign Debt

Most countries would like to be part of global society, so they do things that strictly they do not have to. Something they do is repay sovereign debt even in circumstances where they would be excused from defaulting from a purely economic or legal point of view. They do this because repayment is but a part of the policy choices that nations face. Sometimes sovereign debt policy is a question of state survival, but often it is one of economic management of the political economy that includes international trade and finance. A default can have negative consequences on everything from trade policy to diplomacy to the stock market. It is of course possible to opt out of the global trading system as a country, but that is not really a sovereign debt policy choice. It is rather a political economy decision the government takes that has consequences far above the finance implications. Examples of such isolation include Russia's repudiation of debt in 1917 and China's in 1947 following both countries' communist revolutions. The revolutions meant that the countries became inward-looking economically, and one consequence was complete repudiation of sovereign debt. But in all but the most extreme cases, countries often repay their debt even if legal enforcement mechanisms do not exist.

Because sovereign debt plays an important role in financing a nation, the question why countries repay their debt has been a core question for research in open economy macroeconomics. The focus has often been on elaborate sovereign debt models, some more realistic than others. The implicit assumption in most models is that repayment is a question of willingness to pay, rather than capacity to pay, as first formalised by Jonathan Eaton and Mark Gersovitz in their seminal paper (Eaton and

Gersovitz 1981). The reason is that sovereign debt is paid back most of the time, despite creditors not having many remedies to enforce debt contracts. Countries pay back their loans because they want to be able to borrow again or to avoid financial sanctions. Unlike in corporate bankruptcies, and outside military intervention, no one can force a country to pay its sovereign liabilities. But one extreme and rare exception is that of war reparations, which has often been directly linked to the removal of occupying troops. As a result, sovereigns generally do not directly default on war reparations, as will be shown in the rest of the book. The reason that defaults on reparations are rare is that they have political consequences far and above normal sovereign defaults, which themselves are not costless. Normal sovereign defaults can result in political interference in exchange for financing (as Greece experienced during the Eurozone crisis) or the takeover of critical infrastructure because it had been pledged as collateral for loans (as China has done).[1] But a default on reparations is something different, as it risks state survival.

The most famous example of reparations is probably that of German World War I reparations. Germany defaulted on its sovereign debt in 1933 but did not default on reparations themselves.[2] These were negotiated to a standstill and effectively ended at the Lausanne Conference in 1932, a year before the sovereign debt default. Other reparations have also been repaid under strained financial budgets, such as Iraq's reparations after the Gulf War or Finnish reparations following World War II. In those cases, there was an explicit enforcement mechanism enshrined in a UN charter (Iraq) or a peace treaty (Finland).[3] Reparations are therefore a special case of sovereign debt as they are senior government debt with recourse. Of course, normal unsecured sovereign debt is often raised to finance reparations, so one cannot understand one without understanding the other. Sovereign debt is of paramount importance for paying war reparations and for war finance in general, which is why this chapter is devoted to studying sovereign debt.

Sovereign borrowing by a polity in the form of marketable securities has existed since around 1000–1400 AD (Eichengreen et al. 2019, pp. 8–12). Sovereign debt markets require tax revenues to base repayment on, which

---

[1] An example is Sri Lanka handing over control of its Hambantota Port to China in 2017 (Abi-Habib 2018).

[2] The 1922 refusal to pay reparations is discussed in Chapter 8. The sovereign default is dated according to Hjalmar Schacht (1967, pp. 137–41), but various debts were defaulted on at different times.

[3] The two cases are analysed in Chapters 10 and 12.

requires institutional credibility. Earlier borrowings were in the form of individual loans to sovereign rulers, but Eichengreen et al. show the necessary institutions required for a public debt market (well-defined city states and borders, accounting systems, contract laws, and creditors able to lend enough money) did not exist before 1000 AD. As institutional credibility increased in the first half of the second millennium, sovereign debt was increasingly used to finance wars. From the year 1650, large states also began to borrow to purchase other public goods than military spending. Aided by the rise of financial sectors and diversification of the investor base (to banks and individual investors), sovereign debt stocks rose from that time. British public debt-to-GDP was 190 per cent in 1822 following the Napoleonic Wars while French public debt-to-GDP peaked at 96 per cent in 1896 (Eichengreen et al. 2019, p. 24). Large-scale sovereign borrowing to finance wars was common but so was subsequent repayment. Britain and France reduced their debt stocks in the nineteenth century by running large primary balance surpluses, essentially smoothing out tax rates by paying for wars out of future taxes financed by borrowing.

In the twentieth century, sovereign debt stocks in advanced countries peaked around the two world wars, because of increased public spending and low growth (Eichengreen et al. 2019, p. 29). Sovereign debt before the 1930s was used to smooth taxes but not to manage the business cycle. This was because before Keynes (1936) the prevailing theory was that any increase in government spending would be offset by higher savings elsewhere, as households would anticipate higher taxes in the future to pay for the spending. The idea originated with Ricardo (1821) and is now known as Ricardian equivalence. Barro (1974) reintroduced the idea, which contends that there is no difference between taxes and sovereign debt, and that as such, government spending financed by debt has no expansionary effect.[4] The government might nevertheless see itself running higher than optimal deficits because of political or institutional factors (Alesina and Tabellini 1990) or to smooth out tax rates (Barro 1979).[5] The Great Depression and Keynes changed the argument around fiscal policy. Because output could be constrained by low demand, deficit spending increasingly had a role in business cycle management. It meant sovereign debt was used for more than smoothing out taxes.

---

[4] Barro made no reference to Ricardo, which Buchanan (1976) noted in his rebuttal two years later.
[5] Alesina and Passalacqua (2016) provides an overview of the literature on why governments might deviate from the 'optimal' path of government debt.

A popular interpretation of Keynes' ideas is found in Hicks (1937). He suggested, in what is now called the IS-LM model, that the *General Theory* argument for expansionary fiscal policy applied under very specific conditions: a liquidity trap where interest rates hit the zero-lower bound. At the zero-lower bound for interest rates, monetary policy is unable to return the economy to full employment.[6] In such a scenario, expansionary fiscal policy can return the economy to its capacity, as Samuelson (1947, 1948) popularised in economic textbooks. Increased public spending can increase the overall level of income under the right conditions because of positive fiscal multiplier effects. Recent evidence from the financial crisis of 2008 shows that countries that tightened fiscal policy experienced negative output shocks (Blanchard and Leigh 2013).[7] As a result, throughout the twentieth century, sovereign debt management became an important tool for managing the political economy. Financing for expansionary fiscal policy can come either from the issuance of sovereign debt or money printing but, as Bianchi et al. (2019) show, the presence of sovereign debt risk can complicate matters because increased spending can lead to sovereign debt crises.

Especially in emerging markets, governments tread a delicate line balancing austerity and stimulus because countries can lose market access quickly. The countercyclicality of government spending is only observed in developed countries, while it is non-cyclical in emerging markets (Uribe and Schmitt-Grohé 2017, p. 9). Emerging market governments have historically tried to avoid expansionary fiscal policy in a downturn, but austerity can exacerbate output losses. The risk is that high debt levels might make it hard to service the debt. It is easier to borrow money if you start out with low debt-to-GDP ratios, as shown by Romer and Romer (2019), which is intuitive. The risk of facing a credit constraint and sudden stop in credit availability is therefore juxtaposed with the benefits from smoothing macroeconomic costs, as with countries facing reparations.

The question to ask, then, is whether the benefits of borrowing are worth the costs of incurring more debt. History shows that most countries facing large reparations payments have used sovereign debt markets

---

[6] Hicks' analysis differs from the *General Theory* (see, e.g., Keynes 1937, pp. 222–23) but the important point for this section is that deficit spending (and therefore implicitly sovereign debt financing) has a role in managing the business cycle (for a history of Keynes and Keynesian thought, see, e.g., Carter 2020).

[7] Japanese interest rates hit the zero-lower bound in the 1990s (Krugman 1998), as did most of the developed world in 2008 (e.g., Bernanke 2017).

to smooth the costs over time. In recent times (since 1800), only the minor reparations following World War II were repaid from current taxes. Sovereign debt markets have changed in the last 200 years, but the use and frequency of public borrowing has been ever present. As have sovereign debt defaults. Because if countries borrow money, they must also consider if they can or want to pay back the loans. What happens when they do not is a sovereign debt default, which is what I turn to next.

3.1 SOVEREIGN DEBT DEFAULTS

A sovereign debt default is in essence a broken promise, as suggested by Ams et al. (2019). But it can be surprisingly hard to define. The reason is that sovereign defaults can take many forms. Some events of default, such as not repaying a loan due, are easily identified by debt contracts. But a sovereign default can be economically costly without breaking any legal contracts. An example is a forced renegotiation and restructuring of a debt stock that is undertaken while the debt is still being serviced.

The first thing to do is therefore to define the different types of sovereign defaults. Defaults fall into one of three categories.[8] The first is minor *technical defaults*. They include covenant breaches or administrative errors, which are broadly ignored by creditors and third parties (such as rating agencies). This first category plays a minor role in sovereign debt management. The second category is *contractual events of default*, specified in legal contracts and defined as defaults by rating agencies. An example is failure to pay interest or principal after a standard thirty-day grace period. Contractual defaults include both negotiated defaults (also called 'soft defaults') where payments are missed, as well as unilateral defaults ('hard defaults'). The third and final category is *substantial defaults*, which are not contractual defaults but have the same economic effects. Examples of the latter include distressed debt exchanges, the use of Collective Action Clauses (CACs) to renegotiate debt contracts, or a restructuring of local debt by a change to the local law.

The type of default does not necessarily say anything about why a sovereign might default (unwillingness or inability to pay), the severity of a default (macroeconomic costs, market exclusion, trading restrictions), how the process of a default occurs (negotiated or unilateral), or what the outcome is (repudiation, debt restructuring, financial autarky). Each of these are discussed in the following sections.

---

[8] This is based on the discussions and definitions in Ams et al. (2019).

3.1.1 When to Default

Countries have historically mostly paid back their sovereign debt. This has occurred even though creditors have few remedies to enforce repayment should the debtor choose to default (Gelpern 2016). Countries can avoid attachment of their sovereign assets in a default, unlike private debtors, because there is no bankruptcy regime for sovereign states. Rather, it is a negotiation between a sovereign state and other sovereign or private parties. Courts in a creditor country, say the US, can tell the debtor to pay but have no way of forcing repayment.[9] Historically, military force has often been used (or threatened) to ensure payments, especially before World War I. Following the interwar years, enforcement of debt contracts by military power became less common (Mitchener and Weidenmier 2010). Countries might in theory only pay back war loans if they win, as suggested by Eichengreen (1990), but in practice political uncertainty, international monetary conditions (Ghulam and Derber 2018), or a rise in political popularity (Herrera et al. 2020) are better predictors for default. Politicians are influenced by local factors in deciding when and how to default. The paradox of why countries repay sovereign debt, despite a lack of enforcement options, is prominent in the literature.

Three strands of the literature have come up with explanations for repayment. The first originates with Eaton and Gersovitz (1981). They suggest that countries repay their debt because they want to maintain their reputation for good credit. They offer no distinction between types of default, and a missed coupon payment has the same effect as a full default. Any sovereign default renders a country unable to borrow again because no one wants to lend it money. Because the choice is based on debt incentives, Eaton et al. (1986) propose that a theory of international lending should concern itself with whether the borrower is likely to repay. The second strand suggests that countries repay sovereign debt to avoid facing economic sanctions in the event of default (Bulow and Rogoff 1989a, 1989b). Unlike in the Eaton and Gersovitz framework, legal considerations play a role as debt renegotiations and partial defaults can occur. The sanctions literature makes explicit the assumption that countries in default must have no ability to invest or purchase insurance contracts abroad. If the country can purchase cash in advance abroad,

---

[9] There are exceptions provided by a global financial system. These are discussed later in the chapter.

the reputational model breaks down. Creditors have certain financial remedies to confiscate financial assets and seize exports to incentivise payment. The definition of default is more nuanced than in the reputational strand, but the approach is a bit less common in quantitative studies of sovereign debt.[10] The third strand originates with Grossman and van Huyck (1988). They show that defaults are more likely if the state of the world is bad, which they define as excusable defaults. Inexcusable defaults occur when there is no negative exogenous shock. It is, however, quite hard to distinguish between excusable and inexcusable defaults in practice, even though sovereign defaults tend to come in waves and clusters. Actual debt issuances by governments have almost exclusively come in the form of fixed, non-state contingent debt, despite the theoretical economic benefits of issuing state-contingent debt as proposed by Paul Krugman (1988). If a debt restructuring imposes too harsh conditions on the debtor country, the total resources available to service the debt might decrease as a result. The same is the case for war reparations. If too large a sum is imposed, the chance of repayment goes down because it can create economic and political instability.

In the last 200 years, many sovereign defaults have been caused by a variety of external factors. Sturzenegger and Zettelmeyer (2006, p. 6) point to worsening terms of trade, recessions in creditor countries, increases in interest rates, and a crisis in one debtor country that spreads to other debtor countries. Sovereign defaults through the 1980s and 1990s exhibited several common characteristics as well: output contractions, interest rate spikes, and a deteriorating current account. Aguiar and Gopinath (2006) and Arellano (2008) use these insights to build on Eaton and Gersovitz' framework to create a formalised sovereign debt model. The main feature is that countries default in bad times when incentives for repayment of non-contingent debt is lowest. Mendoza and Yue (2012) provide a general equilibrium model with endogenized output costs, where imports require financing and a sovereign default forces the country to use suboptimal inputs because no such financing is possible from borrowing. The model has been extended to better reflect the data by several authors. Hatchondo et al. (2009) and Chatterjee and Eyigungor (2012) include long-duration bonds, rather than the single-bond framework of earlier studies, while Dvorkin et al. (2021) add maturity extension as an option for countries in a restructuring. They show that

---

[10] There are many exceptions; for example, Asonuma and Trebesch (2016).

because income recovers from the time of default to the restructuring, it often makes sense for countries to negotiate a maturity extension rather than just haircuts to nominal debt.

Na et al. (2018) show that sovereign defaults are typically accompanied by exchange rate devaluations, which adjust the real wage downwards. A default frees up domestic capacity from debt service, while a devaluation lowers the unemployment rate by adjusting the relative real wage. In this model, a capable central bank can isolate an external crisis so that it does not spread to the domestic sector by devaluing the currency. This type of framework became the literature standard for models of the Eaton-Gersovitz tradition. A sovereign essentially defaults when the cost of repaying debt is larger than the benefits from continued market access. One problem with this argument, as we will see when we apply such a model to war reparations, is that it implies more frequent defaults than are found in the real world.

3.1.2 Frequency of Defaults

In the last sixty years, more than half of all nations have defaulted in one way or another. In the last 200 years, the number of defaults has been higher (Beers and Mavalwalla 2018), as shown in Figure 3.1. The figure shows the percentage of sovereign nations in default at any point in time since 1800. The solid line shows the number of defaults measured by their contribution to world output. The dotted line is the unweighted percentage of nations in default at any time. The solid line is interpreted as follows: if, hypothetically, the United States was half of the world economy and only the United States was in default (all other nations were not in default), then the solid line would show 50 per cent. Over the last 200 years, at any point in time, on average about 20 per cent of nations are in default or undergoing a restructuring. The number falls to 7 per cent if measured by output, with considerable parts of the world's nations in default during the Great Depression. Figure 3.1 shows that sovereign defaults are not rare, but reparations-related defaults are rare. Maybe somewhat surprisingly, post-war periods rarely resulted in sovereign defaults, even when countries were strained for economic resources (Shea and Poast 2018).

The willingness to repay sovereign debt is a choice for policymakers and the broader polity. The occurrence of sovereign debt restructurings has increased in recent years, with defaults happening both because of an inability and an unwillingness to repay debt. Sovereign defaults

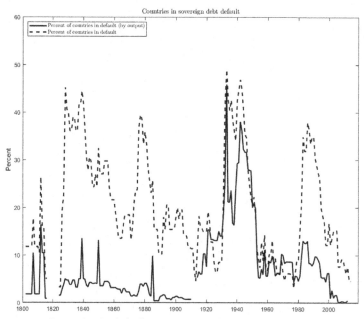

FIGURE 3.1 Countries in default (1800–2020).
Source: Reinhart and Rogoff (2009) online appendix. Replication file,
plot_ltdefaults.m.

and restructurings come in many shapes and sizes: from Russia's full
repudiation of debt after the Bolshevik Revolution in 1918 (Reinhart
and Rogoff 2009, p. 61) to Uruguay's creditor-friendly restructuring in 2003 (Cruces and Trebesch 2013, p. 97). After the Bolshevik
Revolution, bondholders recovered nothing until 1987 when Russia re-
entered international bond markets and offered a nominal settlement
(worthless in real terms). Meanwhile, Uruguay's debt exchange in 2003
was pre-emptive, required no principal haircut on the bonds, and only
extended the maturity by five years. The net present value loss was less
than 10 per cent.

After few sovereign defaults in the decades following World War II,
the Latin-American debt crisis saw a surge of defaults in the 1980s. This
was followed by Russia's default in 1998, the Argentine default in 2001,
and the Eurozone restructuring of Greek debt a decade later (Beers and
Mavalwalla 2018, pp. 11–17). Alongside these well-known sovereign
defaults, there has been a steady stream of smaller, less notable ones.
Figure 3.2 shows the total amount of debt in default at any point in time
since 1960 as a percentage of outstanding debt and world output.

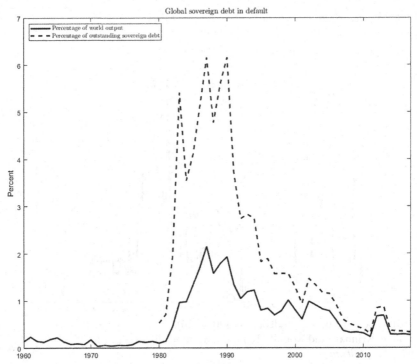

FIGURE 3.2 Global sovereign debt in default since 1960.
Source: Bank of Canada's Credit Rating Assessment Group database on
sovereign defaults. Replication file, *plot_sovdd.m.*

3.1.3 How to Default on Sovereign Debt

Countries can default in many ways. The type of default a country engages
in depends on the debt instrument as well as its creditors. Different types
of default range from full repudiations through to unilateral or negotiated defaults to minor technical defaults. Defaults can either be partial
or on the full debt stock, as well as on domestic debt or on external
debt. Creditors can broadly be defined as belonging to either multilateral
official creditors (such as the IMF, the World Bank, or regional development banks), bilateral official creditors (other countries), or commercial
private creditors.[11] Debtors can discriminate by defaulting selectively on
some creditors or on some debt instruments. This section gives a brief
overview of the myriad of complexities that sovereign defaults can entail.

[11] The breakdown of creditors and types of defaults follow Ams et al. (2019) and Buchheit
et al. (2019).

The doctrine of state succession says that successive governments must honour previous regimes' debt as a matter of public international law. A new government inherits both the assets and liabilities of their predecessor, regardless of differing political philosophy. This historical norm of continuous repayment by states is well covered in the books on sovereign debt by Odette Lienau (2014) and Jerome Roos (2019). The most drastic sovereign default is a full repudiation of debt, but it is rare in modern times. Repudiation of debt is when a country says that its debt is *odious*. Odious debt would be an exception to state succession were it to be recognised in international law (Jayachandran and Kremer 2006). The doctrine of odious debt states that if debt was issued with no benefit and no consent of the people, and the creditors knew it at the time, then a new government should not be responsible for the old regime's debt. Repudiation of debt has occurred throughout history, most famously after the Russian Revolution in 1918, but recent invocations of odious debt have been rare.[12]

Much more normal are unilateral or negotiated defaults, which can both involve a debt restructuring later. The terms 'hard' and 'soft' defaults are hard to define. A hard or unilateral default generally means a payments default combined with a refusal to negotiate with its creditors. A unilateral default often sees the debtor extend a restructuring offer but not in good faith. A soft or negotiated default might not constitute a legal default, as interest rate payments might be made during the negotiation process. Soft defaults might therefore fall under the substantial default definition. Because it is hard to define, it might be that a creditor sees a default as a unilateral default, while the debtor sees unfriendly creditors. As Ams et al. (2019) write, most defaults fall somewhere in the middle. In the last 200 years, the median haircut in sovereign restructurings is below 50 per cent, as shown by Meyer, Reinhart and Trebesch (2022).

The actual event of default can take several forms. Most common is a *payment default*, where the debtor fails to make interest or principal payments. The country can claim insolvency or illiquidity but decides not to pay. Unlike in repudiations, the country does not dispute the validity of the debt but rather decides not to pay for other reasons. A country can also choose to invoke a *moratorium*, where a legal act in the debtor

---

[12] Exceptions include Ecuador in 2008 and the Greek Parliament's Truth Committee on Public Debt.

country suspends payment. In a moratorium, if the creditor agrees, it can negotiate that it does not constitute a payment default (which makes it a negotiated payment suspension). A *covenant default* occurs when the debtor breaches a debt contract. Examples include subordination, false representation of data, or lack of authority to borrow at the time of the contract. *Cross default* is when a default on one instrument triggers a default on another (related) debt instrument. Another recent type of default is a *credit default swap (CDS) credit event*, as defined by derivatives contracts. CDS was invented in the 1990s and pays out the difference between the principal and the recovery value. A credit event can be defined as all three types of default (technical, contractual, or substantial) but is of more interest to investors in derivatives markets, and not to the sovereign itself. Finally, *policy-related defaults* are linked to official borrowing and are usually bespoke. They are more common in corporate borrowing, but can include maximum debt-ratios, sanctions, or ineligibility to borrow from the IMF.

The different types of default can affect different instruments and creditors. The most common distinction is whether the default occurs on domestic or external debt. Local debt and external debt can either differ because they are different currencies (see, e.g., Ottonello and Perez 2019) or because they are governed by different laws (see, e.g., Buchheit and Gulati 2017). A restructuring on local law bonds is easier because the law can be changed by the government. When external debt is governed by foreign law, such as New York law, then the jurisdiction for creditor lawsuits is foreign. Two-thirds of total outstanding debt since 1990 has been local debt (Reinhart and Rogoff 2011a, p. 322), but since reparations were mostly paid in hard currency, the debt raised to pay was mostly in foreign currency.

Default on debt to multilateral official creditors is the rarest because they often have preferred creditor status. It means their debt is senior to other debt. Debt to the IMF in particular is known to be senior because it provides bridge loans if a country experiences a sudden stop (see Section 3.1.4 for details). The World Bank and the regional development banks also have senior status, although sovereigns default on multilateral official creditors sometimes. War reparations are most alike senior, multilateral official debt, except with the added feature that it is often enforced militarily. Sovereign defaults on these types of loans and creditors are the rarest, even if the seniority is not necessarily legally enforced or written into debt contracts.

Once the debtor has defaulted, creditors have certain actions available to them, although specifics depend on the debt contracts. Most sovereign bonds include acceleration clauses, whereby creditors can demand immediate repayment of the remaining principal if a country defaults (see, e.g., Buchheit and Gulati 2002). It is common that 25 per cent of bond holders can accelerate a bond in the event of default and that a majority can reverse the decision if the country starts repaying again. If the default occurs on debt to multilateral creditors, one option is to suspend or cancel further disbursements. If the loan documents state so, it can also result in a refund to the multilateral creditors, but that is specific to the creditor group. Loan agreements or sovereign bonds can be modified if they include CACs. CACs offer a way to restructure sovereign bonds if a stated majority of creditors agree and they are included in many new bond issues. They force the remaining creditors to participate in a restructuring and eliminate any holdouts. The early generation of CACs had bond-by-bond votes. Newer CACs vote on the entire debt stock (or across multiple bonds).

Countries can choose who they want to default on. Sturzenegger and Zettelmeyer (2008) found domestic and foreign holders of debt were treated similarly, but that different debt instruments were not treated equally. Sovereign debt restructurings undertaken at the Paris Club require comparable treatment of all creditors, but this has not always happened. Countries can default in full on all debt instruments or partially on some. Countries also look at who owns the debt, especially if it is the domestic banking sector. It might make sense to spare some debt instruments if a default creates a financial crisis (the so-called *doom-loop* that was a problem during the Eurozone crisis).

Seniority in sovereign debt is therefore complicated. Schlegl et al. (2019) show that since at least 1979, private creditors have been de facto senior to bilateral creditors, while multilateral creditors are senior to both. Banks are generally junior to bilateral creditors and are only ahead of trade creditors. The difference between how creditors are treated is likely to do with the cost of default and enforcement of debt claims by creditor groups. War reparations as sovereign liabilities are therefore senior to other claims because they were almost always enforced by occupation, making it difficult if not impossible to default on them.

3.1.4 Costs of Sovereign Debt Default

The costs of sovereign debt default depend on macroeconomic conditions and what type of default the country engages in. The costs to the country can come from lower economic growth, spill over effects from financial markets, exclusion from sovereign debt markets, or disruption to international trade. The cost to creditors is simply that they will not receive all or some of their investment (loan) back.

The main explanation in the literature for why countries pay back their sovereign debt is that a default is costly for economic growth. Most sovereign debt models therefore assume a direct loss of output because of default, in addition to the inability of smoothing consumption by borrowing. The reason is that most sovereign debt defaults occur when economic growth drops, something that has been empirically determined in a long list of academic papers. The highest estimate of lost output from default is found in De Paoli et al. (2009). They suggest that the median debt crisis lasts ten years and carries a loss of output of over 5 per cent per year. Furceri and Zdzienicka (2012) find that output is 10 per cent lower eight years after a sovereign default. The average cumulative output decline in the three years before a default is similarly high. Sosa-Padilla (2018, pp. 97–99) finds the decline to be around 7 per cent, while Reinhart and Rogoff (2009, pp. 129–30) find it is around 8 per cent. Despite the high output costs around default, there are some arguments against defaults causing output to fall. One is that sovereign defaults generally mark the trough of a contraction, as first suggested by Yeyati and Panizza (2011). The second is the need to differentiate between the types of default. Trebesch and Zabel (2017) show that hard defaults are followed by large output collapses, while negotiated (soft) defaults often have a limited impact on growth. But those growth effects are the immediate output falls around a sovereign debt default.

Another reason that the cost of default can be real and long-lasting is if the country will have to pay more to borrow in the future. Cruces and Trebesch (2013) find evidence of this. They show that defaulting countries pay a higher interest rate on subsequently issued bonds. The higher interest rate compensates for higher risk of default because countries that default once are more likely to do it again. A related channel, albeit a relatively recent phenomenon, is that defaulters carry lower credit ratings (Ams et al. 2019). Lower credit ratings generally increase the risk premium that investors require to lend to a country. A default therefore increases long-term costs of issuing sovereign debt.

A sovereign default can also impact participation in international trade, although the empirical evidence is mixed at best. One theory is that because creditors are less likely to trade with a defaulter, or indeed would want to impose sanctions, international trade is negatively affected by a default. Martinez and Sandleris (2011) show that trade sanctions do not account for any reduction in bilateral trade following a default, because the decline in bilateral trade can be accounted for by the overall reduction in economic activity. The data therefore seem to suggest that there is no causal effect from trade sanctions. One interpretation of Martinez and Sandleris' results, offered by Uribe and Schmitt-Grohé (2017), is that trade sanctions have no effect in the short run but do in the long run. They show that if the time horizon is fifteen years, there is a cost to defaulting that is noticeable in international trade.

One more cost of default comes from potential collateral damage to the economy and the country's economic and political institutions. If a sovereign debt crisis coincides with a banking crisis, economic costs triple compared with a sovereign debt crisis with no banking crisis (e.g., Tomz and Wright 2007 or Reinhart and Rogoff 2011a). Both Hébert and Schreger (2017) and Andrade and Chhaochharia (2018) show that default costs are imputable to disruptions in the financial market intermediation of credit. They measure the cost through stock market declines and exchange rate volatility, where higher probability of default causes stock markets to decline and exchange rates to depreciate. Exchange rate depreciation is a common feature and often coincides with sovereign defaults.

In the area of substantial defaults, a large devaluation can have real costs – and potentially cause a default of external debt as it is more costly to pay debt in foreign currency. Balance of payments crises models show how countries can be forced to devalue their currency by speculative attack. The literature that originates with Calvo (1988) explains how sovereign debt crises are sometimes accompanied by a currency crisis.[13] Calvo posits that a devaluation can be considered an implicit default, albeit on locally denominated debt. The mechanism through which the implicit default happens is that a country over-extends itself financially. The policy leads to capital outflows, as investors expect economic conditions to be unsustainable. The unsustainable policies can either be fiscal policies (Krugman 1979) or happen through balance-sheet effects (Corsetti et al. 1999a, 1999b; Kaminsky and Reinhart 1999; or Burnside et al. 2004). In the latter type of crises (balance-sheet effects), banking crises precede currency crises because firms or households hold assets in local currency and have debt in hard currency (US dollars or euros). If the currency falls, then liabilities increase while assets stay the same, which create imbalances. Devaluations do not mark the trough in output because a devaluation exacerbates the imbalances.

[13] More recent contributions are Da-Rocha et al. (2013) and Corsetti and Dedola (2016).

A final cost of default is a direct cost that stems from lawsuits and holdouts creditors. If a country defaults but does not restructure its debt with all its creditors, holdout creditors might engage in legal action. A cost might be that courts in third-party jurisdictions agree with the creditors. An example could be an attempt to block payments to other creditors (such as already restructured loans), as happened in the case of Argentina (more on which in Section 3.2). Legal disputes in sovereign debt restructurings have become frequent throughout the 1990s and early 2000s because most bonds are issued under New York or English law jurisdiction (Schumacher et al. 2021). The direct and indirect legal consequences of a sovereign default are therefore increasingly high.

3.2 SOVEREIGN DEBT RESTRUCTURINGS

Sovereign debt defaults often, although not always, result in a restructuring of the debt stock. The outcome of a sovereign debt restructuring can be a reduction of the debt stock in nominal or net present value terms. Nominal reduction in the debt stock is through nominal debt haircuts, while a reduction in the net present value of liabilities can occur either through maturity extensions or coupon reductions. This section describes how sovereign debt restructurings occur in general, including the recent history of restructurings, the methods, and the players involved. In Chapter 12, I use this as a background to analyse the Iraqi sovereign debt restructuring, which was one of the largest in history, included discussions of odious debts and war reparations, and also had a geopolitical angle.

Before World War I, sovereign defaults often resulted in blockades or sanctions to ensure repayment of debt (Mitchener and Weidenmier 2010). Famous banking houses played an important role in preventing full scale defaults, because they acted as a liquidity provider for countries that found themselves in a liquidity crisis (Flandreau and Flores 2012). Countries could not be forced to restructure through legal means and often the only remedy was military force (Gelpern 2005, pp. 396–97). This slowly changed throughout the twentieth century, but it was not until the end of World War II that restructurings became formal affairs with a playbook (Sgard 2016), understood in the sense of the same recurring institutions involved; not as in a formal bankruptcy code, such as is seen, for example, in Chapter 11 for corporations in the United States. In the aftermath of World War II, several institutions were set up to manage the new world order, of which two dealt with sovereign debt: the

IMF founded in 1944 and the Paris Club in 1956. Since then, three types of negotiation have occurred frequently during defaults. One, countries negotiate with the IMF to provide balance-of-payment funding for the short term. Two, there are negotiations with official creditors to reduce the debt burden at the Paris Club. Three, private creditors engage to restructure their claims, often via the London Club (Rieffel 1985, p. 2). The three negotiations can happen simultaneously or in steps and are outlined here.

The IMF was set up to provide help to countries facing balance of payments crises. The Bretton Woods system, meant to govern global economics affairs, was designed to avoid competitive devaluations (Boughton 2004, pp. 4–7). The lessons from German reparations and the Great Depression were institutionalised into the IMF, in a framework its creators hoped would avoid autarky, protectionism, and competitive devaluations, and would also foster economic growth. The United States would return to the gold standard, while all other currencies would be pegged to the dollar (and gold). The IMF would govern the system and provide short-term lending for balance of payments adjustments (Bordo and James 2000). IMF lending increased throughout the decades, as debt crises occurred more frequently in emerging markets.[14] The debt crises of the 1980s, the Mexican ('tequila') crisis in 1994–95, the Russian default in 1998, and the Argentinian default in 2001 all involved the IMF (Orastean 2014). As crises changed – from currency and convertibility crises in the Bretton Woods era to sovereign debt and financial crises from the 1980s on – the IMF adapted. It increasingly started to offer large loans and helped facilitate sovereign restructurings (Reinhart and Trebesch 2016).

The Paris Club is an informal group of twenty-two official creditors that has negotiated 463 restructurings with 96 countries between its founding in 1956 and September 2020, as can be seen in Figure 3.3.[15] The Club has been housed at the French Treasury in Paris since the 1970s.[16] The Paris Club has a set of procedures for countries to negotiate debt restructuring, where participants vary depending on the creditors (Rieffel 1985, p. 3). Restructuring of external debt by official creditors is more common

---

[14] For a general history of the IMF since the fall of the Berlin Wall, see Boughton (2012).

[15] www.clubdeparis.org/en (accessed 5 September 2020).

[16] There were discussions in the early days about moving the operation to the IMF or the World Bank, but the French prevailed (Rieffel 1985, pp. 23–26).

When Nations Can't Default

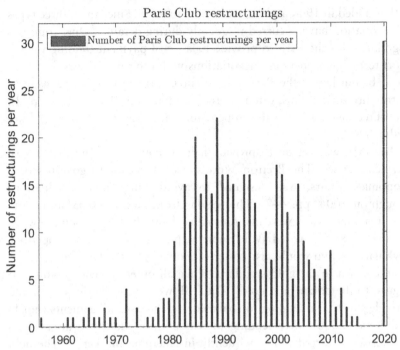

FIGURE 3.3 Paris Club restructurings (1956–2020).
Sources: Cheng et al. (2018, p. 184) online appendix with added restructurings from 2020 from the Paris Club (thirty in total following the COVID-19 crisis, most of which are suspension of repayments). Replication file, *plot_pc.m*.

than with private creditors, with several countries recurring as defaulters (Das et al. 2012). Countries needing assistance can contact the Paris Club to start negotiations, but a prerequisite for engaging in Paris Club talks is an IMF Stand-By Agreement, to provide short-term financing. The Paris Club works on five principles (Cheng et al. 2018, p. 183):

1. Solidarity, meaning the members of the Club act as one creditor (no side deals);
2. Consensus, meaning there is consensus on the restructuring offer;
3. Conditionality, meaning a deal is conditional on the terms of IMF programmes;
4. No boilerplate terms, with each restructuring based on its merits and needs; and
5. Comparability of treatment for non-Paris Club creditors.

Initially, only countries close to default could be considered ('imminent default rule'), and the Paris Club was a last resort (Rieffel 1985, pp. 3–7). From 1956 to 1987, countries could only receive flow treatment; that is, rescheduling maturities and changing coupons, with no nominal haircuts. The Paris Club changed the rules, allowing for stock treatment of debt, in 1994 (the 'Naples Terms'). This allowed for debt stock relief for highly indebted countries with no imminent default in 1996, while the 2003 Evian Approach offered stock and flow treatment to all countries. The first use of the Evian Approach was for the Iraqi restructuring (Rieffel 1985, p. 10). The changing governing structure meant the Paris Club was used frequently from the late 1980s. The change in Club principles coincided with an increase in sovereign debt restructurings in the 1980s (Rieffel 1985, pp. 7–16).

In the 1970s, the London Club was formed to deal with commercial restructurings (Rieffel 2003). It is like the Paris Club, but with a broader scope. The London Club also has a set of procedures but for a group of private creditors. Early on, it consisted mostly of commercial banks and it is more flexible than the Paris Club (Rieffel 1985, pp. 22–23). No IMF Stand-By Agreement is necessary to deal with the London Club; terms are flexible; and the debt relief can be done pre-emptively. The loan providers of external private debt have historically been commercial banks, but as the Bretton Woods system collapsed, new players emerged. Creditors suddenly consisted of hedge funds, asset managers, investment banks, trade creditors, state-owned enterprises, contractors, and suppliers. They could hold a variety of different claims: bonds, loans, notes, bills, or trade credits. Some claims were not even against the debtor, such as credit default swaps. These changes made it hard to find one creditor committee to represent the interests of all the creditors, as they were not necessarily aligned.

All restructurings include a power struggle between debtor and creditors. US policy has consistently been in favour of negotiated settlements, with neither debtor nor creditor obtaining structural leverage (Buchheit and Gulati 2019).[17] Until the late 1980s, creditors had no legal remedies to ensure payments. This changed in the 1990s. In the case of the Argentine restructuring, creditors forced Argentina out of global financial markets through a series of legal victories in New York courts (Buchheit and Gulati 2019, pp. 8–10). The boilerplate legal prospectus

---

[17] See, for example, brief for the United States as Amicus Curiae, NML Capital Ltd v Republic of Argentina, 2012, WL 1150791.

used in most debt contracts included a *pari passu* clause, ensuring equitable payment. Restructurings imply exchanging old claims for new instruments. The rise of 'vulture fund' creditors meant the rise of hold-outs (Fang et al. 2021). These holdouts sued for *pari passu* payments with the new, restructured bonds. The holdouts won (Buchheit and Gulati 2017). Because of the globalisation of financial markets, a legal victory in one major financial centre can cut off market access world-wide. Argentina could not pay interest on any of its bonds until it paid off the old holdouts. Creditors thus gained one way of enforcing sover-eign debt, hitherto impossible. The story of restructurings is increasingly one of creditors having remedies not previously available (Schumacher et al. 2021).

Anil et al. (2018) find that the higher the share of senior bonds in the debt stock, the higher the likelihood of repayment. The reason is that governments are committed to repay because the cost of default increases with the stock of senior debt. Reparations-linked debt is in most cases considered senior and enforceable, so the cost of default is likely higher than in many other cases of sovereign defaults.

3.3 ODIOUS DEBTS

The doctrine of state succession says that successive governments must honour previous regimes' debt as a matter of public international law. A new government inherits both the assets and liabilities of their pre-decessor, regardless of differing political philosophy. One exception to state succession would be the doctrine of odious debt, were it to be recognised in international law (Jayachandran and Kremer 2006). There is an argument, made by King (2016), for example, that the doc-trine of odious debt already exists in international law, but it has never been used in practice.[18] This doctrine states that if debt was issued with no benefit and no consent of the people, and the creditors knew it at the time, then a new government should not be responsible for the old regime's debt. Odious debt, then, would be an exception to state succession.

Even though governments almost always adhere to the principle of state succession, it is almost impossible to legally enforce sovereign debt

---

[18] Changing international law occasionally happens but needs support from powerful nations, see Choi and Gulati (2016).

contracts, and no sovereign bankruptcy regime exists (Gelpern 2016). Following World War I, several attempts were made to formalise model arbitration clauses in sovereign bonds (Weidemaier 2014), but until the 1950s defaulting countries were effectively immune from legal action (Gelpern 2005). Even in the latter half of the century, restructurings were still largely voluntary ad-hoc affairs (Sgard 2016). CACs, which offer a way to restructure sovereign bonds if a majority of creditors agree, were absent from Iraqi debt contracts and most other contracts until recently (Gelpern and Zettelmeyer 2020). Most countries therefore had no way of legally forcing creditors to exchange their claims. This included Iraq, as I show in Chapter 12, and it left Iraq with the option of a negotiated restructuring or a repudiation by declaring its debt odious.

Repudiation of debt has occurred throughout history, most famously after the Russian Revolution in 1918 (Laskaridis et al. 2020), but recent invocations of odious debt have been rare. Exception include Ecuador's default in 2008 (Gelpern 2010),[19] and the Greek Parliament's Truth Committee on Public Debt.[20] As I argue in Chapter 12, the origin of Iraq's debt stock meant invoking the doctrine of odious debt was possible, but it would require a new approach by the institutions involved. A standard sovereign debt restructuring, meanwhile, was up against potentially aggressive creditors who were used to receive generous treatment and who could attach Iraq's assets abroad. The doctrine of odious debt remains largely unused in the sovereign debt world.

3.4 A PRACTICAL GUIDE FOR RESTRUCTURING SOVEREIGN DEBT

Let us leave theory for a moment and assume that we are a player in a sovereign debt restructuring, either as a creditor or a debtor.[21] This is how the process would normally unfold (Buchheit et al. 2019). The underlying assumption for almost all sovereign debt these days is that

---

[19] The Internal Auditing Commission for Public Credit was appointed by the president and found Ecuadorian debt to be illegitimate, leading to a strategic default; see Internal Auditing Commission for Public Credit, *Final Report of the Integral Auditing of the Ecuadorian Debt* (2008). Both Arturo Porzecanski (2010) and Adam Feibelman (2010) argue Ecuador was far from proving its case.

[20] The Truth Committee on Public Debt, 'On Public Debt, Preliminary Report' (2015), www.hellenicparliament.gr/UserFiles/8158407a-fc31-4ff2-a8d3-433701dbe6d4/Report_EN_final.pdf (accessed 1 October 2020).

[21] This section is a lightly adapted version of a piece I wrote for the *Financial Times*, describing how the sovereign debt restructuring process works (Hinrichsen 2022b).

loans will not be repaid fully but rolled over (Phan 2017). Nominal debt stocks tend to rise over time and bullet loans – the standard in sovereign borrowing – are replaced by new loans as they mature. A crisis can therefore happen quickly if it is impossible to borrow new money for whatever reason. Let us assume a country is out of money but wants to remain part of the global financial system (so no total repudiations of debt à la Russia 1918). The country needs to restructure its liabilities, and it might even already have defaulted by not paying a coupon (a contractual failure to pay). Even if it doesn't default contractually, it will do so substantially by forcing a distressed debt exchange. The outcome will be classified as a sovereign debt default regardless of the type of default or severity of outcome.

3.4.1 The Fundamental Problem

A debt restructuring is fundamentally about allocating economic costs to someone. Countries want the burden of adjustment to fall on external creditors. Creditors want the burden to fall on taxpayers. The problem is one of resource allocation and identification of why the debt is unsustainable, and to what degree.

The first step in a debt workout is to figure out what the problem is: chronic low growth, falling commodity prices, no export sector, a bankrupt financial sector, the maturity structure of the debt, too large a debt stock, or hidden debt that wasn't disclosed. Perhaps the debt was manageable at low interest rates, but now interest rates are high and servicing the loans is a budgetary problem. Citizens don't like that, which makes it a political problem.

Sovereign defaults have occurred for all of these reasons (some more often than others, see, e.g., Esteves et al. 2021). Normally it's a mix of factors, but understanding the root cause is a first step in a successful restructuring. If it is a liquidity problem caused by a pandemic, maybe the country just needs temporary help. Perhaps the problem is that the country has a debt stock that is several times its annual export earnings, in which case the problem is fundamental. The restructuring must address the problem.

The second step is to find out what type of debt the country has. Is the debt external? If yes, what kind of external debt – governed by foreign law, issued in foreign currency, or held by foreigners? What share of the debt is domestic? If the debt is governed by domestic law, it is easier to restructure legally, but if all the sovereign debt is owned by your financial system, maybe a restructuring will cause a domestic financial crisis that just makes everything worse. Maybe most of the liabilities are not even directly on the government books but rather guaranteed state-owned enterprises that need to be part of a restructuring. Any initial analysis should answer these questions.

3.4.2 The Restructuring Process

The first issue is whether to go to the IMF or not. The IMF can come in and do a debt sustainability analysis (DSA) and lend credibility to the macro-economic numbers. A DSA is a prerequisite for a restructuring at the Paris Club, but, more importantly, it sets out how much debt a country is likely to be able to pay 'sustainably'. The IMF does an analysis of the balance of payments and the debt stock among other things, and it can provide stop-gap financing if there is a credible way to make debt sustainable. The downside is that IMF programmes often come with strings attached, such as 'reforms' that a country might not find very appealing. The reality is that any IMF programme is a political art, not science. The benefit is that the IMF has done many restructurings before, as have most of the lawyers and bankers involved on either side. A sovereign debt restructuring has no set process – but the players and the tools involved are usually the same.

Restructuring involves an exchange of old claims for news claims, where the new claims have different characteristics: lower principal value, lower coupons, or longer maturity. It's usually a mix, but the composition depends on what the problem is – and what you can get creditors to agree to. If the debt stock is manageable but all the debt is due in the next two months, maybe a 'reprofiling' of the maturities is all that is needed. If the debt stock is too high, maybe principal haircuts are required, or maybe a lowering of the coupon until after any reforms are enacted and growth hopefully picks up. Once this analysis is done – usually behind closed doors together with the advisers and the IMF – the doors are opened and some sort of negotiation starts.

The DSA probably suggest what debt to restructure and what debt to exclude (and what debt to pay!). Generally, you'll want to exclude some types of claims needed to keep the economy going, such as trade credits (to maintain and facility international trade) and Treasury bills (for short-term financing). But it depends on the problem and the debt stock. Trade credits and T-bills are usually excluded from restructurings, but not always – if 80 per cent of a country's debt is T-bills then you can't really exclude them.

The process from here depends on what type of debt the country has and on its creditors. It's a good idea to start where you can get the best deal and have the most friends. Negotiations with bilateral creditors can happen between politicians or at a bureaucratic level. Normally it's done at the French finance ministry (the Paris Club), where most developed countries are members (but importantly not China).

There are generally two ways to go about dealing with commercial creditors: either a creditor consultation via an adviser, which will report back to the country/IMF or a negotiation with creditor committees made up (usually) of the biggest lenders. Committees can verify a deal and might make other creditors comfortable that it's the best deal on the table (after all, no creditor wants to give debt relief only to see someone else repaid in full).

3.4.3 The Players

First the borrower. A sovereign county is a unique debtor. It is very difficult to force a country to do anything. There's no sovereign bankruptcy code, no way to work out defaulted debt, and seizing state assets is very difficult. Do you want to try to seize Russian assets?

What a state has is its reputation and a wish to be part of global society. Countries are supposed to pay their debts under the doctrine of state succession (one of the international laws that are generally adhered to), but states are political entities. The debtor responds to domestic political incentives. A judge in New York might tell a country to do one thing, but getting a country to respond is a different thing. Countries are often not in a rush.

Then there are the creditors. Creditors are important because they lend money, but on the other hand they don't vote. Because most sovereign debt restructurings start out with an IMF DSA, the creditors are already pitted against each other if one or more classes of debt are excluded from a potential restructuring. So it's a zero-sum game. Often, a creditor's main opponent is not so much the debtor but rather other creditors. The senior creditors are normally multilateral institutions (IMF, the World Bank, some development banks), which often have 'preferred creditor status'. The IMF is paid before everyone else. Sometimes preferred creditor status is also given to some wannabe-multilaterals (European Investment Bank, European Central Bank, Korean Development Bank, etc.), but if too many get it that's not great for junior creditors.

Creditors can be bilateral lenders (other countries, which negotiate at the Paris Club or individually), banks or bondholders (which usually form committees), trade creditors (often on their own but with political backing), households, or state entities. Each will argue their case. Some creditors can be more of a pain than others, as some are litigious or prone not to accept a deal.

Each creditor tries to talk their way up the capital structure. If you cannot do this, you want to make sure that everyone else shares the pain. If you're a local bondholder, you say the financial system will go belly-up if you're restructured. If you're an international bondholder, you mutter that the country will never be able to borrow in global markets again if you're restructured. In extremis, you say that you will go bankrupt if there is a restructuring and lobby your own government to help you negotiate – as banks in Europe did with Greek sovereign debt. You argue it's cheaper to extend credit to Greece so they can roll over their debt rather than having to recapitalise some French or German bank.

3.4.4 The Legal Aspects

A legal analysis is needed to figure out the tactical approach. International law is difficult to enforce, but legal analysis still plays a very important role in today's sovereign debt world – mainly because most debt contracts are governed by New York or English law.

The first step is to figure out how much of your debt is domestic law, which is easier to deal with, and how much is foreign law. Then you figure out how many of your bonds have old *pari passu* clauses, what type of collective action clauses govern the bonds, if some loans have weird clauses, and if the overall debt stock invites litigation. Some countries, such as Ukraine, have relatively recently issued debt that is easier to aggregate and thus restructure, while others, such as Zambia, have older contracts that might give creditors or debtors some legal upper hand.

As a creditor, you try to figure out if your bond can be aggregated. Should you accelerate if there is a default? Get a judgment? Can you hold out for a better deal while other creditors restructure? Maybe you have an old, non-performing loan. If you have written it down already, it's surely better to be able to collect on a smaller loan. Of course, if you want to sue, it's important to get your strategy right, but also to remember that lawyers are expensive.

3.5 A SOVEREIGN DEBT MODEL

In this section, I present one sovereign debt model that can produce a default set, where countries would normally default on their sovereign debt. The default sets can then be judged against episodes of war reparations to see if repayment lies outside the norm. The framework is a sovereign debt model like that of Na et al. (2018), where default and devaluation occur simultaneously. It quantifies the gains from continued market access and compares it with the cost of repaying debt. The methodology creates an optimal default policy for the government, which can be compared to historical reparations. The idea is to quantify the benefits of being able to borrow on sovereign debt markets and compare it with the costs of repaying debt. The macroeconomic history is then compared with the model prediction. The importance of enforcement of sovereign debt is inferred as macroeconomic characteristics are similar for defaulters and non-defaulters alike.

The model follows the real business cycle models, with the debt stock considered external rather than local. Reparations were financed largely by debt denominated in foreign currency, and the real economy is therefore more important than suggested in Calvo's models. Obviously, every model has its limitations: This one has no explicit financial sector. Sosa-Padilla (2018), for instance, estimates a standard sovereign debt model, but includes bankers as the transmission shock to the real economy. Such a model has several useful assumptions for more contemporary studies, but those make it less useful for historical comparisons. The main feature is that defaults and banking crises happen simultaneously, where the transmission mechanism is via the financial system. A default causes a loss on banks' balance sheets, which in turn tightens lending standards. While still empirically true, in earlier periods the financial sector was simply smaller, and the financial sector is therefore left out.

Sovereign debt models can provide a framework in which the cost of servicing sovereign debt is quantified against the benefits of repayment. In the model on the following pages, a benevolent government can free up domestic balance sheets by defaulting, but it results in an output loss and removes the country's ability to borrow money.[22] In the model, the government chooses to default or repay sovereign debt, based on a value function. The nominal exchange rate is set unilaterally by the government, which can counteract any (potential) distortions from wage rigidities via monetary and exchange rate policies. The predictions of the

---

[22] As is standard in the literature and an empirical feature of sovereign debt defaults (see, e.g., Borenztein and Panizza 2008; Furceri and Zdzienicka 2012; or Hébert and Schreger 2017).

model can then be used for both the nineteenth century with limited wage rigidities and the twentieth century.[23] In the nineteenth century, wages were flexible, while in the twentieth century, the nominal exchange rate adjusted real wages lower. Because of the adjustment mechanism, if it makes sense to default in a floating exchange rates regime; it makes even more sense in a world of fixed exchange rates.[24]

The model is the optimal monetary policy version of Na et al. (2018). The point of the analysis is to understand if the macroeconomic conditions, with and without reparations, should lead to default. One complicating factor in the analysis of sovereign debt is that defaults are often endogenous. Defaults can be caused by a series of negative shocks to the economy and defaults can cause a loss of output. Both are common, as shown by Esteves et al. (2021), who use a narrative approach to find that historically exogenous causes of default are more common, but endogenous factors are becoming more frequent. They find that 62 per cent of sovereign defaults between 1870 and 2010 can be explained by exogenous factors, with terms of trade shocks and political factors the most regular causes of default. In their sample, they also find evidence that default causes output to fall.[25] The latter evidence is generally, and in this book's model, used as a justification for an exogenous cost of default.

The model allows us to observe certain stylised facts around sovereign debt defaults, with the default set a function of the benefits and costs of repaying debt. The value functions allow for a characterisation of what can be considered optimal policy in terms of whether to default or not. The model can then be measured against the historical setting of war reparations and whether the cases lie in the default set. It is calibrated to the French economy in 1870–73, the German economy in 1930–33, and the Finnish economy in 1945–48. The model helps to quantify if the costs of repaying reparations were above a level at which countries normally default. If the answer is yes, it suggests that countries should have defaulted on reparations and entered autarky, but were unable to because sovereign debt was enforced by occupation. The next few pages present the model and some of the model's insights are then used in the following chapters, which tell the stories of each war reparation.

---

[23] See Eichengreen (2008) for a general discussion of wage rigidities.

[24] To adjust the relative real wage and the price of non-traded goods in a fixed exchange rate system, unemployment would have to rise. A devaluation would adjust this via the exchange rate instead.

[25] Their sample does not include the Iraqi default, which experienced a large negative output loss both before and after the sovereign default.

3.5.1 Government

The model is of a small open economy where the government borrows on international debt markets. The economy consists of the government, homogeneous firms that are perfectly competitive, and households that have identical preferences. The government can either be in default or not. If the country is repaying its debt, $R_{t-1} = 1$, whereas if the country defaults at the start of the period, then $R_t = 0$. Default implies that the country has lost all access to borrowing on international debt markets. If the country is in default, it exits default in $t + 1$ with probability θ and remains in default with $1 - \theta$ probability. A default is defined as a total default on all external debt.[26] If $R_t = 1$ then households receive a lump-sum payment for the debt tax that the government levies, F_t, which is expressed as $g_t = F_t / P_t^T$ in terms of tradable goods, where P_t^T is the nominal price of tradables. If the country is in default, the payments that households would have made to foreign lenders are confiscated and returned to the households. The sequential government budget constraint is then

$$g_t = d_{t+1}q_t^d \tau_t^d + (1 - R_t)d_t, \qquad (3.1)$$

where d_{t+1} is the level of debt at t to be repaid at $t + 1$, q_t^d is the price of one unit of face value debt, and τ_t^d is the tax collected on debt. The debt is denominated in tradable goods so that the effect can be measured in consumption. It follows the standard Eaton–Gersovitz allocation of debt with centralised borrowing and centralised default. Households take the country premium on borrowing as exogenously given, while the government internalises it into the country risk premium it pays on its external debt. The price of debt must satisfy a risk-neutral foreign lender that wants to cover their opportunity cost of capital; that is, lenders are expected to earn the same return abroad as at home

$$\frac{Pr\{R_{t+1} = 1 \mid R_t = 1\}}{q_t} = 1 + r^*. \qquad (3.2)$$

Which means that the country spread is simply the probability of default in the next period.

---

[26] It means there is no recovery value on defaulted bonds. Cruces and Trebesch (2013) show that higher haircuts lead to longer exclusion from capital markets, which can be captured by lowering the parameter θ.

3.5.2 Firms

Each firm will want to maximize profits, Π_t, and produce non-traded output according to

$$y_t^N = F(h_t), \tag{3.3}$$

where the function is concave and increasing. The input is simply labour h_t, provided by the households who are paid nominal wages, W_t. Firms maximise profits according to

$$\Pi_t = P_t^N F(h_t) - h_t W_t, \tag{3.4}$$

which can be rewritten as

$$p_t F'(h_t) = w_t, \tag{3.5}$$

with $w_t = W_t / P_t^T$ being the real wage in terms of tradable goods, and $p_t = P_t^N / P_t^T$ the relative price of non-tradables in terms of tradables.

3.5.3 Households

Households are alike and make decisions based on information available to them at present time, with constant relative risk aversion. Their utility is maximised with respect to

$$E_0 \sum_{t=0}^{\infty} \beta^t U(c_t) = \left(\frac{c_t^{(1-\sigma)} - 1}{(1-\sigma)} \right), \tag{3.6}$$

with c_t being total consumption, the parameter $\beta \in (0,1)$ denotes the discount factor, and U is assumed to be concave and increasing. c_t is a composite of the two types of consumption: traded c_t^T, and non-traded c_t^N, and is given by its CES aggregator function

$$c_t = A(c_t^T, c_t^N) = \left[a c_t^{T^{1-\frac{1}{\xi}}} + (1-a) c_t^{N^{1-\frac{1}{\xi}}} \right]^{\frac{1}{1-\frac{1}{\xi}}}, \tag{3.7}$$

where A is a linearly homogenous function that is concave and increasing, a is the percentage of tradables in the total consumption basket, and ξ is the elasticity of substitution between tradables and non-tradables. The firms are owned by the households in a uniform manner, and they therefore receive the profits from said firms. The household budget constraint is given by

$$P_t^T c_t^T + P_t^N c_t^N + P_t^T d_t = h_t W_t + \Pi_t + F_t +$$
$$(1 - \tau_t^d) P_t^T d_{t+1} q_t^d + P_t^T \tilde{y}_t^T. \tag{3.8}$$

The left (top) side of the equation is each household's spending, which consists of consumption of tradable and non-tradable goods, plus their debt. The right-hand side of the equation is each household's income from their labour, profits from firms they own, the lump-sum payment (F_t), τ_t^d a tax on debt income received from the ownership of foreign debt, with $\tilde{y}_t^T$ being each household's endowment of traded goods, which is given and stochastic. In reality, τ_t^d can be thought of as a tax on capital flows, such as reserve requirements on banks or capital controls.

People in this economy are subject to no-Ponzi conditions. The relative price of non-tradables, p_t, can be written as

$$p_t = \frac{A_2\left(c_t^T, c_t^N\right)}{A_1\left(c_t^T, c_t^N\right)}, \tag{3.9}$$

$$Y_t = U'(c_t) A_1\left(c_t^T, c_t^N\right), \tag{3.10}$$

$$\beta E_t Y_{t+1} = \left(1 - \tau_t^d\right) q_t^d Y_t. \tag{3.11}$$

The household budget constraint therefore uses the Lagrange multiplier, Y_t / P_t^T. Households supply inelastic labour $\bar{h}$ and it is assumed that $\bar{h} = h_t$, meaning the economy is at full employment. The assumption here is that the central bank stands ready to counteract any distortions from nominal wage rigidities by devaluing the exchange rate, to ensure that the real wage is lowered.

3.5.4 Equilibrium

Households optimise their utility subject to their budget constraints and choose the composition of their consumption basket and borrowing. In equilibrium, the market for non-tradables clears

$$c_t^N = y_t^N. \tag{3.12}$$

Each period, the country receives y_t^T endowment per household, stochastically and exogenously decided. To ensure there is a cost associated with default, it is assumed that $L\left(y_t^T\right)$ is a loss-function that is positive and increasing, so that

$$L\left(y_t^T\right) = \max\left\{0, \delta_1 y_t^T + \delta_2 \left(y_t^T\right)^2\right\}.$$

If the country is not in default, output is simply equal to the endowment y_t^T. The loss-function also dissuades countries from defaulting during boom-times. The natural logarithm of tradable output y_t^T, follows the law of motion and is given by

$$\ln\left(y_t^T\right) = \rho\ln\left(y_{t-1}^T\right) + \eta\mu_t, \tag{3.13}$$

where μ is an independent random variable with mean equal to 0 and standard deviation η, while ρ is a positive parameter with a value between 0 and one governing the autocorrelation of output. The total consumption of tradables is chosen according to

$$c_t^T = y_t^T - \left(1 - R_t\right)L\left(y_t^T\right) + R_t\left[q_t d_{t+1} - d_t\right]. \tag{3.14}$$

When the country is not in default, the price of its debt q_t^d must equal what is offered by foreign lenders q_t, otherwise nobody would be willing to offer credit, so that

$$R_t\left(q_t^d - q_t\right) = 0. \tag{3.15}$$

It follows that the law of one price also holds for actual prices, as with the price of money, so that

$$P_t^T = P_t^{T*}\varepsilon_t,$$

where ε_t is the nominal exchange rate from last period to t, so when ε_t goes up, the currency for the donor country depreciates. The price of foreign traded goods is normalised to one for simplicity. Finally

$$\left(1 - R_t\right)\tau_t^d = 0, \tag{3.16}$$

$$\left(1 - R_t\right)d_{t+1} = 0, \tag{3.17}$$

$$R_t\left[q_t - \frac{E_t R_{t+1}}{1 + r^*}\right] \doteq 0, \tag{3.18}$$

$$\frac{A_2\left(c_t^T, F\left(h_t\right)\right)}{A_1\left(c_t^T, F\left(h_t\right)\right)} = \frac{w_t}{F'\left(h_t\right)}. \tag{3.19}$$

Given the assumption of optimal monetary policy, the government can set the exchange rate ε_t and the level of the debt tax τ_t^d. Then the stochastic processes of consumption c_t^T, labour h_t, debt in the next period d_{t+1}, and the price of debt q_t, are given by processes of traded output y_t^T and the choice of default R_t, and initial condition of debt d_0.

3.5.5 Default

The government only engages in default when it is economically beneficial to do so. Default occurs when the loss of output by repayment v^r, is bigger than default v^d, or

$$v^r\left(y_t^T, d_t\right) < v^d\left(y_t^T\right).\tag{3.20}$$

The left-hand side of the equation is the value of being able to access international capital markets and the right-hand side is the value of being in default. Continued repayment $R_t = 1$, has a value of

$$v^r\left(y_t^T, d_t\right) = \max_{\{d_{t+1}, h_t, c_t^T\}}\left\{U\left(A\left(c_t^T, F(h_t)\right)\right) + \beta E_t v^g\left(y_{t+1}^T, d_{t+1}\right)\right\}\tag{3.21}$$

Where the last expression is the value of continued markets access, the optimal level of $h_t = \bar{h}$, and it is subject to

$$c_t^T + d_t = y_t^T + q\left(y_t^T, d_{t+1}\right)d_{t+1}.$$

The value of default $\left(v^d\right)$ and the value of having access to capital markets $\left(v^g\right)$ are

$$v^d\left(y_t^T\right) = \max_{h_t}\left\{\begin{array}{l} U\left(A\left(y_t^T - L\left(y_t^T\right), F(h_t)\right)\right) + \\ \beta E_t\left(\theta v^g\left(y_{t+1}^T, 0\right) + (1-\theta)v^d\left(y_{t+1}^T\right)\right)\end{array}\right\},\tag{3.22}$$

$$v^g\left(y_t^T, d_t\right) = \max\left\{v^r\left(y_t^T, d_t\right), v^d\left(y_t^T\right)\right\}.\tag{3.23}$$

The default set is then given in terms of tradable-output levels of d_t

$$D(d_t) = \left[y_t^T : v^r\left(y_y^T, d_t\right) < v^d\left(y_t^T\right)\right].\tag{3.24}$$

Equation (3.24) can be thought of as the optimal policy reaction of when to default, given the government's wish to maximise the full-employment real wage

$$w^f\left(c_t^T\right) = \frac{A_2\left(c_t^T, F(\bar{h})\right)}{A_1\left(c_t^T, F(\bar{h})\right)}F'(\bar{h}).$$

The probability of default in the next period if the country is repaying is

$$Pr\{R_{t+1} = 0 \mid R_t = 1\} = Pr\{y_{t+1}^T \in D(d_{t+1})\},\tag{3.25}$$

and the price of the country's debt as a function of tradable output and the debt level is

$$q\left(y_t^T, d_{t+1}\right) = \frac{1 - Pr\{y_{t+1}^T \in D(d_{t+1}) \mid y_t^T\}}{1 + r^*}.\tag{3.26}$$

It is therefore possible to give the optimal size of the devaluation, specified by the policy rule that stabilises nominal wages, by

$$\varepsilon_t = \frac{w_{t-1}}{w^f\left(c_t^T\right)}.\tag{3.27}$$

It is assumed that the government sets the optimal level of exchange rates as the regime is that of optimal monetary policy. As shown by Na et al. (2018), the value functions under the assumption of optimal monetary policy are similar to Arellano (2008).

3.5.6 Calibration

The calibration of the model is done to try and capture some of the larger reparations cases in the following chapters. It means that three calibrations are performed: to France in the 1870s (the Franco-Prussian Wars indemnity); to Germany in the 1930s (World War I reparations); and Finland in the 1940s (World War II reparations). The output process of (3.13) is estimated using ordinary least squares for each of the episodes. Figure 3.4 shows real GDP per capita from 1860 to 1960 for the countries studied, with the log of output and the structural trend on the left and the cyclical component obtained by log-quadratic detrending on the right.

The choice is motivated by the fact that a log-quadratic approach explains a lot more of the cyclical deviations than a log-linear approach. The results do not depend on the choice of detrending method. Figure 3.5 shows the cyclical components of output using log-linear detrending method to the left (King et al. 1988), and HP(100) filtering to the right. There are substantial differences in the length of the suggested business cycles, but the contraction in cyclical output in the years after reparations transfers is similar. As an example, for France from 1870 to 1873, the deviation from the secular trend changes by less than 1 per cent across all methods. The other episodes are similar. Quadratic detrending is therefore used throughout the book.

The autocorrelation and standard deviation of the cyclical trend used in the model are estimated from 1860 to 1930 before the German default. It therefore avoids the volatile period of World War II in the standard deviation parameter.[27] The output process yields the following for the three countries

$$\ln\left(y_t^T\right)_{\text{France}} = 0.932 \ln\left(y_{t-1}^T\right) + 0.037 \mu_t,$$

$$\ln\left(y_t^T\right)_{\text{Germany}} = 0.932 \ln\left(y_{t-1}^T\right) + 0.039 \mu_t,$$

$$\ln\left(y_t^T\right)_{\text{Finland}} = 0.932 \ln\left(y_{t-1}^T\right) + 0.043 \mu_t.$$

[27] Autocorrelations of the cyclical component of real GDP are 0.958 (France), 0.941 (Germany), and 0.907 (Finland) for annual data. To avoid unrealistic distributional assumptions in making the number into quarterly to fit the model, the standard parameter in the literature is used for ρ. The standard deviations would be 0.072, 0.083, and 0.042 if the full period to 1960 was used.

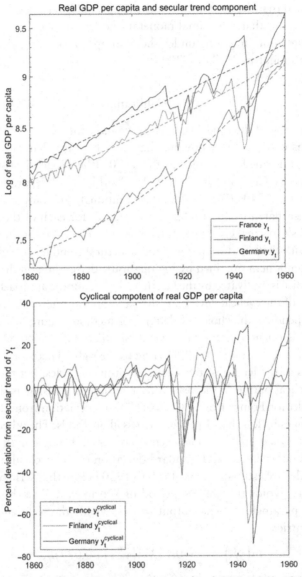

FIGURE 3.4 Secular and cyclical components of real GDP (1860–1960).
Note: log-quadratic detrending used to obtain cyclical trend. The dashed line
is the secular trend (left-hand). Replication file, *lqtrend_p2.m.*
Source: Bolt et al. (2018) data for output.

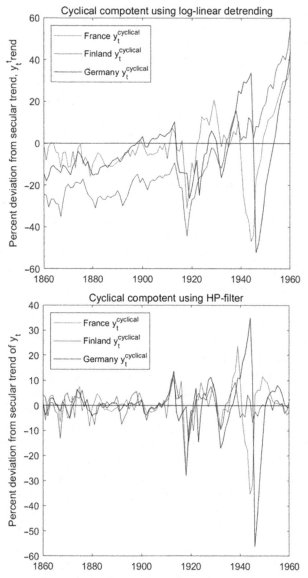

FIGURE 3.5 Log-linear detrending and HP-filter of real GDP (1860–1960).
Source: Bolt et al. (2018). Replication file, *alt_trends.m*.

In addition to the autocorrelation of output, several parameters are used across the three episodes. All are standard in the literature and follow Na et al. (2018). The inverse of elasticity of intertemporal substitution of consumption is set at $\sigma = 2$, while the elasticity of consumption between traded goods and non-traded goods is $1/\sigma = 0.5$. The share of tradables in consumption is $a = 0.26$. Steady state traded output y^T and the labour endowment $\bar{h}$ are both set at unity. The value of the subjective discount factor $\beta = 0.85$, which might seem low, but higher values of β worsen the overall fit of the model.[28] The range for traded output is set between 0.7 and 1.5. Following Na et al. (2018), 200 grid points are assumed for both output and debt. Their simulation approach for computing the transition probability matrix for tradable output is used. Figure 3.6 shows the density distribution of external debt for the calibrations. Germany's debt level is assumed to fall between 0 and 200 per cent of tradable output, while France and Finland have an upper limit of 150 per cent, which are well outside each country's actual minimum and maximum debt levels, as I will show in later chapters. The time unit of the model is in quarters of a year.

The rest of the model parameters are episode specific. For the calibration of the French economy between 1870 and 1873, I follow Devereux and Smith (2007). The labour share of the non-traded sector is $\alpha = 0.64$, which is slightly lower than the literature. It is justified by a larger share of profits and rents to fixed factors than is the case in more recent studies. The annual world risk-free interest rate at the time was 3.7 per cent. The time-unit of the model is a quarter, so $r^* = 0.0092$. It is the average interest rate of UK prime bank bills between 1870 and 1873, which was the largest bond market at the time.[29] Because France did not default, the parameter setting the length of default is $\theta = 0.0385$ following Chatterjee and Eyigungor (2012). The value implies that the country is in default on average for around 6.5 years.[30] The first loss-function parameter, δ_1, is calibrated to −0.35 while the second is estimated, $\delta_2 = \dfrac{(1-\delta_1)}{2} / \max(y^T)$. Taken together with $\beta = 0.85$, it implies an average debt-to-GDP ratio

---

[28] The next section shows the sensitivity of output for various values of β.

[29] Chiţu et al. (2014) show the US dollar overtook sterling as the dominant currency for bond issuance around the Great Depression. Accordingly, the United States is used as the risk-free rate for Germany and Finland.

[30] A default of 6.5 years is around the average for 100 systemic crises (Reinhart and Rogoff 2014, p. 50).

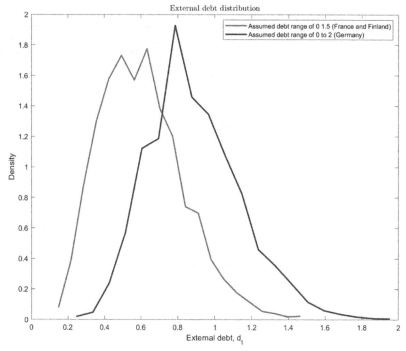

FIGURE 3.6 Distribution of external debt.
Note: Depending on the country being in good financial standing. Replication file, *debt_dist.m*.

around 72 per cent for France when it is not in default, close to its actual debt-to-GDP in 1871 (Table 3.1).

For the German 1930–33 calibration, labour's share of income is set at $\alpha = 0.60$ as the aggregate labour share of national income was close to 0.6 leading up to the default (Ritschl 2002, table b.5). Imputed wages would have to be calculated in trade and agriculture, but given the lack of data and a low degree of mechanization in these sectors, it is assumed they are close to the aggregate. The average annual risk-free rate on US 3-month Treasury bills was 1.4 per cent, so that $r^* = 0.0035$. $\theta = 0.0312$, which implies a length of default of around eight years. Germany first defaulted on its sovereign debt in 1932 and was in default until the end of World War II, but forcibly regained access to borrowing in 1940 (Klug 1993, pp. 9–12). The loss-function parameters $\delta_1 = -0.32$ and $\delta_2 = 0.42$ are calibrated for a debt-to-GDP ratio of close to 110 per cent,

TABLE 3.1 *Model parameters*

			France (1870–73)	Germany (1930–33)	Finland (1945–48)
Episode specific	α	Labour share in the non-traded sector	0.64	0.6	0.75
	a	Share of tradables	0.5	0.26	0.26
	r^*	Risk free return (quarterly)	0.0092	0.0035	0.0024
	θ	Probability of escaping default	0.0385	0.0312	0.0385
	δ_1	Loss-function	−0.35	−0.32	−0.31
	δ_2	Loss-function	0.44	0.42	0.40
	η	Standard deviation	0.037	0.039	0.43
Standard parameters (same across)	ρ	Autocorrelation of output	0.932		
	σ	Inverse of elasticity of substitution in consumption	2		
	ξ	Elasticity of substitution between traded and non-traded	0.5		
	y^T	Steady-state traded output	1		
	$\bar{h}$	Labour endowment	1		
	β	Discount factor	0.85		
Discretisation of state space		Traded output range	0.7–1.5		
		Debt range	0–1.5		
		Grid points for output	200		
		Grid points for debt	200		

as German debt-to-GDP exceeded 100 per cent in 1931 (Papadia and Schioppa 2015, p. 6).

For the calibration of the Finnish economy from 1945 to 1948, $\alpha = 0.75$, which is standard in the literature. The world risk-free rate is still the US three-month Treasury bill rate, which averaged 1.0 per cent, so that $r^* = 0.0024$. As in France, given no default $\theta = 0.0385$. The loss-function parameters $\delta_1 = -0.32$ and $\delta_2 = 0.40$ are calibrated for a debt-to-GDP ratio of close to 65 per cent.

3.5.7 Sensitivity

Table 3.2 shows the model's sensitivities to changing various parameters. The baseline model is the German calibration, which is denoted by a star. The table shows model statistics for the frequency of default, d/y denotes the average debt-to-GDP ratio in per cent, $r - r^*$ is the credit spread in annual per cent, y is detrended output, and tb is the trade balance. Sigma denotes the standard deviation and corr the correlation.

Figure 3.7 shows the model estimates for different values the subjective discount factor β for the German calibration. As the discount rate is lowered (higher β) the present cost of default goes up. For $\beta = 0.95$, the median output loss before default increases to over 20 per cent. A higher value of β worsens the fit of the structural credit spread across episodes.

3.6 STYLISED MACROECONOMIC FACTS ABOUT SOVEREIGN DEBT DEFAULTS

The model allows for the characterisation of certain stylised facts that typically accompany a sovereign debt default. It is simulated under optimal monetary policy, where the government can freely choose the exchange rate and the debt tax, across 1.1 million quarters for each of the

TABLE 3.2 *Model statistics*

	Default frequency	d/y	$r - r^*$	$\sigma(r - r^*)$	corr$(r - r^*, y)$	corr$(r - r^*,$ tb/y$)$
$\beta = 0.85^*$	1.90	86	2.33	2.18	−0.48	0.81
$\beta = 0.90$	0.96	112	1.05	1.31	−0.47	0.82
$\beta = 0.95$	0.29	150	0.31	0.61	−0.49	0.81
$\rho = 0.91$	0.08	200	0.09	0.26	−0.56	0.51
$\rho = 0.932^*$	0.96	112	1.05	1.31	−0.47	0.82
$\rho = 0.95$	1.98	52	2.40	2.77	−0.45	0.79
$\rho = 0.97$	3.94	17	6.19	7.26	−0.30	0.42
$\eta = 0.035$	0.53	177	0.55	0.79	−0.56	0.86
$\eta = 0.039^*$	0.96	112	1.05	1.31	−0.47	0.82
$\eta = 0.045$	1.62	56	1.84	2.09	−0.43	0.82
$a = 0.10$	0.95	112	1.05	1.31	−0.47	0.82
$a = 0.26^*$	0.96	112	1.05	1.31	−0.47	0.82
$a = 0.50$	0.98	112	1.05	1.31	−0.47	0.82
$\alpha = 0.30$	0.94	112	1.05	1.31	−0.47	0.82
$\alpha = 0.60^*$	0.96	112	1.05	1.31	−0.47	0.82
$\alpha = 0.75$	0.94	112	1.05	1.31	−0.47	0.82

Source: Tables can be replicated by running *statistics_model_germany.m* with the varying calibrations from the German model, which is used as baseline and denoted by star.

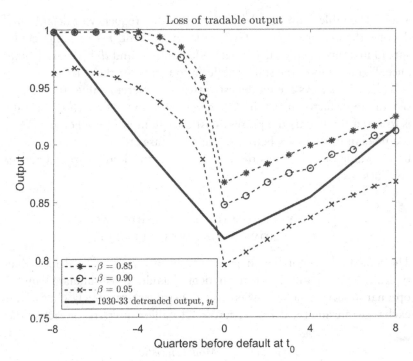

FIGURE 3.7 German model output for different values of β.
Source: Bolt et al. (2018). Replication file, *plot_b.m.*

three calibrations, where the first 0.1 million simulations are discarded. The approach follows that of Na et al. (2018). The median values are calculated for y_t^T, c_t^T, d_t, w_t, ϵ_t, p_t, and the credit spread on external debt. The time of default is then normalised at t_0. Figure 3.8 shows the median of each macroeconomic indicator in the two years before and two years after default at t_0, for the French, German, and Finnish calibration. The time scale is again in quarters of a year.

Three stylised facts can be observed: first, as in most models of sovereign debt, a default occurs after a continuous contraction in tradable output across a short period of time. y_t^T falls 12 per cent (France), 13 per cent (Germany), and 14 per cent (Finland) in less than one year before the government defaults at t_0 which triggers the loss-function $L\left(y_t^T\right)$. The government chooses to default when the cost of debt service is higher than the benefits of continued ability to borrow, as specified by the value functions (3.20) to (3.24). As the risk of default increases, the risk premium on external debt goes up. Higher interest rates discourage

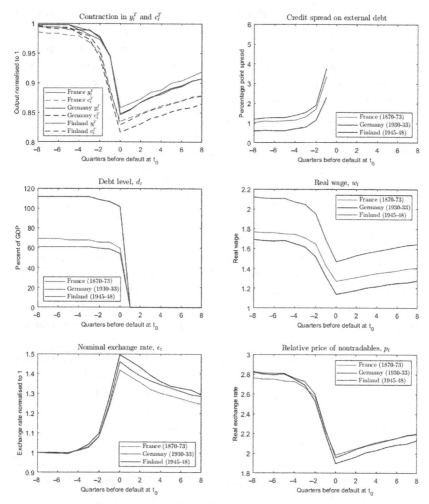

FIGURE 3.8 Stylised sovereign debt defaults.
Note: Replication file, *plot_model.m*.

borrowing so that the consumption of tradables c_t^T falls more than y_t^T. Second, default is accompanied by a large devaluation of both the nominal exchange rate ϵ_t, and the real exchange rate, shown by the relative price of non-tradables p_t. The devaluation is not followed by a bout of inflation as nominal prices remain stable. Third, the reason there is no inflation is that the real wage w_t declines, which lowers the real labour costs of firms. The three stylised facts are all characterised in equilibrium.

The output contraction that leads to default is mostly a function of subjective discount factor β, the volatility of the economy η, and its auto-correlation ρ. With a higher level of β, households will be more patient and ready to forego current for future consumption. The cost of default goes up with a higher β, which makes countries default less often. Fewer defaults decrease the country risk premium and increase the level of sustainable debt. An increase in the level of volatility in the economy η has the reverse effect. A higher permanent volatility of output drives up the default frequency because there are more large negative income shocks, which increases the risk premium on external debt. The level of desired savings increases to protect against the volatility, which lowers the level of debt. Increasing the autocorrelation of output ρ increases the default frequency and lowers the level of debt. The reason is that output costs of default are present at high levels of output. The lower ρ is, the more likely it is that output will be higher soon, which lowers the frequency of defaults. The level of real wages and the relative price level are affected by changes to a and α, but the direction of the adjustment before a default is not, neither is the frequency of default. The loss-function parameters (δ_1, δ_2) are calibrated to ensure the model matches the level of debt-to-GDP as observed.

The central bank can set the nominal exchange rate ϵ_t, which ensures that the external crisis does not spread to the non-traded sector. The government can also set the level of taxes on external debt τ_t^d, which in a historical setting is best interpreted as the introduction of capital controls. Using the same estimation for τ_t^d as for the other macroeconomic indicators, Figure 3.9 shows the median level of capital controls in the two years before a default. The model thus captures the introduction of capital controls in the years leading up to a sovereign default, as was the case in Germany in the 1930s.

The model as outlined here assumes optimal policy from the government with respect to the default decision and in setting the exchange rate and capital controls. A central theme of this book is that governments have not always had the option to do that. Countries might not have had the option to default or devalue their exchange rate or they have been discouraged from levying capital controls from their neighbours or creditors. Why assume optimality in policymaking? It is certainly possible to include wage and currency rigidities alongside explicit financial sanctions. But the point of the analysis is to explain *optimal* sovereign debt policy and compare it with reparations policy. By judging the historical episodes through a sovereign debt framework, it is possible to

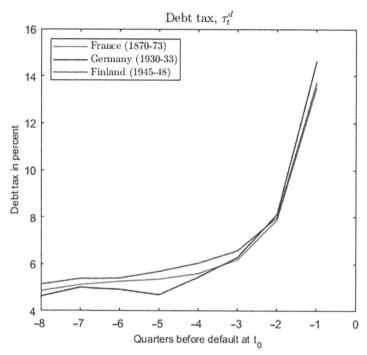

Debt tax, τ_t^d

FIGURE 3.9 Estimate of capital controls.
Note: Replication file, *plot_tau.m*.

understand how extraordinary times of war reparations were. If the macroeconomic conditions are far worse than when countries default, it tells us that the enforcement mechanism for reparations debt is more binding than for other types of sovereign debt.

3.7 THE SOVEREIGN DEBT DEFAULT SET

The stylised facts of sovereign debt default presented in Section 3.5 can help analyse the special case of war reparations. To apply the analysis to historical cases, the following chapters provide the context around how the reparations were paid. The default set (equation 3.24) is shown graphically in Figure 3.10 for each of the three calibrations, with the level of debt on the y-axis and tradable output on the x-axis. The colour white denotes the area in which the government repays debt, while the grey area denotes where the government defaults. The figure shows how to interpret the model and compare it with the repayment of war reparations.

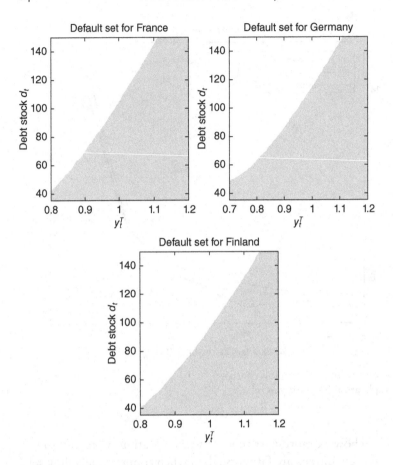

FIGURE 3.10 Default sets.
Note: The grey area is the state denotes repayment while the white area is default. Replication file, *plot_default_sets.m.*

To apply the model to historical data, the reparation is interpreted as an unexpected increase in the state variable d_0. At t_0 the country learns that it must pay the reparation, which is captured by a decrease in net output by the term $y_0 - d_0$. It is then possible to see where the level of net output lies in the default set, given historical data for the other macroeconomic variables. It will allow us to understand the costs of paying reparations and whether the optimal policy would have been to default. The model output is compared with historical data in Chapters 6, 8, and 10, for which I collected data for real GDP, credit spreads, debt levels, real wages, nominal exchange rates, and real exchange rates for the three cases.[31] This is where the book changes tack, with the remaining chapters leaving theory and looking at the large reparations cases since 1800. The first one is the reparation France paid following the Napoleonic Wars, which was paid in full ahead of time thanks to France's ability to issue large amounts of sovereign debt.

---

[31] Because of the lack of sectoral GDP for the period, tradable output is proxied by detrended real GDP per capita, available yearly.

4

Napoleonic Wars Reparations

By 1814, the Napoleonic Wars had been ongoing for eleven years, and France had been in political and economic turmoil for some time before that. War-weary and still without a decisive victory, Britain suggested a defensive alliance with Austria, Prussia, and Russia in 1814. Initially, the goal was peace; war reparations were not discussed. The Treaty of Chaumont of 1814 suggested a peace alliance of twenty years, threatening continued war if Napoleon did not agree to a cease-fire and the reversion to pre-revolution borders. The British would subsidise all expenses (Artz 1934, pp. 110–18). The settlement risked peace with Napoleon still on the throne of France, but almost certainly ensured a victory for the Allies (Schroeder 1996, pp. 501–14). Reparations were not part of Chaumont, and the offer suggests the goal was not to destroy France. On the contrary, ending the war was prioritised over full surrender. This proposal, however, was rejected. Napoleon ordered his army to continue fighting, forcing the Allies to assault Paris on 31 March 1814. Their assault was successful, and Napoleon was expelled to Elba on 11 April (Treaty of Fontainebleau, 1814). The armistice was signed on 23 April, followed by the Treaty of Paris on 30 May. According to the Treaty of Paris, French borders returned to their 1792 lines, allowing France to keep some revolutionary gains in Belgium, Italy, and Germany. The Allies' soldiers left Paris three days later (White 2001, p. 338).

These treaties managed the wars' immediate end. However, the alliance between the four major powers that had ended the war (Austria, Britain, Prussia, and Russia) did not last long. Prussia and Russia had agreed in the 1813 Treaty of Kalisz to divide up Saxony and Poland, substantially altering the balance of power in Europe. The Congress of Vienna was convened for 1 October 1814, to settle the peace more durably. In January 1815, Austria and Britain aligned with their former French foe to force them to abandon it. The issue was settled with all five countries recognised as the Great Powers of Europe (Chapman 1998, p. 16). It was during these negotiations that Napoleon escaped from Elba, raised an army, attempted to launch an attack on Britain – and was promptly defeated at Waterloo, ending what became known as the Hundred Days War.

This escape had nearly allowed France to become the European hegemon once more. The following peace settlement was therefore renegotiated on much less generous terms. In total, 150,000 Allied soldiers occupied France. Each nation provided 30,000 men and commanders, with an additional 10,000 soldiers from Bavaria and 5,000 from each of Denmark, Saxony, Hanover, and Württemberg. The French government paid all their expenses, including 50 million francs for wages (Veve 1989, p. 99). Louis XVIII was allowed to return to France to rule, with backing from the Allies. The Second Treaty of Paris reduced France's borders even further, to their 1790 limits (Chapman 1998, pp. 33–60). Reparations were introduced, this time with a dual purpose: to ensure there was no third attempt at war and as an incentive to gradually reintroduce France into the balance of power in Europe. Occupation would only end upon full repayment (White 2001, pp. 355–56).

The Second Treaty of Paris set out a payment schedule for the war reparations, indemnities, and occupation costs. War reparations were set at 700 million francs, as a punishment for Napoleon's failed Hundred Days War. Reparations were to be paid in four-month instalments over five years, beginning in December 1815. Late payment would carry an interest rate of 5 per cent (White 2001, p. 340). Reparations were not the sole expense France had to shoulder; it also had to bear the costs of occupation for as long as repayment lasted.

In 1815, the reparation cost was 180 million francs, with 150 million francs each subsequent year until 1821. The occupational costs were structured as a bond: France delivered 7 million *rentes*, that is 140 million francs face-value consols, carrying a 5 per cent coupon, for the duration of the occupation. The bond could be sold in case of non-payment (Vuhrer 1886, pp. 59–100). If France was able to repay ahead of schedule, occupation costs would be reduced. Actual occupation costs therefore amounted to 660 million francs as France repaid early, instead of 930 million francs, including 27 million francs for the removal of troops from France. Finally, indemnities worth 321 million francs were specified

TABLE 4.1 *French reparations (million francs)*

	Second Treaty of Paris	Payments made
War reparations	700	686
Occupation costs (five years)	930	660
Indemnities	321	501
Penalties	–	17
Foregone foreign debt	–	43
Total	1.951	1.907

Source: Second Treaty of Paris (1815); Nicolle (1929, pp. 186–89); White (2001, p. 341).

in the Treaty. Originally, each country had claimed far higher numbers, citing pre-war debt, wartime borrowing, and requisitions. Over 1.5 billion francs of claims were submitted which France managed to negotiate down to 321 million francs (Vuhrer 1886, p. 96).

The French legislature approved the indemnity payments in May 1818, alongside a more centralised control of taxes and expenditures (Oosterlinck et al. 2014, p. 1086). In addition, France ended up paying a further 180 million francs in indemnities to foreign individuals (Nicolle 1929, pp. 186–89). Table 4.1 summarises the required and actual payments made between 1815 and 1819.[1]

The French paid reparations quicker than set out by the Second Treaty of Paris, with very little difference between the agreed and actual sums. Given the speed of repayment, France incurred lower occupational costs, but indemnity payments turned out higher than initially anticipated. In terms of size compared with the French economy, data for France's total output is somewhat unreliable. The best estimates are found in Oosterlinck et al. (2014) and Toutain (1997). Average GDP for the period (1815–19) is estimated at around 8.6 billion francs. This figure is used throughout the book, but is not useful to measure model fit because it is an estimate and no time-series is available.[2] With this in mind, total reparations payment represented around 22 per cent of average GDP. A sizeable expenditure to finance for a government whose share of output was only estimated at around 9 per cent of the economy – even more

[1] As noted by White (2001), France also had a range of (domestic) budgetary arrears related to Napoleon's 1815–16 campaign. Revolutionary-related confiscations were settled between 1816 and 1825.

[2] Levy-Leboyer and Bourguignon (1990, p. 322) estimate 9.1 billion GDP and White (2001) use 9.2 billion francs as a yearly average GDP estimate throughout the period.

sizeable when one considers the need to rebuild infrastructure after years of war.[3] The payment is visible in French trade and government budget balances (Figure 4.1), where the dotted lines are the balances net of reparations payments.

The French paid a combination of reparations, indemnities, occupational costs, and penalties from 1815 to 1819, meaning that the average annual expenditure was just under 4.5 per cent of GDP per year. As Figure 4.1 shows, France was initially close to financing the payment from the government budget and the trade balance, although as payments grew it had to raise debt as well. The solid lines are the actual trade and government budget balance. The trade balance is net of specie flows. One interpretation of the gap between the lines is that it is the forgone net domestic investment amount from financing the transfer, which was as high as 9 per cent in 1818.

Regarding the government budget balance, France ran an austere policy. When indemnity is discounted, the fiscal balance was positive. Both the trade and fiscal balances show that funding was available without borrowing; that more goods were sold than bought; and that more taxes were collected than money spent. If the combination of the trade and fiscal balances were higher than reparations, no debt would need to be raised. France needed little external financing in the early years of the repayment, as fiscal revenues increased by 20 per cent from 1816 to 1817 (Oosterlinck et al. 2014, p. 1077).[4] The full reparations amount is included in the figure, even though most of the indemnity was structured as an off-balance sheet issuance of *rentes* (White 2001, p. 343). While it had the effect of circumventing the government budget balance, the macroeconomic effects are the same: interest must be paid and net foreign assets shift accordingly. Consequently, French debt-to-GDP doubled from under 20 per cent in 1815 to over 40 per cent in 1819, as seen in Figure 4.2.

The French Revolution had destroyed France's credit profile, and Napoleon had financed the war mostly by taxes rather than debt or

---

[3] Total government expenditures were 799 million francs in 1815. General government finances are found in Séguin (1824), Vuhrer (1886), and Mallez (1927), available at the Banque de France and Bayerische Staatsbibliothek online archives. Calmon (1870) is available at the Banque de France online archive. Fiscal expenditures from 1816 are found in Oosterlinck et al. (2014, p. 1077).

[4] A chicken and egg problem, as the figure can also be interpreted to mean that balances went negative *because* France raised money internationally. As these are accounting identities, the causality can be argued both ways.

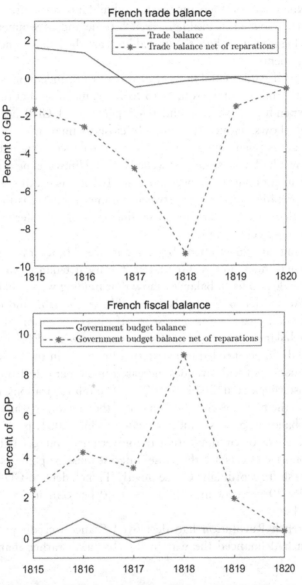

FIGURE 4.1 French trade balance and fiscal balance (1815–20).
Note: The entire reparations payment is used for the dotted line, even if
financed off-balance sheet. Replication file, *plot_france_tbg.m*.
Source: Nicolle (1929, pp. 186–89) for reparations; Toflit18 database as presented in Charles and Daudin (2015) for the trade balance, where I have netted
out specie flows; Oosterlinck et al. (2014, p. 1077) for the fiscal balance; for
GDP, see text.

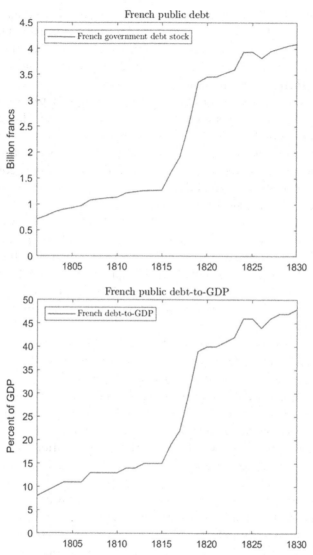

FIGURE 4.2 French government debt stock (1800–30).
Source: Debt data shared by Oosterlinck et al. (2014, pp. 1074–75); for GDP
data, see text. Replication file, *plot_french_d.m.*

money printing (Bordo and White 1991).[5] The French ability to borrow internationally had returned somewhat during the war, but large-
scale borrowing was not initially undertaken to finance the payments

---

[5] This was in stark contrast to the British, whose fiscal and monetary capacity to raise
funds had been key to victory (Antipa and Chamley 2017).

(Greenfield 2016). The long war (and preceding revolution) had impoverished France. Raising large loans in addition to increasing taxes was 'ridiculed' by French bankers at the time, who said that the market would not absorb loans to France (White 2001, p. 345). The initial outlays were therefore mostly funded by attempts to run balanced budgets, which meant that the government had to run large, net-of-reparations surpluses. As Figure 4.1 shows, this was mainly the case. However, the pay-as-you-go budget policy of using incoming taxes to pay for expenditures meant that the government ran into trouble when taxes were not forthcoming. Interest rates were not exorbitant, but debt could only be issued in small amounts. France issued some debt in 1816 and 1817, but not enough to pay the reparations, and jobs were cut while taxes were raised (White 2001, pp. 342–43).[6] In 1815, 36 million francs of *rentes* were issued at 9.8 per cent yield, and a further 70 million was raised abroad in London and Hamburg in 1816. Additional funds were raised from shorter-term bills, but at significant cost of 12 per cent (Calmon 1870, pp. 139–230). As a comparison, during the same period the British issued debt with a yield below 5 per cent (Homer and Sylla 2005, p. 192).

France still missed payments, which resulted in penalties and arrears. Some of the occupational forces threatened to increase the number of their soldiers, which would have worsened the fiscal outlook even further. As it became clear borrowing would be required, the interest rate France would have to pay on longer-term bonds increased (Figure 4.3), with markets unwilling to offer large loans. Negotiations were happening with foreign banks but broke down because of opposition to repayment by French Ultras, the conservative landholders (Oosterlinck et al. 2014, pp. 1081–83).

It was not until two international banks, Barings Brothers in London and Hope & Company in Amsterdam, offered to underwrite a debt issue that large-scale debt financing was attempted (Oosterlinck et al. 2014). Until early 1817, large debt issuances were considered impossible. As Greenfield (2016) shows, higher interest rates, lower placed amounts, and domestic politics made such issuances impossible. In February 1817, the French government tried anyway and went to the market to raise 100 million francs. It succeeded, paying an average yield of 8.6

---

[6] For example, because of austerity-imposed hardship and a failed harvest, the government was forced to subsidise the price of bread in 1816 (White 2001, p. 344).

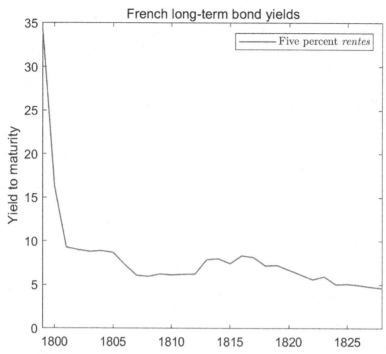

FIGURE 4.3 French long-term bond yields (1799–1830).
Source: Homer and Sylla (2005, p. 217). Replication file, *plot_france_r.m.*

per cent. Perhaps surprisingly given the previous statement by French bankers, over half of the issue was sold on the Paris Bourse. The bond sale was followed by another 100 million francs in March, and a further 115 million francs in July (Calmon 1870, pp. 139–230; White 2001, pp. 346–49). The issues were successful, with over-subscription for a 292 million francs loan in May 1818. This enabled a full settlement of the reparations in 1819.[7] French interest rates came down after the war, as Figure 4.3 shows. The figure shows the long-term interest rate, which is the most important, as it was in the bond markets that France financed reparations.[8]

---

[7] It oversimplifies the story, which includes attempts to corner the market in government debt, failed negotiations, and extensions. See White (2001) and Oosterlinck et al. (2014) for more.

[8] The short-term rate interest rate (not shown) was the interest that the central bank, Banque de France, offered to discount paper overnight. In practice, the short-term rate

French public debt levels increased significantly during the period, as expected, with an annual interest rate cost of around 1.4 per cent of GDP (White 2001, pp. 351–52). It is doubtful that France had many assets left after the war, which made raising debt or selling assets more difficult. A question is therefore what if anything in the French economy changed that made it possible to issue debt. I make two arguments. The first is that the ability to raise debt was always better than proposed by French bankers at the time, as the successful issuances showed. The second argument is that the end of the war coincided with the improved terms of trade, which generated an economic windfall. This meant France's economy improved a lot. To understand how much, Section 4.1 will look at French trade during the time, relying on the terms of trade model from the technical appendix in Chapter 2 to estimate the gains from the terms of trade shock.

4.1 TERMS OF TRADE

The end of the Napoleonic Wars coincided with a dramatic improvement in the French terms of trade. The improvement came with significant volatility, as seen in Figure 4.4, which shows the terms of trade for the period from 1805 to 1820.[9] The changes to the relative price level suggest a fall in the demand for imports and an increase in the demand for exports. The change in prices did not simply take place because of the end of the war, but was caused by a structural change to French trade that occurred during the war. Especially the Continental Blockade between 1806 and 1814 was influential in changing the French structure of trade, of which Crouzet (1964), Davis and Engerman (2006), O'Rourke (2006), and Juhász (2018) have all offered detailed accounts.

The Continental Blockade from 1806 affected international trade structures and relative prices. Import prices in France went up a lot during the blockade. The relative price of imports from non-European countries (such as sugar or raw cotton) was particularly elevated during the blockade. The linen industry was already suffering before the war, but the loss of export opportunities accelerated the decline. Marseilles went from producing industrial output worth 50 million francs in 1789 to 12

---

corresponds to the price at which firms can finance themselves in the money markets. Throughout the first half of the nineteenth century, it was generally static (Homer and Sylla 2005, pp. 224–25).

[9] Data quality is poor, as would be expected for the period, and several of the data points require some or full interpolation. However, different estimates for commodity prices show similar behaviour for the terms of trade (O'Rourke 2006, 2007).

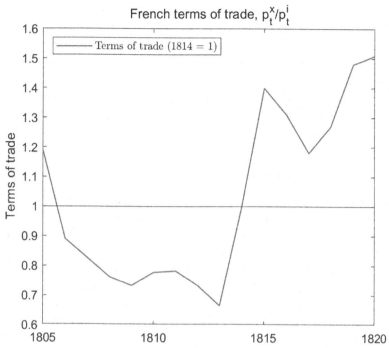

FIGURE 4.4 French terms of trade (1805–20).
Note: The export price index for 1817 is extrapolated from 1816 and 1818.
Replication file, *plot_france_tot.m*.
Source: Estimates based on Esteban (1987).

million francs in 1813 (Crouzet 1964, p. 571). O'Rourke (2006) suggests a welfare loss of between 3 and 4 per cent for France in the years during the blockade because of higher import prices. The structural changes to the economy were significant, as exemplified by the important sector of textiles. Juhász (2018, pp. 3372–73) shows that France turned from a net importer of cotton manufactures at the start of the war to become a net exporter by the end of the war.

The blockade was officially lifted in 1814 having collapsed a year earlier. French (and other continental) industries were hurt by the loss of overseas trading owing to the blockade, and European ports lost a lot of trade. If the changes to import and export prices were simply brought about by the end of the war, the relative level would not necessarily change as the same effects would be present to France's trading partners. As France turned from a war to a peace economy, the terms of trade turned in its favour. Peacetime demand for French luxury products, an improved manufacturing export sector, and a reopening of the global trading system all acted as positive catalysts for a large positive economic shock to France. This coincided with the negative shock from the reparations transfer.

In recent empirical studies, Schmitt-Grohé and Uribe (2018) find in thirty-eight emerging market economies between 1980 and 2011 that terms of trade shocks explain less than 10 per cent of movements in output. But the terms of trade improvement in France was large and coincided with the reparations transfer.

4.2 HOW FRANCE PAID REPARATIONS

The chapter has so far outlined how France experienced a positive terms of trade shock as the war came to an end and has given a historical overview. It is now time to try and put those two together to suggest how France was economically able to repay the entire reparation ahead of time. I show that the gain from the terms of trade improvement is approximately similar to the cost of the reparation. I attempt to explain the French history in a theoretical setting to infer the reaction of missing historical variables such as the level of output, investments, and consumption, but some assumptions are needed. The historical context provides the backdrop for many assumptions and modelling choices as outlined in Chapter 2, Section 2.4, but the most important choices are restated here. First, data availability for the period is less good than for reparations in the twentieth century.[10] Second, France is treated as a small open economy: in 1820, it only made up about 5 per cent of the world economy (Maddison 2007, p. 379). This means France was likely a price-taker on international markets, with exports accounting for less than 10 per cent of its economy (Levy-Leboyer and Bourguignon 1990, pp. 322–27). Third, the economy had no significant capital controls or frictions. France increased tariffs in 1815 and 1819, but the magnitude was minor (Pahre 1998, p. 487), and all indications are that capital flowed freely across borders.[11] Fourth, it is assumed there were few

---

[10] As described earlier, output data is static and consumption data is not available. Reliable data on the total investment share of the economy are hard to come by. Toutain (1997) and Levy-Leboyer and Bourguignon (1990) suggest that investments did not expand but with little elaboration.

[11] Capital controls in small open economy models are often modelled as a tax on external borrowing (e.g., Schmitt-Grohé and Uribe 2016), but as earlier in the chapter capital flowed into France with few restrictions. The sovereign debt model presented in Chapter 3 has explicit capital controls.

product varieties, which allows for some simplifying assumptions about the structure of the economy. Fifth, because of no detailed consumption and output data, I am looking for predictions that can be compared with historical data available (terms of trade and the trade balance). Other studies, such as Eugene White (2001, p. 360) estimate a sharp contraction, with consumption falling by 19 per cent over five years, while I suggest a more mixed picture.

It is possible to imply certain macroeconomic reactions from the model in Section 2.4 that fit the historical setting (see Figure 2.5 in Chapter 2). After decades of war and blockade, French infrastructure needed rebuilding. The wars did not see the same degree of physical destruction as wars in the nineteenth century, but expenditures on roads, housing, and utilities were likely neglected in favour of war-related spending. In addition, the blockade caused a structural change to the manufacturing sector. It is possible to imagine that in response to a large positive trade shock, households exchanged leisure for work. The increase in investments is similarly believable, as the marginal product of capital increases, which follows results in Juhász (2018) who finds that the capital-labour ratio did not change. France's export sector expanded as described earlier to take advantage of new opportunities that occurred following the transition to a peacetime economy and expansion of international trade. The economy was not booming for households, which had to pay higher taxes to finance the reparations transfer.

There is no explicit government sector in the model, so government consumption does not feature explicitly. But data is available for government expenditures, which can be used to disaggregate the reparations transfer from normal consumption. Overall government spending saw a sharp increase from 1815, as shown in Figure 4.5. The figure breaks government spending into non-reparations related ('normal') expenditures and reparations-related expenditures. Regular expenditures were relatively stable, with the entire rise in government consumption being payment of reparations. The predicted increase in consumption from the model is around 20 per cent of GDP. We know from this chapter that the transfer was around 22 per cent of GDP. It would imply that the entire gain in terms of consumption from the improved terms of trade goes towards paying the reparation.

Imagine a counterfactual where France did not experience an improvement to its terms of trade at the end of the war. In this, demand for French exports does not increase and does not generate an economic windfall. It means that to pay the reparation, the trade balance must

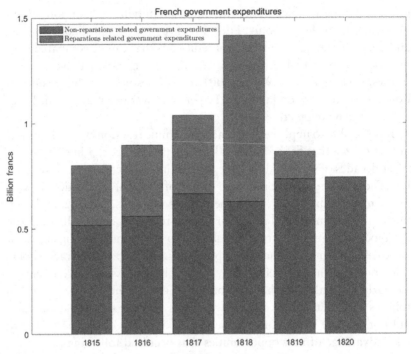

FIGURE 4.5 French government expenditures (1815–20).
Source: White (2001, p. 343). Replication file, *plot_france_gc.m.*

adjust upwards by lowering the level of imports, to repay the higher level of debt. Figure 4.5 would likely look the same, but with no improvement in the terms of trade, the transfer would have to be paid without higher levels of economic activity. The economic hardship of households would therefore be even worse. The formal model comes up with roughly the same as a simple back of the envelope exercise would. If the openness rate of the economy (imports and exports as a share of GDP) is 10 per cent, as suggested earlier, and the terms of trade improvement is roughly 75 per cent, as per Figure 4.4, it would imply roughly a 4 per cent gain a year. As the terms of trade was permanently improved, the 4 per cent gain a year equals around 20 per cent total gain over the five years the reparation was paid, similar to the formal model.

The suggested interpretation is therefore that the Napoleonic Wars reparations were paid out of the terms of trade improvement that followed the end of the war. That is not to say that it is measurable directly in the national accounts, but the economic windfall helped drive output and exports higher, which generated money to repay the transfer and help with debt sustainability. The incentives to repay quickly were considerable, as France was occupied from Calais to the Swiss border for as long as payment was outstanding (Veve 1989, p. 99), but it might not have been possible to have the relaxation of the credit constraint in 1817 without the terms of trade improvement. It was the relaxation of the credit constraint that ultimately allowed France to pay the transfer ahead of schedule, but borrowing is always a function of a country's ability and willingness to repay its debt.

5

Haiti Indemnity and Sovereign Debt

Not all indemnities or reparations lend themselves to short-term economic analysis because some are paid back over many years. The indemnity Haiti paid to France is such an indemnity. It still had very important implications for both the economy and political structure of Haiti many years later. It was a watershed moment in transfers between nations, the indemnity forced issuance of large amounts of sovereign debt, and it left a trail of costs in Haiti that a book such as this at least must mention, albeit briefly: other scholars have done the story more justice. The reasons for imposing war reparations are usually a combination of wanting damages for war, to punish another state, or to gain a geopolitical advantage in the aftermath of the war. The Haitian indemnity was imposed for those reasons, but not by the winner of a war against the loser. No, it was the former French masters that demanded a payment that was many times Haiti's GDP to allow Haiti to maintain independence.

France imposed a reparation on Haiti in 1825 after the former colony gained its independence in 1804 (James 1938; Blackburn 2006). The reparation was justified as compensation for loss of slaves and land, with France conditioning the recognition of Haiti as a sovereign state only against such payments. The imposed indemnity was 150 million gold francs in 1825. The amount is significant when compared with the Haitian economy at any point in time, and Piketty (2020, p. 473) estimates it as being equivalent to 300 per cent of 1825 GDP, while Oosterlinck et al. (2021) estimate it at a slightly lower 270 per cent of GDP. The outstanding reparation was reduced to 90 million francs in 1938, but it was not until 1947, over a century after the initial settlement, that all loans related to the indemnity were paid off (Munro 1969,

p. 25). In the end, Haiti paid the equivalent of 21 billion 2015 US dollars to France (Sommers 2015, p. 124).

Indemnities are by default demanded and not voluntary, but in the case of Haiti, the French came to Haiti in 1825 with a navy. The navy had orders to negotiate but to require reparations (Bruffaerts et al. 2021), although Alex Dupuy (2020) has recently argued that it was in the interest of the Haitian elite to gain recognition of the property rights they had claimed in the years since the revolution and that the indemnity was not entirely a product of French aggression. The size of the indemnity was so big that Haiti did not have the money to pay the reparation, set at 150 million francs to be paid in five instalments. This meant Haiti had to borrow the money, which it did – with France as the creditor. The first loan was negotiated in France just after Haiti agreed to pay. Three diplomats travelled back with the French to seal a financing deal for 30 million francs for the first instalment. Six million francs went to the bankers, which included the Rothschilds, leaving Haiti with 24 million francs in cash. It was a crippling debt Haiti had to borrow, even as 60 million francs of the debt was cancelled in 1838. To pay indemnities, more loans were required, which indebted Haiti because of the size of the indemnity. The outcome is known as the 'double debt' of indemnity payments and increased sovereign debt stock. In some years, more than 40 per cent of government revenues went to pay France (Porter et al. 2022).

To pay interest on its high debt stock, Haiti undertook many revenue generating efforts. These included sales of government land, the issue of domestic loans, and exorbitant taxes on households and exports such as coffee, a main export. But because of the size of the debt, it meant little if any money was left for domestic investments in Haiti, which was lagging behind neighbouring states. While states' fiscal capacities grew across the world during the nineteenth century, Haiti was caught in a death spiral where all available cash went to pay off the French state and its bankers. Critical infrastructure investments in health care, bridges, or roads were neglected as a result. In 1874, there was still 12 million francs of debt outstanding. In 1875, another loan was taken out, this time with a 40 per cent commission to investors and bankers. It paid off the old outstanding debt, but the new debt was also to France.[1]

The impact of the debt is seen in many of the country's financial institutions as well. The National Bank of Haiti was set up by French bankers

---

[1] The history here follows Porter et al. (2022) and Oosterlinck et al. (2021, 2022).

and was headquartered in Paris (it was the bank that financed the Eiffel Tower). This was a profitable enterprise for its French owners, but less so for the domestic economy. By 1915, France was no longer the primary country interfering in Haitian affairs, as the United States was the dominant foreign political actor. National City Bank of New York, today's Citigroup, by this point owned the National Bank of Haiti alongside most of the country's external debt. The New York bank managed to extract enormous payments, with Porter et al. (2022) estimating that 19 per cent of Haiti's government revenues went to pay off the foreign debt between 1825 and 1957. Oosterlinck et al. (2022, p. 1270) calculate that if the indemnity had instead been invested with a real return equal to Haiti's GDP (2.1 per cent between 1825 and 2020), it would have been equal to 160 per cent of current GDP. This is a conservative assumption given that the money could have gone into domestic investments.

By 1957, Haiti was debt free for the first time in 150 years. But the debt had been a contributing factor to ensuring that no good institutions had been built in the country, which had spent most of its fiscal budget on debt and the military. During the period, there were a total of seventeen revolutions or coups. One disaster was followed by another, as the family of François and Jean-Claude Duvalier (Papa Doc and Baby Doc) took over. History can never be explained by one factor, but the indemnity and accompanying debt was a contributing factor to the difficulty in building good institutions, as elites stole money and had incentives to maintain status quo.

Enforcement of Haiti's sovereign debt was threefold. Initially, it was enforced by the gunboats France sent to 'negotiate' the indemnity. As with other indemnities, there was a military component. But unlike most other transfers, there was an incentive for local elites to agree to the transfer to enshrine the political structure that emerged after independence. Finally, in the decades after the original agreement, Haiti's sovereign debt was enforced by international financial institutions by first France and later the US, who had large monetary incentives to keep the country indebted.

Does this mean that Haiti's sovereign debt can be considered odious in hindsight? Oosterlinck et al. (2021, 2022) argue that the answer is yes, and not just in hindsight: they note that Haiti has a possible legal claim today. The length of repayment is unique among indemnities, as not many transfers are longer than a decade. The larger ones (such as Germany's World War I reparation) or longer ones (such as Germany's reparation to Denmark after World War II) often end up being negotiated away or simply ignored. It is difficult to see how Haiti's sovereign debt was in the interest of its people, as it was in essence a debt to pay for independence it had already won. As is the case in many of these cases, however, the debt is paid if the creditor can enforce its claim. In the case of Haiti's long debt, how the debt was enforced and by whom changed – but there was always someone abroad or internally who benefited from not writing off the debt. It was just never the citizens.

6

Franco-Prussian War Indemnities

France was forced to pay an indemnity to Germany after losing the Franco-Prussian War in 1871. The origin for war was a power struggle between the great nations of Europe. Prussia was victorious in its 1866 war against Austria, which put it in a dominant position over France. A diplomatic dispute led France to declare war in July 1870, with the first battle in August the same year. By September, Germany had won a series of decisive military battles, and the war ended in early 1871 with Germany as winner. Germany annexed Alsace-Lorraine, and as part of the peace settlement Prussian Chancellor Otto von Bismarck imposed an indemnity of 5 billion francs starting in 1871. The indemnity had the purpose of curbing French power.[1]

The indemnity had to be paid in four instalments over three years, with the majority (3 billion francs) due by March 1874. The total size of the indemnity amounted to around 25 per cent of French output (Monroe 1919, p. 269). It was slightly larger in terms of output and taxes collected than the Napoleonic Wars reparations, with annual debt service costs and repayment of the indemnity amounting to 9 per cent of output per year. The first payment of 500 million francs was due thirty days after the Treaty of Frankfurt (1871), which meant France had to borrow money quickly. In June 1871, France opened subscriptions for a 5 per cent *rentes* perpetual bond, which was issued at a price of 82.5, equivalent to an

---

[1] The history provided here is neither complete nor conclusive, but is meant to offer a brief context for why the indemnity was imposed. This section follows Monroe (1919) for how the indemnity was financed and paid. For a general history of the period, see, e.g., Kindleberger (1993, pp. 241–50).

interest rate of 6.1 per cent. The bond was over-subscribed, and the total size of the loan was 2 billion francs, covering the first three of four instalments. In July 1872, a second bond was announced, this time targeting 3 billion francs to repay reparations fully. The loan was over-subscribed twelve times and issued at a price of 84.5 with a notional of 100 (which equals an interest rate of 5.9 per cent). By then, France had raised enough money to pay back the indemnity in three years.

According to Gavin (1992, p. 176), France had 13 billion francs in net foreign assets by the end of 1869. Between 1871 and 1874, when France paid the indemnity, its foreign investments fell but net exports rose, as money was diverted towards the bond issues (Monroe 1919, p. 273). These bond issues had high subscriptions from foreign investors, but the primary financiers of the loans were via Paris. At the same time, the French current account was consistently positive, and French accumulation of net foreign assets continued in the 1980s. The loans issued were general purpose bonds guaranteed by the government. The indemnity was de facto senior to these loans, as the indemnity was linked to the removal of German troops, but there is no indication that a default was seriously discussed. Because the investor base for the loans was largely domestic, a subsequent default would hit French investors. Devereux and Smith (2007, p. 2392) show that the French terms of trade deteriorated during the repayment from 1871 to 1873, but conclude that the ability to borrow the money meant the impact on consumption was muted. The primary cost was a lower stock of net foreign assets.

Just over a quarter of total output was paid over three years, again mainly financed in sovereign debt markets (Kindleberger 1993, pp. 241–50). The French held many foreign securities that were easily sold, providing liquidity for loans issued to repay the indemnity (Taussig 1927, pp. 266–68). The sale of securities allowed for debt financing on rather attractive terms. The indemnity was considered too big to pay by many at the time, but easy issuance of loans and asset sales meant it was actually repaid quickly (Gavin 1992, p. 175). The debt issuance changed savings and investments for the period between 1871 and 1873, as a large share of domestic savings went to pay the reparation, but it was temporary. Figure 6.1 shows French savings, investments, and current accounts. The dotted line represents the current account net of indemnity, while the solid line represents the difference between savings and investments (on the left) and the French current account (on the right).

France's status as a net creditor might have influenced its debt and repayment strategy. Figure 6.2 shows the French default set as defined

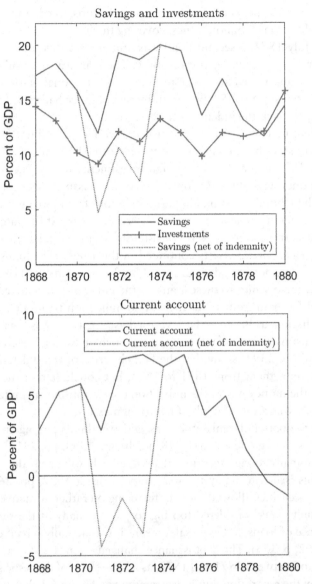

FIGURE 6.1 French savings, investments, and current account (1868–80).
Sources: Jones and Obstfeld (2001) online dataset for savings and investments;
Lévy-Léboyer and Bourguignon (1990, table A-III) for the current account;
Devereux and Smith (2007, p. 2380) for the reparation. Replication file,
plot_sica.m.

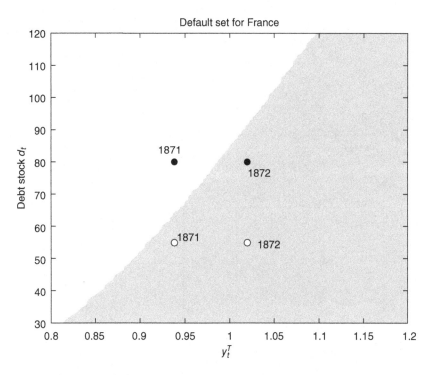

FIGURE 6.2 French default set, debt stock, and detrended output.
Note: The white area is the state denotes repayment while the grey area is
default. The dots denote French debt excluding the indemnity (hollow dots) and
including the indemnity (black dots) on the y-axis and detrended output on the
x-axis. Replication file, *plot_default_set_france.m*.

in Chapter 3. The figure shows where France was in 1871 and 1872. On
the x-axis is deviation from trend real growth and on the y-axis is the
debt stock. The grey area denotes areas where the sovereign debt model
considers default to be optimal, while the white area denotes areas
where repayment is optimal. The hollow dots are French output and
gross debt stock excluding the indemnity, while the black dots include
the indemnity. As can be seen, once the indemnity is included in France's
debt stock in 1871, it seems to be in the default area because of high debt
and low output. Yet France did not default and did not seem to seriously
consider it. I propose four reasons why this was the case, even though,
as we will see, some macroeconomic indicators suggest a default was
optimal.

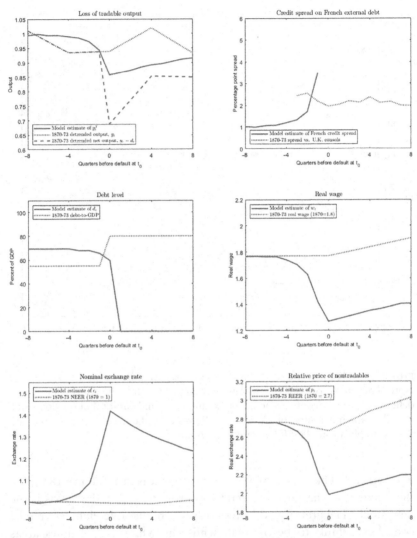

FIGURE 6.3 Model estimate and French historical data (1870–73).
Sources: Bolt et al. (2018) for output; Ljungberg (2019) for nominal and real
exchange rates; Insee and Bank of England for bond yields; debt calculated from
Oosterlinck et al. (2014), White (2001, p. 351), and Ritschl (1996a, 2012a).
Data on real wages is an estimate based on BL (1898, p. 668) for Paris wages. A
similar trend is found in Bowley (1898, p. 488). Replication file, *plot_france.m*.

Before discussing the reasons why France paid the indemnity, Figure 6.3
compares the macroeconomic predictions of the model to historical data,
collected for the years 1870–73. The figure shows historical data two

years prior to the announcement of the indemnity at t_0 and two years after. The two years prior to a hypothetical default coincides with the end of the war (1871). Detrended output falls during the war but expands afterwards, with GDP increasing by 10 per cent from 1871 to 1872 back to 1870 levels. In the upper left of the figure is detrended output, where the median default occurs when output is 12 per cent below its trend. French growth was below trend by around 6 per cent, but the fall in net output y_0-d_0 is significantly bigger. Unlike in the model, the credit spread on French government bonds during the period was static, trading around 5 to 6 per cent from 1870 to 1873, with no spike as the risk of default did not increase. The level of debt in the model before default is around 65 per cent, close to the pre-indemnity level of 55 per cent debt-to-GDP but below the 80 per cent ratio in 1871 after the indemnity was announced.

The level of real wages in the nineteenth century was generally flexible, but for the period 1870–73 both nominal and real wages were stable. Monroe (1919, p. 278) provides evidence that wages went up in the mining industry, which benefited from higher exports, but the aggregate wage level was generally stable during the period according to the sources cited for Figure 6.3. The nominal exchange rate was stable because France was on the bimetallic standard (Flandreau 1996). The indemnity was paid in gold, silver, notes, and bills of exchange, with the latter being the primary way of payment. It meant that there was a large flow of specie underlying the indemnity as France were to provide bills of exchange in Germany, and therefore sold gold and silver in the market for bills, which influenced prices of both goods and money. However, because of the bimetallic standard, the overall level of nominal and real exchange rates fell relatively little.

Despite a large loss of output, higher interest rates than in the model, and a large increase in debt, France nevertheless repaid both the indemnity and its debt. France borrowed 5 billion francs (25 per cent of GDP) in thirteen months and Devereux and Smith (2007) suggest that consumption was largely unaffected. I suggest four reasons for how France was able to repay without entertaining the idea of default.

The first is that France was in an exceptionally good position to borrow large amounts of money because of its large stock of foreign assets at the end of the war. The Franco-Prussian War was over in less than a year and France did not have to sell all its foreign assets to finance the war. According to Ritschl (1996a, p. 185), the French debt stock was around 55 per cent of GDP in 1869, which is around 11 billion francs. Gavin (1992, p. 176) notes that at the same time French foreign assets were around 13 billion francs, which is estimated to yield around 5 per cent. We know that the current account, net of the indemnity, was negative of around 2 billion francs. It means that at the end of the war, France had no net debt, as its gross debt roughly equalled its foreign assets.[2] The debt stock in Figure 6.2 might therefore be overstated substantially because it is gross debt. In fact, it provides an additional incentive for repayment. A default might induce sanctions on France. Because France had little net debt, it might be especially vulnerable to sanctions or confiscations of its foreign assets, which might yield a higher return than the cost of its debt.

The second reason is that France could borrow enough money quickly to pay the indemnity, which meant the costs could be smoothed over many years. The type of debt that France used to borrow was a *rentes* bond, which is a perpetual bond with no maturity. The speed at which it issued debt meant that the upfront costs were minimal. The ease was shown both by the speed and by the large over-subscriptions to its loans, from both domestic and international lenders.

The third reason is related to how the bonds were issued. The bonds were underwritten by de Rothschild Frères (the Paris house), N. M. Rothschild & Sons (the London house), and the Barings Brothers in London.[3] In addition to underwriting the loan, the London house of Rothschild also guaranteed foreign exchange stability to facilitate the transfer to Germany. The loan required the combined effort of the Rothschild and Barings families, as outlined by its private documents (Ayer 1904, p. 55). The underwriters lent France credibility and enhanced scrutiny of the loans. Underwriters played an important role during the time, as has been outlined by in a series of papers by Flandreau et al. (2009) and Flandreau and Flores (2012). The underwriters helped to place the bond and made the financing operation possible, but they also played a role in monitoring and enforcing repayment. Because the underwriters were heavily involved, the likelihood of being able to borrow money went up. It also increased the probability of repayment because the banking houses enforced market access.

---

[2] The timing might even underestimate the level of net foreign assets a little because the French current account was around 1.1 billion francs in 1870 and the indemnity only started in 1871. But since the indemnity flows were known by then, it can be assumed that they were included in the debt strategy.

[3] The source for the loans is Ayer (1904, pp. 54–57), which was a privately published book on the history of the London house of Rothschild.

The fourth reason is that France might have taken the optimal trajectory in terms of output, consumption, and wages. Looking at Figure 6.3, French output grew in the year after the war. It might have been clear to the French government that output losses in 1870–71 were war-related and it would be costly to default. If the government knew that it could smooth out one bad year, it would not make sense to take the output loss associated with default (neither in the real world nor in the model). The trajectory and stability of French wages and nominal and real exchange rates would seem to confirm this view.[4] Had France defaulted on the indemnity in 1871, two things would likely have happened. The first is military intervention. Germany annexed Alsace-Lorraine but in the event of no payment, it might have intervened militarily, either to confiscate the money or grab more land. The second is that a default would have cut France off from borrowing internationally. The international banking houses and its neighbours would have stopped the flow of credit, possibly confiscated French foreign assets, or placed sanctions on France.

All four reasons for repayment can be true at the same time. The lower level of net output and the use of export proceeds to pay the indemnity, rather than accumulate foreign investments, suggests there was a real cost of resources to France. But France's external position meant it was well positioned to repay the indemnity quickly, and France would have incurred large political and economic costs had it attempted a sovereign default. So even if enforcement of the transfers was not binding by creditors who militarily occupied France, which it was, it was a case in which incentives to repay were large. The indemnity therefore stands out as unique, in that France's role in the European political landscape and economic situation both suggested that repayment of its indemnity made sense.

---

[4] It is also possible that the economy adjusted by lowering the level of real wages, but that it does not show up in the limited data source on French wages for the period.

7

Smaller Nineteenth-Century War Reparations

The nineteenth century saw several war reparations that, like the Haitian indemnity covered in Chapter 5, do not lend themselves easily to short-term economic analysis – in this case because national economic data is lacking in all three cases. I describe three episodes briefly in this chapter, because they show that war reparations can be very different depending on the political institutions and intentions of the winning nation. The first did not have much of an impact because of its small size. The second fundamentally changed the fiscal structure of the Greek state. The third left China with more than thirty years of debt that had to be repaid. Each case is only mentioned here to enforce the central message of this book – namely that reparations are repaid as long as the creditor wants or can enforce them.

Neither China nor Greece has reliable nominal GDP figures to compare the size of the indemnities. In context, however, they were undoubtedly large and required significant sovereign debt issuance (in the form of bilateral loans) to finance. But with no dependable output number, is it difficult to put this in perspective. It is the reason that the reparations are left blank in the overview that appears in Table 1.1.

7.1 MEXICAN–AMERICAN WAR REPARATIONS

The United States paid indemnities to Mexico from 1848 to 1881, after the Mexican–American War.[1] In national income terms, this reparation was minor. The Treaty of Guadalupe Hidalgo of 1848 stipulated the

---

[1] The war ended in 1848. I am indebted to Eugene White for pointing out that it contained reparations.

United States pay 18 million US dollars, of which 15 million dollars was indemnities and 3.25 million dollars was transferred debts. Using data from the Federal Reserve to convert the indemnity to 2011-equivalent US dollars and comparing that with the chained real GDP per capita multiplied by the population at the time (Bolt et al. 2018), I find it is the equivalent of less than 1 per cent of GDP. The economic impact of this reparation was minor, but it was nonetheless paid over thirty-three years.

7.2 CRETAN WAR REPARATIONS

In 1897, Greece lost the Cretan War to the Ottoman Empire. Greece had been overrun and asked the Great Powers of Europe to broker an armistice, which they did just before Athens was invaded. Greece was at the time highly indebted and defaulted on some of its outstanding sovereign bonds. In the negotiations that followed, sovereign debt payments were directly linked to indemnities by creditors. The Ottomans had required 10 million lira but were negotiated down to 4 million lira and loss of some territory (Waibel 2015, pp. 14–17). The amount was considered so high that the Greek capacity to pay was in question, but with no reliable GDP figures this is not possible to quantify directly. Creditors forced an intervention in Greek fiscal decisions, to make sure there was capacity to pay. The final agreement included a loan of 6.8 million pounds from the UK, France, and Russia to Greece (Waibel 2015, pp. 14–17). The loan was thus larger than the indemnity, but ensured Greece could repay existing private creditors too. Greece did not have much choice in the matter: enforcement of sovereign debt happened under the threat of invasion. The terms included the de-facto takeover of fiscal affairs and made indemnities and existing creditors *pari passu* (meaning equal ranking of claims), ensuring repayment. In the end, Greece paid the equivalent of 94 million francs in indemnities.

7.3 CHINESE REPARATIONS TO JAPAN AND BRITAIN

China paid reparations twice in around 1900: first between 1895 and 1901, when China paid 230 million taels of silver to Japan following the Sino-Japanese War (Dong and Guo 2018, pp. 17–18); second between 1901 and 1939, when it paid 669 million taels of silver as reparation for the Boxer Rebellion (Hsu 2000, pp. 477–91). The Treaty of Shimonoseki of 1895 stated that China owed indemnities to both Japan and Britain. The payment was too large to finance without a loan, which China obtained from Russia, France, Britain, and Germany (Dong and Guo 2018, p. 18). The loss of the Boxer Rebellion in 1901 doubled indemnity payments, as all eight invaders had to be compensated.[2] China was thus shackled with significant indemnity payments for the next thirty years, which it financed with European loans.

---

[2] The Eight-Nation Alliance: Austria-Hungary, Britain, France, Germany, Italy, Japan, Russia, and the United States.

8

German World War I Reparations

The Treaty of Versailles of 1919 stipulated that Germany pay reparations for World War I. The size of reparations was to be negotiated after Versailles by the Reparation Commission, but the Germans expected 30 billion gold marks to be an upper limit.[1] In 1920, news leaked of a larger-than-expected reparations bill of around 80 billion gold marks. It sent shockwaves through the German public. In 1921, the London Schedule of Payments set the total reparations bill at 132 billion gold marks, far above initial estimates. It would be payable in three tranches: A-bonds (for war damages) worth 12 billion marks or around 25 per cent of 1913 gross national product (GNP); B-bonds (for inter-Allied war debt) worth 38 billion marks or around 75 per cent of GNP; and C-bonds, the majority, at 82 billion totalling 150 per cent of GNP. The implicit understanding was that the C-bonds would not need to be repaid (Ritschl 2012a, p. 945). The total size of the A-bonds, the war reparations, added together with the existing German debt stock in 1920 of around 50 per cent of GNP was equivalent in size to the French indemnity and debt stock of 1871 in terms of GDP. There is reason to believe that the size of the reparation was negotiated with the historical precedent in mind. According to Marks (2013), who surveys the literature on the negotiations of the Versailles Treaty, diplomats and politicians made numerous references to the Franco-Prussian War indemnity. The French would be intimately aware of the cost they bore, which shows up in discussions at the time to be found in French archives. The initial enforcement mechanism was different, but the value of

---

[1] See James (1986), Schuker (1988), or Ritschl (2002) for a comprehensive history. The history part of this chapter follows from their work.

the reparations was estimated to be payable by Germany, as indeed it had been for France. The difference was the additional war debts and C-bonds. Adding in the B-bonds for inter-Allied war debts took German debt levels well above historical precedents, but total debt levels were close to those of Britain and France after the war, even though Germany had relied more on debt and less on taxes to finance the war than Britain (James 1986, pp. 49–50). Reparations (A-bonds) were around 24 per cent of output, which is close to the value of the indemnity France paid in 1871.

As a share of output, the combined A- and B-bonds, which covered reparations and inter-Allied debts, were around 100 per cent of German GDP (Ritschl 2012a, pp. 945–46). If the entire proposed reparation is included, the bill represented 300 per cent of pre-war GNP. The further 200 percentage points of debts included C-bonds, a debt that was added for political reasons to maintain a grip on Germany and avoid further aggression. However, there was no real expectation of repayment of the C-bonds, at least according to dip-lomatic cables from the time. In addition to monetary payments, the United States confiscated German patents, such as chemical patents, through the Office of Alien Property (Steen 2001). The confiscation of patents helped develop a US domestic chemicals industry, and while not classified as reparations, this altered the structure of trade in both countries through the 1920s.

8.1 GERMANY AFTER THE WAR

Debt levels for everyone coming out of World War I were large. Britain's debt was 144 per cent of GDP and France's was 135 per cent (Ritschl 2012a, pp. 945–46). Even taking reparations into account, Germany's debt burden was comparable with that of other European nations. But it was a large reparation payment that required the issu-ance of bonds because not enough foreign currency was available, and Germany ran persistent current account deficits throughout the 1920s (Figure 8.1).

Investments were consistently higher than savings, even when repara-tions payments are netted out, and wage growth and expenditures con-sistently outpaced revenues. There was a 'general wage push' in the late 1920s in Germany, as Harold James (1986, p. 68) put it. The consistent deficit financing of the public sector meant that resources were scarce in the private sector, resulting in low and falling investments throughout the 1920s (James 1986, pp. 110–61, 132–46).

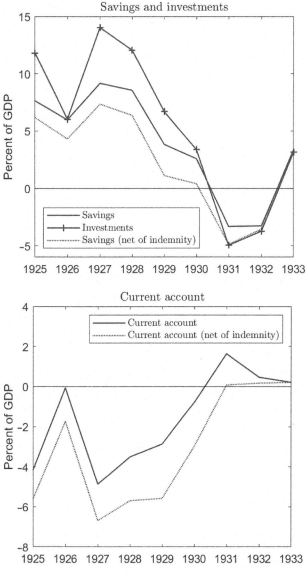

FIGURE 8.1 German savings, investments, and current account (1925–33). Sources: Jones and Obstfeld (2001) online appendix; Ritschl (2012a, p. 953) for reparations figures. Replication file, *plot_sicag.m*.

Germany experienced an extremely volatile business cycle in the interwar years as the economy swung from hyperinflation to deflation and depression. Figure 8.2 shows German real GDP per capita as well

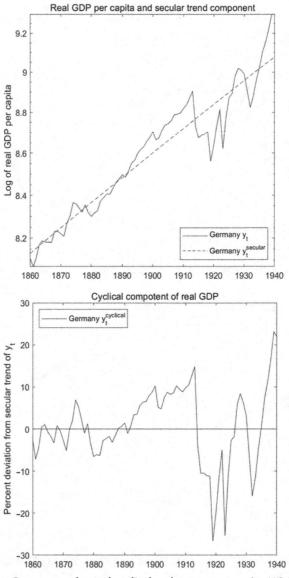

FIGURE 8.2 German secular and cyclical real output per capita (1860–1940). Source: Bolt et al. (2018). Replication file, *lqtrend_p2a.m.*

as detrended GDP (to the right) for the period 1860 to 1940: the period from the start of World War I until the mid-1930s saw large output swings. Albrecht Ritschl (2012a) suggests that Germany had three distinct economic phases during the interwar years, which are shown in

TABLE 8.1 *German economic phases between 1921 and 1933*

	1921–23	1924–29	1930–33
Real growth (deviation from trend)	–14.0	0.8	–7.7
Current account	–	–3.1	0.4
Inflation regime	Hyper inflation	normal	deflation

Note: The numbers are mean deviation from trend growth and mean current account in per cent of GDP for the years in each column.
Source: Bolt et al. (2018); Jones and Obstfeld (2001).

Table 8.1. Each phase saw different growth rates, capital flows, and inflation regimes – and reparations played a key role in each economic phase.[2]

The initial phase from 1921 to 1923 was characterised by hyperinflation. During 1920, the German economy had stabilised, but after the size of the reparations bill became clear, tax revenues plunged. The much higher than anticipated reparations bill resulted in tax 'boycotts' from the German public (Ritschl 2012a, p. 950).[3] The government had to make up for lower tax revenues from the boycotts, so the central bank had to print money. During this period, only the minimum required transfers were forthcoming as the financial system collapsed, external creditors saw their claims reduced in real terms, and political instability increased alongside unemployment. Germany's capacity and willingness to finance reparations on international capital markets was limited. Its debts in 1921 were mostly foreign debt, which increased its incentives to default. By late 1922, Germany refused to pay what it considered an intolerable and odious debt, as output losses made the debt burden worse. Germany was forced back to the negotiation table in January 1923 when the Allied occupied the Ruhr to enforce payment of reparations.

[2] There are different ways to break down Germany's economic phases. Harold James (1986, p. 213) suggests a different breakdown based on the structure of German wages after the stabilisation of the mark: 1924–25 saw rapid wage growth from a low base; mid-1925–26 saw a temporary slowdown in wage pressures; 1927–28 saw wages increasing with the civil service leading; 1928–30 saw wages continuing to rise while employers resisted unsuccessfully; and from 1931 wage rates fell dramatically.
[3] The literature also suggests that distributional conflicts and delayed stabilization played key roles in stoking hyperinflation. This section focuses on reparations as the key issue, but I do not suggest that to be the definite cause of hyperinflation. See, for example, James (1986, pp. 126–32) for a discussion about the role of industry and investments on inflation.

8.2 THE DAWES PLAN

After Germany went into default on reparations in 1922, the Ruhr was invaded to enforce repayments. Out of the occupation came the Dawes Plan in 1924 to formalise the payment schedule (Schuker 1988; Yee 2020, p. 49). This included a feature that gave commercial creditors preferential treatment to reparations and resulted in a debt-to-GDP ratio of around 68 per cent in 1925.[4] Germany had a need to attract capital in the form of debt to finance its expenditures and reparations. Commercial international investors, particularly American investors, lent money to Germany that helped finance reparations. Capital outflows from Germany during the 1920s were significant, but were matched by external investments, which allowed Germany to keep rolling over debt at reasonable interest rates (Farquet 2019).

The second phase occurred from 1924 to 1929. The period was the mirror-imagine of the earlier years (see Table 8.1) as growth rebounded, inflation stabilised, and capital started to flow into Germany, which increased debt levels. Output was still more than 10 per cent below trend in 1924, but by 1925 output had almost recovered. In 1924, the Dawes Plan settled the reparations question and ended Allied occupation of the Ruhr (see, e.g., Lutz 1930, pp. 41–48 or Yee 2020). The payment scheme included only reparations (the A-bonds) but did not provide any explicit debt relief. The liability of reparations was therefore still significant, with the present value of the Dawes Plan annuity almost equal in size to the combined A- and B-bonds (Ritschl 2013, table 4.1). The Dawes annuity was considered unpayable by many at the time, even though the German commercial debt stock had been inflated away and was negligible by 1924 (see, e.g., Costigliola 1976).[5] Germany had to attract large capital inflows from 1924 to finance the reparations transfers, something that it was successful in doing until 1929. The reason it was successful was that the Dawes Plan embedded investor protections into reparations, as shown by Ritschl (2002, pp. 193–217). The protections were in the capital structure under the Dawes Plan. This stipulated that reparations remained junior to corporate debt claims in the central bank's foreign exchange window, providing a remedy to enforce commercial debt claims. The protections were needed in 1924 to ensure that Germany could borrow

---

[4] Using the present value of the Dawes annuity, as per Ritschl (2013).

[5] Fleisig (1976) argues that Germany would have defaulted even without a global depression. Neto (1986), on the other hand, suggests that the German government never tried to raise taxes or cut spending to produce the required primary surplus.

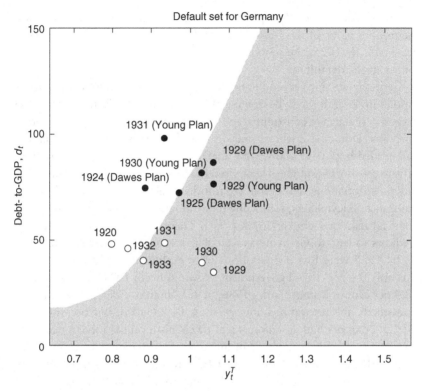

FIGURE 8.3 German default set, debt stock, and detrended output.
Sources: Ritschl (2012a, pp. 945–46) for commercial debt in 1920; IMF
data for commercial debt in 1924–25 (negligible); Ritschl (2013) for the net
present value of Dawes Plan annuity and GDP in 1924 and 1925; Papadia and
Schioppa (2015, p. 6) for data from 1928 to 1933. The x-axis is deviation from
trended output. Replication file, *plot_default_set_germany_all.m*.

abroad to finance the transfers, as German debt was not sustainable. By
1924, German detrended output was 11 per cent below trend and the
present value annuity of the Dawes Plan was almost 75 per cent of GNP.
The combination of low output and high debt put Germany in the default
set, as can be seen in Figure 8.3. The figure shows the default set of
Germany, with the grey area denoting default and the white area denoting repayment, as a function of the debt-to-GDP stock and deviation
from trend growth (the white areas are outside the grid of the model). The
hollow dots show German commercial debt excluding reparations. After
the stabilisation of the currency in 1924, German commercial debt was
negligible and is left out of the graph for the years 1924–25 (James 1986,
pp. 40–43). The black dots in the figure show German total liabilities,

which are commercial debt plus reparations annuities (the black dots are the present value of the Dawes Plan and the Young Plan for the years in brackets). By 1925, the rebound in output meant that Germany was no longer in the default set.

Germany was incentivised to borrow from foreign creditors to pay reparations in several ways. Borrowing the money externally naturally eased domestic budgetary constraints and freed up money to be used for other purposes. Domestic credit expansion was difficult because hyperinflation had eroded both trust and wealth. Increased external debt also meant that private creditors would be incentivised to ally with Germany in future reparations negotiations. The end of reparations was the primary stated goal of economic policymakers, something they thought worth taking considerable financial risk for (Schuker 1988, p. 35). There were incentives for foreign creditors to lend to Germany as well. The first was that German debt levels by 1925 were low if reparations were excluded. German debt service was only 0.6 per cent of government expenditures in 1925, compared with 28.4 per cent in Britain (James 1986, p. 48). In an overall creditworthiness assessment, the reparations annuity must be included, but because commercial creditors had an enforcement mechanism on the foreign exchange reserves at the Reichsbank, it meant they were senior debt claims (Yee 2020). The invasion of the Ruhr in 1923 had showed that enforcement of reparations was binding, even though France and Belgium experienced high political costs for military intervention. As a result, the commercial debt stock increased from 1925 as Germany borrowed abroad and money was recycled from the United States in what Stephen A. Schuker (1988) terms 'American "Reparations" to Germany'. From 1924 to 1929, Germany issued corporate and sovereign bonds across Europe and private foreign credit flowed into Germany, which was used to finance reparations transfers (Accominotti and Eichengreen 2016, pp. 476–78). The borrowing meant there was no transfer of resources between 1924 and 1929 because the current account matched the reparations flow. Germany paid 2.5 per cent of national income every year from 1925 to 1932 in reparations, which peaked at 3.5 per cent in 1929 (Machlup 1964, pp. 374–95). In present value terms, the transfer was quite real, of course, because debt increased.

8.3 THE YOUNG PLAN

The third phase from 1929 to 1932 was marred by austerity and deflation. Already in 1927, the first financial troubles had started. The government issued a 500 million Reichsmark loan with a 5 per cent interest, which had to be converted to a 6 per cent loan to avoid the price of the loan falling too drastically in the secondary market (James 1986, pp. 50–52). By 1929, the issue of financing began to dwarf other economic problems. The government tried and failed to issue the full 500 million Reichsmark of the Hilferding Loan despite big tax concessions to investors, and at the same time tax revenues started to fall, which led to a budget crisis in late-1929. The post-war economic structure was under pressure, as calls for both tax and spending cuts intensified with support from the Reichsbank. The problem of loan financing got worse throughout 1929, as Germany tried and failed to obtain long-term credit from international banking houses J.P. Morgan and Dillon Read (James 1986, pp. 54–59). The government increasingly had to rely on short-term treasury issuances, which increased the rollover risk when the debt matured. The cause of the crisis was not simply a reversal of capital flows. James (1986, pp. 39–110) has argued that the difficulty the government had in financing growing public expenditures stemmed from distributional effects. A larger bureaucracy, increased the level of spending on agriculture and social welfare, and as there was no reform of the many levels of government (Reich, Länder, and communes), wealth and income were not redistributed away from pre-war rentiers (James 1986, p. 51). The public financing issue was worsened by the weakness of the banking system, which turned into a full-blown banking crisis in 1931 (see, e.g., James 1986, pp. 281–323). The economic crisis thus had domestic as well as global origins, because when the domestic economy started to weaken it did so alongside the start of the Great Depression. Germany's reliance on foreign debts hit a wall, and with it a looming balance of payments crisis.

The Young Plan negotiations occurred simultaneously with the increased financing troubles. There were signs of a run on the foreign exchange reserves in the spring of 1929 during the negotiations as it looked as if there was no agreement (James 1986, p. 284), but a deal was reached in August 1929 and formally approved in 1930. The economic and political impact of the Young Plan was big. It was expected that the plan would offer some relief, but as Ritschl (2002) shows, the outcome was instead a change in the structure of debt. The present value of the new reparations annuity under the Young Plan was slightly lower than the Dawes Plan, but the debt seniority of commercial creditors over reparations transfers was reversed. The implicit understanding during the Dawes years, as argued by Ritschl (2002) and earlier by Schuker (1988), was that reparations would be reduced dramatically. In the context of Figure 8.3, the implied belief during the Dawes years was that de facto debt levels were the hollow dots (commercial and sovereign debt) but not the black dots (which includes reparations annuities). The Young Plan made clear that German liabilities included reparations. The Young Plan was accompanied by an official loan ('the Young bond'), but private credit access dried up during 1929 (Ritschl 2012a, pp. 954–57). Foreign loans became unavailable and domestic credit expansion was not possible under the Young Plan, as at least parts of the annuity payments became senior to commercial debt (Schuker 1988, p. 52). The debt sustainability of Germany became an acute problem because the total stock of reparations was not written down but only reprofiled. Short-term creditors began to demand austerity policies to roll over existing loans, and because the government had lost access to long-term foreign credit, the Brüning government engaged in austerity policies to regain long-term debt solvency. Until the reversal of capital flows, high real wages in Germany had not affected the unemployment rate but after 1929 they did. The Young Plan ruled out a devaluation and made Germany unable to alleviate the pressure from high real wages, which translated into a sharp output contraction, as first outlined by Borchardt (e.g., in 1990).

8.4 ENFORCEMENT OF REPARATIONS

The last French troops did not leave Germany until 1930, so there was very likely still a binding enforcement mechanism on reparations in 1929. A hard German default in 1929 might therefore not have been possible, which goes some way to understand why the Young Plan was agreed by both sides. A second reason is found in Figure 8.3. The present value of the Young Plan annuity in 1929 was 42 per cent of GDP, while its outstanding commercial debts was 35 per cent of GDP, for a combined 76 per cent debt-to-GDP. The Dawes Plan annuity had a present value of 52 per cent in 1929. Even though the German economy slowed during 1929, it was still above its long-term trend. Germany was therefore still outside the default set in 1929, even with a debt stock of 86 per cent of GDP under the Dawes Plan and 76 per cent under the Young Plan. An outright reading of the model affirms the view that by 1929, it was still in Germany's interest to have access to capital markets, which a unilateral default would have cut off. Germany gave up transfer protections from reparations in exchange for some debt relief and 300 million US dollars in loans, which was hoped to be followed by additional credit. Instead, loans from US and Canadian banks dried up in 1930 following the Young Plan (Schuker 1988, pp. 50–63). With no new loans available to pay off existing interest and reparations, the money had to come from domestic sources.

The result was austerity and deflation, which came at extremely high social and political cost. By 1930, as Ritschl (2002) has argued, if Germany was committed to repaying reparations while not defaulting on its commercial creditors, it had no other options than austerity policies because of years of external debt-financing. But austerity policies led to deflation, high unemployment, and a collapse in growth. These policies came in the form of decrees from Brüning from December 1930 to December 1931, and the policies were a mix of tax increases (explicit and implicit), cuts to state welfare, and reductions in civil service pay (James 1986, p. 36). It is easy to see that Germany ends up in the default set by 1931, with a high debt stock and much lower growth. In that sense, much economic and political pain was for nothing. The foreign credit constraint was self-fulfilling, as it made it impossible for Germany to escape its debt-deflation regime. The remedy for previous periods of high debt and low output was to borrow money, but by 1929 that was no longer possible. Schuker (1988, p. 63) notes that Brüning hoped to engage in foreign credit expansion in the spring of 1932, as it was expected the reparations issue would be resolved. The end of austerity was never enacted by Brüning, despite the Reichstag passing a law allowing more borrowing. The effect of austerity was a vicious cycle of lower revenues and problems of financing increasing deficits (James 1986, pp. 60–73).

The public financing issue was a problem because of the structural weaknesses in the low-growth economy. Even small increases in nominal debt could not be sustained because output fell dramatically and increased the debt burden. The difficulty in rolling loans forced a tightening of credit and a reduction in the money supply (James 1986, p. 293), and continued austerity fuelled the economy into a debt-deflation crisis. By 1931, the political and military situation in Europe had changed and was markedly different from 1923. Germany pushed for and received a moratorium on reparations payments from US President Hoover in 1931 as the financial and economic situation deteriorated (James 1986, pp. 34–35). At the same time, Germany obtained a 100 million US dollar loan from a consortium of central banks as private credit flows stopped, to keep up payments on its other debt (Clement 2004, p. 36).[6] The central bank loan was the only real option for long-term credit because political uncertainty made financing German deficits difficult, even though the deficits were relatively small compared with its European neighbours (James 1986, pp. 71–73).[7] The

---

[6] The New York Federal Reserve, the Bank of England, the Banque de France, and the Bank of International Settlements.

[7] In 1931, German debt service as a share of public expenditures was 2.9 per cent (James 1986, p. 48).

other European nations and the United States had no appetite for a costly enforcement of reparations amid an economic crisis. The Hoover moratorium had not cancelled reparations, but according to Schuker (1988, pp. 64–65), the debate within the German business community throughout 1932 was whether to service foreign debts or default. The economic situation did not improve in 1932, and Germany negotiated a standstill with its short-term commercial creditors. At the Lausanne Conference in July 1932, reparations were de facto cancelled. The conference did not result in a German default on its sovereign debt, because Article 7 explicitly protected bond holders. But the agreement removed the direct repayment from reparations annuities that was previously embedded and meant that the debt had to be serviced out of the government's general-purpose finances (James 1986, pp. 71–73). As can be seen from Figure 8.3, Germany was by 1932 well into the default set even without reparations (the hollow dots), as autarky policies became optimal to repayment of debt.

8.5 GERMANY'S SOVEREIGN DEBT DEFAULT

The standstill and de facto cancellation of reparations removed an important obstacle to a German sovereign debt default. Domestically in Germany, both the Nazis and the Communist Party advocated for a default, which was an alternative to the austerity policies of the Brüning cabinet. The outcome of the Lausanne Conference meant that the capital structure of German debt changed once again, as the long-term debt prioritised during the Young Plan years became junior to shorter term debt. Most of the long-term debt was to commercial creditors in the United States (Papadia and Schioppa 2015), but Germany could engage in discriminatory debt policy because US sanctions were no longer effective owing to its trade policy (see Ritschl 2002). Germany meanwhile prioritised reducing its debt to England because London banking houses continued to offer certain short-term credit arrangements. The Brüning cabinet's policies were to reduce the credit constraint, but once the Nazis took power, a policy of default was explicit (Clement 2004, p. 49). Already by then the debate on whether to service commercial debts was, according to my analysis, redundant. By 1931, autarky was preferable to repayment of debt, as output losses were severe and the benefits from some access to borrowing were outweighed by the cost of servicing debt.

The stylised facts accompanying sovereign defaults were by 1932 all present in Germany, as shown in Figure 8.4. The policy of default was optimal, if late. The figure shows model output as specified in Chapter 4

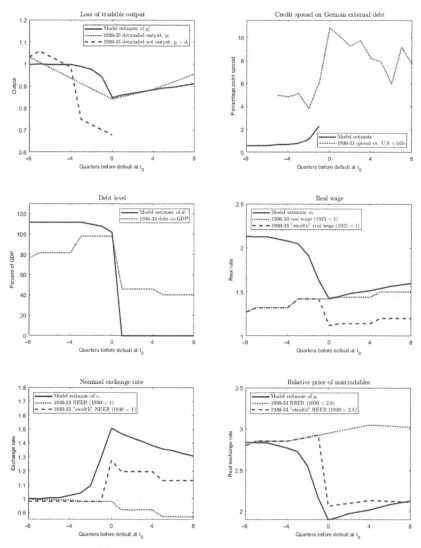

FIGURE 8.4 Model estimate and German historical data (1930–33).
Sources: Bolt et al. (2018) for output; Ljungberg (2019) for exchange rates;
Ritschl (2012b, p. 40) for wages; Papadia and Schioppa (2015, p. 15) for debt
and German bond yields; the Federal Reserve for US yields; and Klug (1993,
p. 18) for the estimate of the stealth devaluation, where the lower part of the
range (30 per cent) is used. Replication file, *plot_germany.m*.

and historical German data from the end of 1929 to 1933, with t_0 being
1932 in this figure (a discussion of the default dates follows). German
detrended real output per capita y_t collapsed 18 per cent between 1930

and 1932, while net output y_0-d_0 was 35 per cent lower. The level of sovereign debt after the Lausanne Conference was 49 per cent of GDP. The credit premium on German bonds over US treasuries more than doubled in the year before the sovereign default. In the model, it occurred as the probability of default rose. The middle-left figure in Figure 8.4 shows that the German debt stock after the default fell to 45 per cent in 1932 and then to 40 per cent in 1933. By 1938, its debt stock was down to 14 per cent of GDP. Even though the government was unable to pursue an outright devaluation of its currency, it nonetheless did so by stealth methods. Klug (1993, p. 18) estimates that exports subsidies meant German exports could be purchased abroad at a 30 to 60 per cent discount. De facto German currency policy was therefore in line with equation (3.27). In the figure, the real wage, the nominal exchange rate, and the real exchange rate are plotted with their actual values and with the stealth devaluation. Nominal wages fell but inflation fell more, and real wages rose despite mass unemployment. By 1932, real wages were more than 40 per cent above their 1925 index, while productivity had risen by less than half (Ritschl 2012b, p. 40).

The German sovereign debt default can be dated in different ways because of the different types of external debt. The political debts of reparations and war debts were suspended for a year by the Hoover moratorium in June 1931, which was followed by the standstill agreement on short-term debt (Ritschl 2012a, p. 956). Reparations were de facto cancelled in 1932 at the Lausanne Conference, but it did not include the sovereign loans issued (Dawes and Young bonds). The standstill agreements led to a rally in the bond prices in early 1932 as cash was perceived available to repay those bonds, as can be seen in Figure 8.5. The Nazis came to power in early 1933 and had an explicit policy of not paying long-term external debts. The 9 June law of 1933 (see Schacht 1967, pp. 137–41) created a foreign exchange clearing office, through which all external interest and amortisations payments were to flow, which in effect meant money would be intercepted by the office. Additional defaults occurred in 1933 as Germany revoked the Gold Clause and announced it would only honour the nominal value of its debt (Clement 2004, pp. 37–38). In 1934, a full moratorium on debt payments was announced alongside capital controls (Schuker 1988, pp. 47–82). In 1934, another spike in interest rates occurred in the lead up to the full default in 1934 (Ritschl 2001, pp. 329–30).

Albrecht Ritschl (2002) has argued that because sovereign debt policies and trade policies were interlinked, it was not possible to default while maintaining open trade with all its creditors. Where this research

FIGURE 8.5 Yields on German external bonds (1931–35).
Note: Bonds converted to yields, using stated coupon, maturities in 1949 for the Dawes and 1965 for the Young bonds (Clement 2004, p. 47). Replication file, *plot_gdr.m.*
Source: Papadia and Schioppa (2015, p. 15).

diverges from previous authors mentioned in this chapter is in estimating the policy of repayment before 1932. As is shown in Figure 8.3, German austerity policies proved to be more costly than continued debt service already in 1931, because of its effect on real growth. A sovereign default would have meant a return to financial autarky and likely trade sanctions, but it would have allowed domestic credit to expand and Germany to leave the stated policy of long-term debt sustainability. The argument here is therefore that the cost of austerity policies was larger than the gain from continued market access, limited as it was to short-term loans. In the model presented here, sovereign debtors only pay their debts if the cost is not higher than financial autarky. Unlike much of the literature, I find that the point of optimal default had already come by 1931, even assuming the Great Depression did not reduce the costs of autarky policies.

9

Russian and Bulgarian World War I Reparations

German interwar reparations are well documented in the literature because of their importance in the lead up to World War II and their role in the Great Depression. But German interwar reparations were not the only ones following World War I. Two other lesser-known reparations transfers were agreed in 1918, neither of which were repaid in full because they were negotiated away by subsequent treaties.

The Bolshevik government in Russia ended their involvement in World War I with the auxiliary Treaty of Brest-Litovsk on 3 March 1918. Russia gave up territorial control over the Baltic states and defaulted on previously incurred debts to the Allies. A subsequent financial appendix was agreed on 27 August 1918, which set out financial terms of the Treaty. Soviet Russia was to pay 6 billion marks to Germany in five instalments from 1918 to 1920, with parts of the transfers consisting of commodities and gold.[1] Russian pre-war output was 16 billion Russian roubles (Markevich and Harrison 2011, p. 680),[2] which at the prevailing exchange rates in 1918 meant the reparation was around 37 per cent of GDP. Only the first two instalments were paid in September 1918, according to Smele (1994, p. 1319), who investigates the flow of Imperial Russian gold reserves. The later transfers were not made because the Treaty was subsequently annulled by the Armistice of 11 November 1918 that ended fighting between Germany and the Allies.

---

[1] Memorandum Appendix XXI (Russian–German Financial Agreement) to The Treaty of Brest-Litovsk, signed on 27 August 1918, published in *Izvestia* on 4 September 1918 (accessed 13 February 2021).

[2] The GDP number is for Soviet interwar territory in 1913.

FIGURE 9.1 Bulgaria net debt-to-GNP (1921–39).
Source: Tooze and Ivanov (2011, p. 37). Replication file, *plot_bdgdp.m*.

Bulgaria was initially given a bill of 2.25 billion gold francs to France, which took its debt-to-GNP to over 200 per cent (Tooze and Ivanov 2011, pp. 37–43). Bulgaria's reparations burden cannot be easily untangled from its war debts, but assuming the increase in foreign public debt from 1919 to 1921 was entirely reparations, the initial imposed transfer was over 150 per cent of output (Dimitrova and Ivanov 2014, p. 239). After the first payment was missed in 1921, the French forced the Bulgarian government to prioritise debt payments. Under great strain, reparations payments were made through 1923. The League of Nations mediated a deal, which postponed most reparations. Of the 2.25 billion francs, 550 million francs was extended to 1935 with the additional 1.7 billion francs postponed to 1953. From 1923 to 1935, only 28 million francs was paid (Dimitrova and Ivanov 2014, p. 221). As shown in Figure 9.1, Bulgaria's debt burden was massive but was negotiated down. No explicit default happened, outside the missed initial payment. It was a story of extreme economic hardship and repayment under duress and diplomacy, albeit more the former than the latter.

The cancellation of reparations, not only in Russia and Bulgaria, but also the later cancellation of reparations and sovereign debt default in Germany, had wider implications for the issue of inter-Allied war debt following World War I. Italy had significant external debt to the United States and the UK as it had borrowed money from the Allies, which was to a large extent paid off from external inflows. Italy received reparations from Germany, and it was understood the two were linked (Astore and Fratianni 2019, pp. 200–10). Italy managed to get significant debt relief in 1926, but nonetheless defaulted in 1934 (Reinhart and Trebesch 2016; Astore and Fratianni 2019). Until then, loans had been forthcoming. One cancellation of reparations therefore had repercussions on other sovereign debt, as the cross-border flow of money fell in the 1920s.

World War II Reparations to the Soviet Bloc

After Germany's defeat in 1945, there was a legitimate claim for reparations from an unjust war, as specified in the Hague Convention of 1907. Reparations were therefore demanded and agreed as part of the settlement at the Potsdam Conference in August 1945. Claims demanded by Soviet Union and Poland were allocated to be taken from the Soviet occupied areas of Germany and Eastern Europe, while the claims from the US, UK, and the rest of the Allies were to come from the Allied occupied areas. This chapter looks at the Soviet Bloc reparations, while Chapter 11 deals with reparations to the Allies.

Reparations to the Soviet Bloc were governed by the Paris Peace Treaties, signed on 10 February 1947 between the victors and Italy, Romania, Hungary, Bulgaria, and Finland. The Peace Treaties of Paris specified reparations should be paid by Hungary, Romania, Bulgaria, and Finland, mainly to the Soviet Union. Italy had to pay reparations to the Soviet Union, as well as Greece, Yugoslavia, Albania, and Ethiopia totalling 360 million US dollars. The amounts for Romania, Hungary, and Finland were 300 million US dollars from each, while Bulgaria had to pay 70 million US dollars. The payments were meant to be paid in kind (i.e., in non-monetary goods) but because all countries but Finland and Italy fell under the Soviet umbrella, reparations were later officially cancelled for Hungary, Romania, and Bulgaria (Nevakivi 1996, pp. 95–97). While the Italian absolute amount was higher, the economy was much larger, and it represented a small amount of GDP (see Chapter 11). Kramer (2009) notes there was a large flow of money from the periphery to the centre of the Soviet Bloc in the years following World War II, regardless of whether the transfers were regarded as reparations. The only reparation to be paid in full was therefore the one from Finland. It is analysed in detail in Section 10.1, as it is a case of a very large transfer that was militarily and politically enforced, despite being damagingly large. It made no economic sense for Finland to repay if the analysis is done through a standard sovereign debt model. If the transfer is thought of as ensuring the survival of the Finnish state, it is another matter entirely.

10.1 FINNISH REPARATIONS TO THE SOVIET UNION

The Paris Peace Treaties (1947) set up the Allied Control Commission and the War Reparations Commission allocated the Finnish accumulated debt to the Soviet Union. In addition to incurring the cost of the Commission, Finland faced significant reparations and lost territory to the Soviet Union.[1] Reparations were to be paid entirely in kind, at an estimated cost of 3 per cent of output per year between 1945 and 1952 (Pihkala 1999, pp. 26–37). The total size of the reparation was 300 million US dollars, which was specified in the Paris Peace Treaties (1947). This was paid primarily to the Soviet Union and the money-equivalent was around 20 per cent of GDP (Pihkala 1999, p. 32).[2] Most of the goods were produced thanks to loans from abroad. As Figure 10.1 shows, internally generated financing was not available because the Finnish the trade balance was negative. While the Finnish level of savings increased dramatically, so did the level of domestic investments, which meant that net goods export was negative from the end of the war until 1951.

From 1944 to 1947, Finland received loans from the US worth 126 million US dollars while paying out the equivalent of 232 million US dollars in reparations. Pihkala (1999, p. 32) estimates that the required dollar funding, had Finland bought only American goods and used them to pay the in-kind reparations, would have been between 546 and 570 million US dollars. It corresponds to around a third of total industrial production in 1945, though by 1952 it had fallen to 4 per cent as the economy had grown. Finnish reparations were mostly funded by loans and foreign debt, which increased from 229 million US dollars in 1945 to 661 million US dollars in 1951 (Pihkala 1999, p. 46). During the period,

---

[1] The Marshall Plan helped rebuild Europe but was politically offensive to the Soviets, and Finland was pressured not to participate by them, an added indirect cost.

[2] The uncertainty around pre-war GDP and GDP levels during the first repayment means that the reparations-to-GDP can only be estimated at somewhere between 17 and 30 per cent. I will use the most reliable GDP number, implying a 20 per cent reparations-to-GDP.

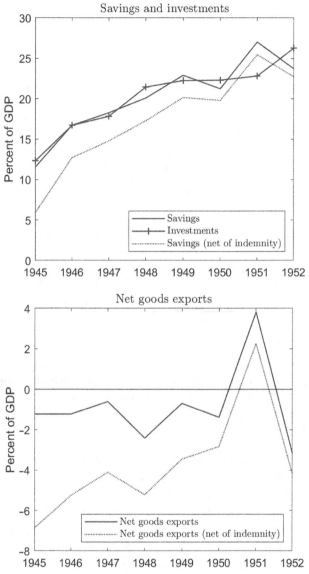

FIGURE 10.1 Finnish savings, investments, and net goods exports (1945–52). Sources: Official Statistics of Finland; Pihkala (1999, p. 35). Replication file, *plot_sicaf.m.*

Finland paid its sovereign debt and reparations despite exhibiting all the characteristics of a sovereign default, as explained in the model in Chapter 3.

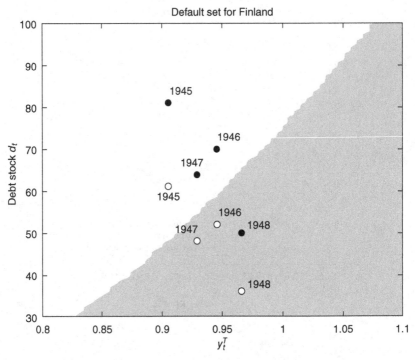

FIGURE 10.2 Finnish default set, debt stock, and detrended output.
Note: The grey area is the state denotes repayment while the white area is default. The dots denote Finnish debt excluding the reparation (hollow dots) and including the reparation (black dots) on the y-axis and detrended output on the x-axis. Replication file, *plot_default_set_finland.m.*

Figure 10.2 shows the default set of Finland for the years 1945 to 1948. The hollow dots denote Finnish sovereign debt excluding reparations on the y-axis, while the black dots are total liabilities including reparations. On the x-axis is detrended real output per capita. Finland came out of the Second World War with low output and a high debt stock. The level of Finnish debt-to-GDP was 60 per cent in 1945 before the announcement of reparations. It jumped to 80 per cent of GDP in 1945 as reparations were 20 per cent of GDP. Only 28 per cent of Finland's debt stock was foreign in 1945, but it grew to more than half by 1949 (Pihkala 1999, p. 46). Because Finland experienced such output loss in the immediate years following the war, Finland was in the default set from 1945 to 1947 if reparations are included in the debt stock. Only by 1948 did output rebound and was sovereign debt reduced, placing it in the repayment area. Unlike in the French case earlier, the period from 1945 to 1947 was marred by economic crises in which wages fell drastically and the exchange rate was devalued.

Figure 10.3 plots the model predictions against Finnish historical macroeconomic data collected from 1945 to 1948. The largest output loss came in 1945 at the end of the war, when detrended real output per capita fell 9 per cent. Net output y_0-d_0 decreased 25 per cent as initial reparations were announced in 1945, before recovering slowly from 1946 onwards. The level of debt after the announcement of reparations was significantly above the level of d_0 in the model. The Finnish debt stock was negotiated at the end of the war and was therefore unchanged before 1945. Until the end of 1946, interest rates did not move much, hovering between 6 and 7 per cent, using Helsingfors municipal bonds as a proxy. But in 1947, the price of the 5 per cent government bond maturing in 1961 dropped, which increased interest rates. Real wages fell by 50 per cent from 1945 to 1948 and Finland devalued its currency the *markka* three times in 1945. Like the real wage, the real exchange rate (bottom right) overshoots the prediction of the model significantly.

The Finnish economy performed worse in terms of exchange rates and real wages than the model would predict for a default. In the model, the government's goal is to maximise full employment real wages, and a default marks the trough in real wages and output. An economic crisis does not spread to the domestic sector, because the government uses optimal monetary policy (by devaluing the currency and increases tariffs) alongside a default. Finland's output, credit spreads, debt stock, real wages, nominal, and real exchange rates all performed worse in the years 1945 to 1947. One reason could be that the country was unable to default on its sovereign debts, which meant that increased levels of domestic resources went to debt service. The only policy option was to devalue the currency, but because its debt was foreign debt, devaluations increased the value in domestic currency. While its loans were in foreign currency, however, reparations were paid in kind.

The reason Finland was unable to default on reparations was the political economy realities of its close relationship with the Soviet Union. Similarly, it was in the interest of Finland to have closer relations with Western Europe and the US, which meant a default on its debt to the United States was impossible. The only policy option was a devaluation and export growth, especially to Western Europe. It meant that as reparations were paid, Finland could grow its way out of its debt problems,

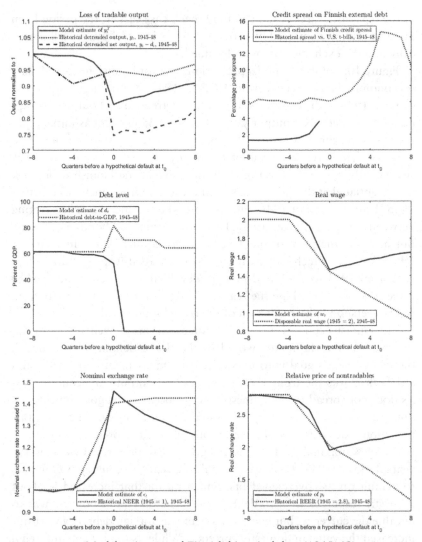

FIGURE 10.3 Model estimate and Finnish historical data (1945–48).
Sources: Bolt et al. (2018) for output; Ljungberg (2019) for exchange rates; Federal Reserve for bond yields; Pihkala (1999) for wages and debt. Replication file, *plot_finland.m*.

which meant that by 1948 it was no longer in the default set. When Finland joined the IMF and the World Bank in 1948, debt-to-GDP was already declining. It was, however, a path that did not include a default because it was impossible politically, even though it might have been a better economic policy.

World War II Reparations to the Allies

World War II reparations to the Allies were smaller than reparations from previous wars and much smaller than reparations demanded by the Soviet Bloc. The geopolitical landscape had changed since the disastrous World War I reparations, and with the end of the war came a new economic doctrine. Instead of claiming reparations that had a significant economic impact, the United States produced the Marshall Plan, which provided loans to Europe. The reconstruction policy after World War II absorbed the lessons of Keynes (1919, 1929a) and the focus was on 'industrial disarmament', not punishment, to ensure the peace (Cohen 1967, p. 270).

The reparations question for the Allied was decided at the Paris Conference on Reparations (21 December 1945).[1] There were some smaller reparations and damages awarded because the brutality and destruction of the Nazi regime was vast. The Final Act of the Conference divided reparations into two categories: monetary restitution (Category A) and asset forfeitures (Category B). The eighteen signatories divided the total among themselves, which was based on a compilation of claims from each country. The main recipients of German reparations were the US, UK, and France. Each country's share is noted in Table 11.1.

The agreement listed the share of reparations each country would receive, which was direct damages and claims received from each country.

---

[1] The source for the history in this chapter is the text of the Final Act of the Paris Conference on Reparations (1945) and archives from the Danish Foreign Ministry, found in the Danish National Archives (journal number 6.Y.Tyskland.1). A summary of the archives was published by the Foreign Ministry in response to a question from Parliament (Udenrigsministeriet 2007).

When Nations Can't Default

TABLE 11.1 *Recipients of reparations from Germany*

	Category A (reparations, percentage)	Category B (assets, percentage)
Albania	0.05	0.35
US	28.00	11.80
Australia	0.70	0.95
Belgium	2.70	4.50
Canada	3.50	1.50
Denmark	0.25	0.35
Egypt	0.05	0.20
France	16.00	22.80
UK	28.00	27.80
Greece	2.70	4.35
India	2.00	2.90
Luxembourg	0.15	0.40
Norway	1.30	1.90
New Zealand	0.40	0.60
Netherlands	3.90	5.60
Czechoslovakia	3.00	4.30
South Africa	0.70	0.10
Yugoslavia	6.60	9.60
Sum	100.00	100.00

Source: Final Act of the Paris Conference on Reparations (1945).

It also listed the rules for asset forfeitures that a country could claim. Category B assets were property that Germany left in occupied areas that could be sold, industrial assets inside Germany, and German ships. The assets left in occupied areas would be subtracted from the reparations claim. Actual German reparations came in the form of explicit payments (reparations) from 1953 to around 1965. All payments amounted to 5.2 billion US dollars, which was around 3 per cent of 1960 German output (Cohen 1967, pp. 282–88).[2] In addition to the explicit monetary transfers, Germany also paid indemnities to prisoners, indemnities for expropriated property, and forfeited assets. In many countries, the money available for damages under the agreement was less than the actual damages.

Japan similarly paid reparations, largely in the form of de-industrialisation. In total, Japan paid around 4 per cent of output to

---

[2] GDP data is from World Bank Indicators. Germany also paid significant restitutions, largely domestically, under the Restitution Act, so the amounts here are specific to the period before 1965. East Germany is not included but paid substantial amounts.

the Allies, but this was largely offset by American economic assistance (DeLong and Eichengreen 1993). Japan was, like Germany, forced to dismantle its war industries in order not to pose a threat. The Japanese Peace Treaty of 1951 considered that Japan did not have the capacity to pay reparations. In the end, only minor transfers to poor Asian countries were made – to Burma, Cambodia, Indonesia, Laos, Philippines, South Korea, Vietnam, and Thailand (DeLong and Eichengreen 1993). In total, Japanese reparations in goods and money came to 1.5 billion US dollars, or about 4 per cent of GDP (Cohen 1967, pp. 272–73).

Finally, there was Italy, whose reparations were part of the Paris Peace Treaties (1947) discussed in Chapter 10. Italian reparations were paid in kind and amounted to around 1 per cent of GDP. The transfer was paid to Yugoslavia (125 million US dollars), Greece (105 million US dollars), the Soviet Union (100 million US dollars), Ethiopia (25 million US dollars), and Albania (5 million US dollars). An additional payment of 6 million US dollars in interest brought the total to 366 million US dollars, with some minor payments to other countries (Cohen 1967, pp. 272–73). The smaller World War II reparations to the Allies are the only recent reparations not funded by the issuance of sovereign debt. The reason was that sovereign debt was not needed to finance relatively minor liabilities. Reparations following World War II were small in value and targeted specifically to deter industrialisation.

The post-war period included significant non-monetary transfers. Gimbel (1990) argues that the United States took reparations from Germany in the form of intellectual property. Patents and scientific know-how were transferred from Germany to the Allies, this including visits to Germany and the migration of scientists especially to the United States. The value of the transfer is hard to estimate because it consisted of both people and information. O'Reagan (2019) shows that the flow of information from Germany to the Allies in the post-war period was significant and had an impact on diplomacy, as well as industry and science. Fisch (1992) argues that the inability to obtain large reparations meant that the Soviet Union did so indirectly through Eastern Germany, although this does not show up as war reparations in the national account.[3] Finland alone followed the example of previous reparations and issued sizable amounts of sovereign debt to finance the payment.

---

[3] One curious side note is that in 1946, the United States offered France debt relief but with conditions: In three of every four weeks, French cinemas had to show American movies. They were allies, so this is not considered reparations, but a condition for loans. After two years, the French reneged (Ulff-Møller 2001, p. 144).

World War II reparations also depart from other reparations transfers when it comes to enforcement of claims. Even if peace settlements and treaties assign damages, the actual collection of transfers depends on the will of the creditor to enforce the agreements. The will of the West, and here it was primarily the US, was to stand together in opposition to the Soviet Union during the Cold War. Enforcement of reparations claims were not important because the United States supported West Germany anyway. Once the process of dismantling the German and Japanese war machines was done, the relatively minor collection of money was left untouched. This did not just happen with regard to the United States. Smaller countries' claims were either negotiated away or de-facto written off, because it was more important to maintain a good relationship to a close ally. As an example of how reparations are only damaging when enforced by military or political force, Section 11.1 provides a detailed view of how German reparations to Denmark were largely written off, despite still being official debt.

11.1 GERMAN REPARATIONS TO DENMARK

The total Danish claim amounted to 11.6 billion Danish kroner for damages during the occupation from 1940 to 1945. The two main claims were 4.6 billion kroner, which was used by Germany to build defence bunkers on the west coast of Denmark, and 2.9 billion kroner from the clearing account, which had been used to 'pay' for Danish exports to Germany. This was relatively minor compared with most other nations' claims, but the enforcement of the claim is of wider interest when analysing sovereign debt.[4] The Paris Conference on Reparations resulted in Denmark having a claim of the overall transfer for 0.25 per cent of Category A and 0.35 per cent of Category B. It also allowed for the liquidation of German assets in Denmark, which was institutionalised in Denmark by the 30 March 1946 law on confiscation of German and Japanese property. A special position and commission was created to find and liquidate said property, which was in effect until 1960.

Denmark received machines and ships from Germany in accordance with its percentual claim, which amounted to a total of 13 million Danish kroner. Liquidated assets left in Denmark after the war amounted to another 30 million Danish kroner, and the commission found another 237 million kroner worth of goods and property. After costs of enforcement, the income was around 200 million Danish kroner or 2 per cent of

---

[4] The story is told from the Danish National Archives and Udenrigsministeriet (2007).

the total claim. Instead, the Danish state took over private claims and paid them out, and then the money received from sales of German assets went to the central bank. In 1953, Germany paid another 160 million Danish kroner as part of the London Agreement on German Debts (known as the London Debt Agreement), which was a payment for expenses that the Danish state had incurred to house refugees after the war. The London Debt Agreement lowered Germany's external debt dramatically, extended maturities, and made transfers conditional on ability to pay. Denmark agreed to lower its claim to 5.7 billion kroner during the conference. Galofré-Vilà et al. (2019) find that the debt agreement contributed to Germany's subsequent growth by creating fiscal space, restoring currency convertibility, and ultimately reintegrating West Germany into global markets. Another 16 million kroner of damages was paid in 1959, with the last minor rate paid in 1983. The transfer in 1983 is, as far as I can tell, the last payment from Germany to Denmark.

Reparations paid by Germany to Denmark therefore amount to a small percentage of the actual claim (5.5 per cent). The reparations agreement never set a money amount of reparations, only a percentage share claim for each country. Denmark's claim was worth 0.25 per cent of the total, but it was not possible to know what the total amount of reparations paid out were. The agreement also stated that creditors could not claim anything alone but had to work with the rest of the signatories. In effect, the 1953 London Debt Agreement settled the reparations question. In 1977, the Danish Prime Minister Anker Jørgensen stated that he would not take the initiative to claim the rest of the money, despite domestic political pressure and continued questions from Parliament. The 'German debt' (*Tysklandsgæld*) is still on the books but was de-facto written off. The reasons given were twofold: Danish claims were minor in the larger scheme of reparations, and Denmark did not want to relitigate a reparations questions after the disastrous effect of World War I reparations. Instead, citizens of Denmark could apply for restitution directly from the state.

The enforcement of German World War II reparations was significantly different from other reparations. Unlike many previous reparations, Germany re-entered the alliance where it was a debtor, and the minor debts were not significant compared with the geopolitical priorities. Given Germany's military status after World War II, it would not have been difficult for the United States or UK to enforce the claims, but it was not considered politically important.

12

Iraq Gulf War Reparations

The most recent war reparation is also the biggest. For more than thirty years, Iraq paid reparations for the damages it inflicted during the Gulf War. As a share of output, reparations were more than 400 per cent of 1991 GDP alone, but even in absolute terms the transfer was large at 52 billion US dollars. What is even more remarkable is that the reparation was repaid even as the country went through a financial meltdown, complete economic isolation because of international sanctions, the 2003 invasion, and a sovereign debt restructuring that wrote off almost nine-tenths of its debt in net present value (NPV) terms. Through all this, reparations were repaid. This chapter focus on how Iraq incurred its large stock of sovereign debt, was forced to pay reparations, and how the enforcement mechanism worked that made reparations de facto senior liabilities of the state.[1]

In 1979, Iraq was a net creditor to the world, owing to its large oil reserves and lack of external debt. Fifteen years later, its government debt-to-GDP was over 1,000 per cent and it possessed few assets to speak of. At the time of the US invasion in 2003, Iraq was saddled with around 130 billion US dollars in external debt, which made it the most indebted nation in the world. Can a country incur so much debt, so fast, without some of the debt being considered odious? Can you have an odious debt stock but still pay war reparations? I argue that in the case of Iraq, some of its debts were odious (or illegitimate). Odious debts are loans that are

---

[1] This chapter is an adaption of two papers I have written for *Middle Eastern Studies* and *Capital Markets Law Journal* (Hinrichsen 2021, 2022). This chapter brings the story together with other case studies for context and formulates the thesis of the book.

not approved by, nor for the benefit of, the people.[2] The story of Iraqi debt, defaults, and the subsequent restructuring has been scantily covered in the sovereign debt and economic history literatures, with no full historiography of Iraqi debt. Earlier studies of the rise of Iraqi indebtedness were undertaken before sovereign debt restructuring between 2003 and 2006, which decided what claims were considered legitimate. Iraq's history is therefore ripe for re-examination.

The chapter brings together many of the theories of this book. The build-up of Iraqi debt occurred during war time and I will argue that much of the debt was odious. The story involved geopolitics, where easy financing was available to Iraq for as long as it was an ally of the West. Once the friendship ended during the Gulf War, large reparations were imposed, with an enforcement mechanism that is akin to older types of transfers. The debt was repaid over decades, and once it was time to restructure Iraq's sovereign debt, after the invasion, reparations were left out. The sovereign debt restructuring is explained in detail here to account for how reparations were left out, but also to show how restructurings occur in practice. This chapter builds especially on Chapters 2 and 3 to weave together a story that illustrates how, even in recent times, reparations are repaid no matter what.

The story requires some history, and it has not been written about fully until now. Earlier attempts to write about reparations and the Iraqi debt history include Morrison (1992) and Alnasrawi (1994), but most mention reparations as a side note to other, Iraq-related research, such as Caron (2004) and Momani and Garrib (2010). Studies such as Chaney's (2008) that detail market reactions to Iraqi political developments from 2006 based on bond yields are impossible for earlier periods because of data gaps. I therefore had to piece together the story before it could be told. The history is important because it is not possible to understand the status of Iraq's debt and reparations without understanding where the debt originated. The sovereign debt world developed fast during the 1980s and the history and concepts explored in Chapter 3 are therefore required to understand much of what was going on.

The Iraqi sovereign debt restructuring featured some new and unprecedented legal tools to get a deal. Most Iraqi oil assets were abroad, which meant that they could be attached by creditors, which is normal in corporate bankruptcies. To avoid Iraq losing some of its assets abroad, they

---

[2] A full discussion of the history and definition of the term 'odious debt' is found in Chapter 3 and in King (2016).

were all immunised from creditor attachment as part of UN Resolution 1483 (2003b). No one had ever put a comparable blanket stay in place. The closest historical precedent was during the Iranian revolution in 1979, when Tehran repudiated all foreign debt and President Carter froze all Iranian assets in the United States in retaliation. In the Iranian case, there were subsequently 400 lawsuits against Iranian property (Christopher and Mosk 2007, pp. 165–67). The executive branch of the US government immunised certain assets based on national security interests, to ensure they could not be attached as judgments. As part of the negotiated settlement following the 1981 hostage crisis (the Algiers Accords), Iranian assets were unfrozen and all lawsuits dropped (Buchheit and Gulati 2019, pp. 6–7).[3] But even the earlier case does not come close to the Iraqi immunisation case in scope and political significance. All these things make it worthwhile to look at the Iraq case in detail.

The methodology of this chapter is a bit different from the rest of the book, as I use both archival and oral sources to write the history of Iraqi debt. The chapter begins in 1979 as Saddam Hussein took power. During the build-up of debt throughout the Iran–Iraq War (1980–88), I use primary and secondary sources to trace the sovereign debt stock. Primary sources are mostly government reports, press releases, official documents, laws, resolutions, and annual reports of creditors. The second half of the chapter uses oral history and primary sources to put together the history of the restructuring as it occurred from 2003 to 2006. I conducted interviews with the key players of the restructuring, including US and UK government officials, lawyers for the Iraqi government, the bankers involved, and civil society activists who were involved in the debt jubilee movement. The chapter does not rely on models such as those used in the first part of the book because they require data that are simply not available from the period. By helping to create a database for Iraqi debt, this provides a wealth of information for future studies.

I show that the rise of Iraqi indebtedness was a consequence of geopolitical trends, in particular American political and commercial interests

---

[3] It ended up in the Supreme Court, which sided with the Executive (Dames & Moore v Regan, 1981). In 1999, another case involving a Swiss company, Compagnie Noga, won a judgment against Russia in Swedish courts. After Russia's 1998 sovereign default, it stopped payments on a deal to Noga. The jurisdiction went through New York where Noga tried to seize assets related to uranium, stored in Kentucky, that Russia had given up as part of an arms deal. Uranium linked to the HEU Agreement was immunised by President Clinton (see Timbie 2004, pp. 183–84; Buchheit and Gulati 2019, p. 6). Noga managed to seize less protected assets in France, but not many other examples come close.

in the region. Political lending trumped solvency concerns, and loans were given on terms more favourable than those of the US government, with no reform conditionality except the need to fight a war against Iran. I argue that much of the debt can be considered odious as a result. To show this, I reconstruct the build-up of Iraqi debts through the 1980s and 1990s. I identify debt levels at four key points in time: in 1979 as Saddam Hussein took power; in 1988 at the end of the Iran–Iraq War; in 1991 at the end of the Gulf War; and on the eve of the US invasion in 2003. I work backwards from claims submitted in the 2003–06 restructuring and trace the loans to the time of their origin, creating a time series of the Iraqi debt stock going back to 1979. It enables, for the first time, the creation of a continuous time series of Iraq debt-to-GDP going back to 1979. It also shows just how large the imposed war reparation was.

12.1 HISTORICAL BACKGROUND

The literature on Iraq's political economy and security situation is rich, but Iraqi debt history is insufficiently covered in the literature. Studies do exist, of course, but none has set out to trace the debt from 1979 all the way to the sovereign debt restructuring in 2006. Earlier studies, such as Abbas Alnasrawi (1994), Ahmed M. Jiyad (2001), and David Caron (2004), tell parts of the story, but they did not have the benefit of knowing which loans were considered legitimate in the 2003–06 sovereign debt restructuring. Other studies, such as Rangwala (2013), did not focus on the debt. There are some studies that concentrate either narrowly on reparations (Morrison 1992) or follow the reconstruction of the economy (Momani and Garrib 2010). Studies such as Eric Chaney's (2008) detail stock market reactions to Iraqi political developments from 2006 based on bond yields, but such studies are impossible for earlier periods because of data gaps. The era leading up to one of the largest sovereign debt restructurings in history is therefore not covered as well as it could have been.

The Iraqi sovereign debt restructuring occurred between 2003 and 2006 and included around 130 billion US dollars of debt, but excluded war reparations transfers from the Gulf War. Most of the debt can be traced back to the early 1980s, even though Iraq had no external debt in 1979. Table 12.1 shows who Iraq owed money to in 1979, but with foreign exchange reserves at 65 per cent of GDP and little debt, Iraq was a net creditor – not a borrower.

Saddam Hussein took power in 1979 after a decade of strong economic growth, but prosperity in the 1970s was followed by economic

TABLE 12.1 *Iraqi debt by creditor, 1979*

	Outstanding debt (US dollar billion)	Per cent of GDP
Paris Club	2	3
Gulf States	–	–
Soviet and allies	–	–
Reparations (non-debt)	–	–
Commercial debt	1	2
Foreign exchange reserves	–35	–65
Total	–33	–60

Note: The negative number denotes creditor status for Iraq. The negative number remains the consistent format, appearing again in later tables, all tracing Iraqi debt.
Sources: Caron (2004, p. 131); Jiyad (2001, p. 19); and Alnasrawi (1994, p. 152).

collapse in the 1980s. The Iran–Iraq War started in 1980 and continued throughout the decade to 1988. Throughout the war, Iraq enjoyed broad international political support for its efforts. The support came both in the form of public support and covert support and loans. Almost all Iraqi debt was incurred during the war, which was helped along by both the West and the East. The United States and Europe did not want a post-revolution Iran to win the war, and happily provided money and weapons to Iraq. Halfway through the war, it became clear the country was insolvent as contractual payments were deferred and rescheduled. New external money kept coming in nonetheless, because the loans and credits were politically motivated and not given on market terms. A full default on Iraq's external debt followed in the late 1980s.

In 1990, after the end of the Iran–Iraq War, Iraq invaded Kuwait in what became known as the Gulf War. But the political winds had shifted: this time the United States led a coalition to defeat Iraq. After the war, the UN forced Iraq to pay war reparations and placed it under international sanctions in 1990. This left Iraq isolated from the global economy for much of the 1990s. The outcome was a phenomenal rise and fall in Iraqi debt-to-GDP from 1979, which can be seen in Figure 12.1 for the first time.[4]

The increase in the debt-to-GDP ratio between 1979 and 1995 comes from both the numerator and the denominator: the absolute level of debt soared as output also collapsed at the end of the war, as international sanctions were introduced and Iraq's oil exports fell.

---

[4] Technically, the figure first appeared in Hinrichsen (2022).

FIGURE 12.1 Iraq government debt-to-GDP (1979–2020).
Source: See text.

The following sections trace the build-up of debt in Iraq over the decades after 1979, culminating with the sovereign debt restructuring in 2003–06. The method, where possible, is to take the restructured debt amounts and work backwards, identifying where the loans originated and reconstructing a loan chronology. There is an attempt to give a best guess of debt levels in 1988, 1991, and 2003. The data in this section are drawn from primary sources (government reports, investigations, declassified intelligence reports, historical data) and secondary sources.

12.2 THE IRAN–IRAQ WAR (1980–1988)

The year 1979 brought momentous change to the Middle East. Saddam took power in Iraq and the Iranian Revolution overthrew the US-backed shah in favour of Ayatollah Khomeini.[5] Change in Iraq came on the back

---

[5] The two countries did not get along. Iranian-backed militias attempted to assassinate several Iraqi ministers and Iraq deported thousands of Iranians: see Kennington et al. (2004, p. 1).

TABLE 12.2 *Iraqi growth rates, 1970–89 (yearly average in percentage)*

	1970–79	1980–89
Government consumption	13.6	–2.9
Private consumption	13.2	–6.1
Investments	27.6	–0.9
Exports	4.4	–5.0
Imports	22.5	–5.6
Domestic trade	16.8	–4.8
GDP	11.7	–4.9

Source: Alnasrawi (1994, p. 101).

of the roaring economy of the 1970s, when output growth had averaged 12 per cent a year after the nationalisation of the Iraq Petroleum Company and a rise in oil prices. Oil production increased fortyfold (Alnasrawi 1994, pp. 79–80). Iraqi petroleum fields were among the largest in the world, producing 3.5 million barrels a day in 1979, with revenues from oil totalling 26 billion US dollars in 1980 (Alnasrawi 1994, p. 93; Mehdi 2018, pp. 1–36). Two-thirds of output came from oil-related activity and the country relied on fuel exports. The economy was controlled by the state and almost all activity ran through the state bureaucracy, from oil policy to control over imports and the allocation of capital (Alnasrawi 1994, pp. 79–103; Foote 2004, pp. 47–70). In 1979, Saddam took over a virtually debt-free economy and 35 billion US dollars in foreign exchange reserves. However, the roaring 1970s were replaced by the miserable 1980s, and the Iraq economy plunged into war and disaster. Table 12.2 shows the average yearly growth rates for the periods. From more than 10 per cent growth rates on average in the 1970s, the Iraqi economy contracted on average about 5 per cent a year in the 1980s.

This was because of the Iran–Iraq War. After months of political attacks and skirmishes, Saddam invaded Iran on 22 September 1980. Almost all countries in the world supported Iraq. During the Iranian hostage crisis at the US embassy in Tehran in 1979, the United States had frozen all Iranian assets and, in turn, the new Iranian government had repudiated all foreign debts (Christopher and Mosk 2007, pp. 165–75). The United States went to the International Court of Justice in The Hague, which ruled in its favour shortly afterwards, ordering Iran to return the embassy and release the hostages. Iran was massively out of international favour.

Consequently, after the Iraqi invasion of Iran, the United States designated Italy as a go-between during initial discussions with Baghdad, which was for the United States to avoid being seen as favouring Iraq (Kennington 2004, p. 3). Neutrality was just for show, though. Iranian objections to the invasion fell flat – owing to its low standing following the hostage crisis – and its petition to the UN went nowhere. The international community was on the Iraqi side, either explicitly or implicitly, with few countries even daring to sell arms to Iran. From early in the war, Iraq had access to politically motivated borrowing from its Gulf State neighbours, the US, and the Soviet Union, with everyone under the understanding that further arms purchases would require a debt restructuring or payment in oil (CIA 1984, pp. 9–19).[6] The Soviet Union would supply weapons to Iraq worth 3 billion US dollars financed by loans and indicated it was willing to restructure Iraq's debt early on in the war.

In 1981, Italy started selling vessels to Iraq worth 1.8 billion US dollars; the Soviet Union supplied arms (initially through its Eastern European satellites); Britain signed a trade pact; and French nuclear physicists arrived on the ground to help build a nuclear reactor near Baghdad. The Iraqi government might have thought a quick victory was possible but as Iran started to fight back, the Iraqi economy began to hurt. Oil exports collapsed by 75 per cent, as export facilities and terminals were destroyed by bombs. Iraq had relied on two oil pipelines – one through Syria, one through Turkey – that quickly dwindled to one: Syria declared support for Iran and cut off access. Iraq quickly depleted its foreign reserves and was forced to borrow money. Loans from the Gulf States totalled 16 billion US dollars through 1981. The Gulf States backed Iraq throughout the war, lending a total of 40 billion US dollars, considering this money a loan; but Iraq considered it to be grants.[7] Iraq also began to request deferral on contractual dues early in the war, mainly on money owed to European suppliers. Creditors agreed to reschedule 85 to 90 per cent of the debt that was to be repaid in 1983 and 1984. The rescheduled debt was to be repaid in equal instalments over four years, starting in 1985. The remaining debt (the 10 to 15 per cent) was repaid either in cash or financed by commercial credits.[8]

---

[6] The CIA report was declassified in 2011 but is originally from 1984.

[7] The disagreement is still outstanding today (as are most of the loans), but the US Treasury pushed (unsuccessfully) to include them in the 2003–06 restructuring.

[8] Commercial credit is a short-term credit facility at a bank, usually paid back quickly.

The United States removed Iraq from its list of countries sponsoring terrorism in 1982, which made it easier to undertake commercial transactions. Arms sales to Iraq increased as a result, both directly from the United States and through proxies. In June 1982, President Reagan issued a secret directive to make sure Iraq would not lose the war, which put the Central Intelligence Agency (CIA) in charge of supplying Iraq with weapons (Hersh 1992). The decision came after the CIA warned that from a military perspective, Iraq had essentially lost the war (CIA 1982). Fighting escalated throughout 1983 and the UN was unable to negotiate a ceasefire. Iraq continued to have easy access to weapons and credit. Jordan joined in, extending loans worth 125 million US dollars to Saddam (Kennington et al. 2004, p. 19). The total eventually reached 1.3 billion US dollars.

In 1982, the Central Bank of Iraq issued about 50 million Iraqi dinars worth of bonds, which were mostly bought by domestic commercial banks (IMF 1983, p. 5). In 1983, the Eurobond market was still open to Iraq's state-owned enterprises. Rafidain Bank issued 500 million US dollars of loans and the Iraq National Oil Company issued 120 million US dollars. Debt service at the end of 1983 was around 1 per cent of exports (IMF 1983, p. 7). The IMF was unable to satisfactorily assess the balance of payments because the quality of data provided was poor, but stated that interest rates on external debt to a subset of creditors (excluding the Gulf States) amounted to about a third of the principal (IMF 1983b, pp. 28–33 and 53).

US support for Baghdad became explicit in 1984 – even after Iraq started using chemical weapons – and the CIA stepped up its war effort (Woodward 1986). France provided 500 million US dollars in new loans and refinanced 1.4 billion US dollars of maturing debt. The international community – via bilateral negotiations by the United States with the Soviet Union and the UN – pushed to end the conflict in 1985, but had no luck. Instead, Iraq went on the offensive in early 1986 via air raids, which had secretly been urged on by the Reagan administration, but to little effect.[9] Despite Iraq's best efforts, the war was being fought on Iraqi soil now, and the military situation was deteriorating. Oil prices halved in 1986 and the oil-reliant Iraqi economy continued its downward spiral. The fall in oil removed the last ability of Iraq to self-finance the war

---

[9] The apparent contradiction between the official negotiation position of the United States and its covert operations, later acknowledged, was likely a consequence of the desire to see Iraq victorious (Frantz and Waas 1992).

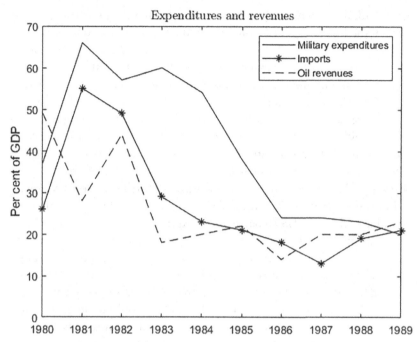

FIGURE 12.2 Iraqi expenditures and revenues (1980–89).
Source: Based on data from Alnasrawi (1994, pp. 93–96).

(Al-Marashi 2018). The economy of 1980s Iraq was a war economy. Military expenditures and imports related to the war effort took up a large part of the national economy. This coincided with declining oil revenues. To sustain the war, Iraq went into debt. Figure 12.2 shows military expenditures, oil revenues, and imports as a percentage of output. It shows how revenues declined at the same time as all spending was directed to the war effort. A natural consequence was that money was directed from social spending to the war effort.

During 1987, the UN passed several resolutions calling for an end to the conflict. As no agreement was reached, the West ramped up pressure to force a negotiated peace and arms sales to Iraq continued unabashedly in parallel to efforts to contain Iran via sanctions and embargoes. In early 1988, the Soviet Union and China agreed to UN sanctions, forcing Iran to the negotiating table. The cease-fire was signed on 20 August 1988. Iran had had little international support and initially could only buy weapons from Libya. In 1982, the Soviet Union, Syria, North Korea, and Israel had started to supply Iran, mostly in return for oil. Iraq, on the other hand, had, as we have seen, plenty of help from across the globe. Loans came in the form of grants, transfers, commercial lending, or covert arms deals. From 1983 to 1993, for instance, Iraq received 2 billion US dollars in loans from the US Department of Agriculture (CIA 2004; Weiss 2011, p. 2).[10] Underpinning the loans was a strong geopolitical desire for Iraq not to lose the war to Iran.

The largest commercial claim submitted in the restructuring in 2003–06 exemplifies the interconnectedness, and shows how Iraq was able to maintain market access until the end of the 1980s. Between 1985 and 1990, a small Atlanta branch of the state-owned Italian bank Banca Nazionale del Lavoro (BNL) extended loans worth 4 billion US dollars to Iraqi individuals and entities. This included 1.6 billion US dollars of loans backed by the US Department of Agriculture's Commodity Credit Corporation (SSCI 1993, pp. 8–9). Officially, the loans were designated for agricultural imports, but the money was used for weapons (illegally). The Department of Justice prosecuted the Atlanta branch manager, arguing he had acted without approval from BNL headquarters in Rome. However, the District Court judge, Marvin H. Shoob, wrote in an opinion that the CIA had likely known about the illegal financing of arms. He also noted that BNL Rome was not a victim, indicating that they had been aware of the loans (Stich 2005, pp. 94–95). The CIA intervened and withheld certain information, which triggered a Senate investigation. Recall that President Reagan had secretly put the CIA in charge of arming Iraq.[11] Thus, the BNL was owned by the Italian state; received loan guarantees from the US Department of Agriculture; and extended loans worth 4 billion US dollars from a small branch in Atlanta, with US intelligence services involved in the court case.[12] Regardless of whether it was officially sanctioned, two governments were implicitly involved.[13]

---

[10] The CIA suggested Iraq had spent 22 billion US dollars on weapons halfway through the war, while Iran had spent 5 billion US dollars. Schmidt (1991, p. 12) suggests total Iraqi weapons imports during the war were 63 billion US dollars (in 1990 US dollars).

[11] The US Senate in its report cleared the CIA of any direct knowledge of illegality; see Kerry and Brown (1992).

[12] Another bank, the BCCI, was investigated simultaneously by the US Senate Committee on Foreign Relations. Senators Kerry and Brown showed in their report how BCCI was a criminal empire that facilitated money laundering and weapons smuggling in Iraq. BCCI provided loans to Iraq, as well as holding deposits and providing funding for BNL (Kerry and Brown 1992, pp. 69, 579). The CIA was involved and knew about the criminality at BCCI (Kerry and Brown 1992, p. 9).

[13] The point being that the Department of Agriculture guaranteed loans were used for weapons (Kerry and Brown 1992, pp. 69, 514, and 578–79).

TABLE 12.3 *Iraqi debt by creditor, 1988*

	Outstanding debt (US dollar billion)	Per cent of GDP
Paris Club	29	95
Gulf States	40	129
Soviet and allies	11	36
Reparations (non-debt)	–	–
Commercial debt	6	19
Foreign exchange reserves	–	–
Total	86	278

Sources: Alnasrawi (1994, pp. 109, 159); Metz (1990, p. 126).

Eventually, the loans were defaulted on and restructured along with all other commercial claims, but the episode underscores how Iraq obtained financing in the 1980s. The loans were made to pay for a war that was supported by most of the Western states, at a time when Iraq had lost the ability to borrow on commercial terms without subsidies.

Iraq emerged from the Iran–Iraq War a country in crisis. After ten years of conflict, Iraqi external debt was a staggering 86 billion US dollars. In less than ten years, the country had gone from being a net creditor to a net debtor, with a debt-to-GDP ratio of 278 per cent. Debt service in 1989 was more than half Iraqi oil revenues (Alnasrawi 1994, pp. 93–109). Table 12.3 shows the breakdown of Iraqi debt at the end of 1988.

There is to this day disagreement over whether the Gulf State loans in fact constituted a grant. Iraq considered the money grants, but Saddam also tried to get the loans cancelled, which is inconsistent with that story. Since there were attempts to restructure all debts at some point in history, I treat it as debt throughout this chapter. The overall level of debt is murky, timelines do not match up, and Gulf States debt levels range from 30 to 60 billion US dollars in the literature. Considering known debt levels three years later in 1991, approximate lending in the ensuing years, and the quality of sources, the best estimate is 40 billion US dollars. Neither contemporary nor historical sources have been able to pin down the dates and conditions of the loans, as contracts were not kept or at least not published (Momani and Garrib 2010, p. 168). Financing from the Gulf States mainly took place at the beginning of the war, but the exact years of the loans are an estimate and interest rates for the loans are unavailable. Debt to commercial creditors is estimated at 6 billion US dollars, but this obscures the role of the US government. The overall level

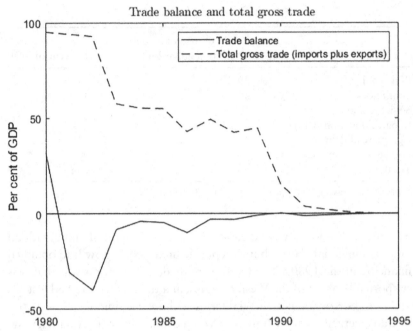

FIGURE 12.3 Iraqi trade balance and total trade in percentage of GDP (1980–95). Source: World Bank Development Indicators.

of indebtedness is clear, however. Iraq spent more money on weapons and imports, while exports collapsed. As Figure 12.3 makes clear, the trade deficit was almost 50 per cent of GDP, while total trade (exports plus imports) collapsed completely.

In the mid-1980s, the first 'soft' default happened (Caron 2004, pp. 131–32; Chung and Fidler 2006). The initial default can be traced to non-payments on contractual goods and services during the war, which extended payments for as long as forty months. Iraq also rescheduled various loans but remained current on others. A small amount of hard currency bonds and bank loans went into default, but most of the credit extended during the Iran–Iraq War continued to be serviced for the rest of the decade.[14] Interest rate and amortisation payments made by Iraq during the war totalled over 24 billion US dollars, mainly to Paris Club creditors, which suggests a prioritisation of payments to friendly creditors.[15]

[14] According to Bank of Canada's Credit Rating Assessment Group database on sovereign defaults, as outlined in Beers and Mavalwalla (2018).

[15] It is also possible payments were made to others but not noted down in any documents, or that payments had been made in barter for oil.

Official creditors in the UK and the United States were paid ahead of other creditors, with the previous loan from the US Department of Agriculture being serviced until 1990 (Rangwala 2013, pp. 101–02). It allowed Iraq to maintain access to new credit, with willing political lenders standing by. Everyone could see that Iraq was insolvent, with debt payments more than half of oil revenues, but if everyone pretended the debt would either be forgiven or rolled over, Iraq could keep borrowing to repay maturing debt. Problems began when the political and financial winds shifted.

12.3 THE GULF WAR AND REPARATIONS (1988–1991)

The cost of war for Iraq was very high. Reconstruction costs have been estimated to be as much as 230 billion US dollars (Alazemi 2013, pp. 97–98), yet the oil sector produced revenues of only 15 billion US dollars in 1989, 55 per cent lower than in 1980. Iraq's net external debt increased by some 120 billion US dollars over the course of the war. In 1990, inflation reached 40 per cent and cash reserves were just enough to cover three months' imports (Alexander and Rowat 2003, pp. 32–36). Despite the economic issues, Iraq did not reduce its military expenditures. Saddam saw himself as a strongman who had defeated Iran on behalf of all the Gulf States. He wanted to use the Iraqi military to bully neighbouring states, foremost Kuwait and to a lesser extent Saudi Arabia, and consolidate his power (Parasiliti 2003, pp. 151–65). Kuwait was owed 14 billion US dollars for loans during the war and refused to cancel the debt, leading to strained relations between the two countries in 1989. The price of oil fell in early 1990 and the Iraqi economy worsened. Saddam blamed Kuwait for low oil prices and accused his neighbour of attempting to drill in Iraqi oil fields. This was the pretext used for war: on 2 August 1990, Iraqi forces invaded Kuwait. Iraq quickly gained control of the territory and annexed Kuwait on 28 August.[16]

Unlike during the war with Iran, this time Iraq did not have the backing of the international community. The United States swiftly sent military support to avoid an invasion of Saudi Arabia by Iraq, and the UN passed Resolution 661 (1990) on 6 August imposing economic and financial sanctions on Iraq. The sanctions contained very few exceptions (humanitarian aid) and forbade any financial transaction with Iraq, including payments under existing contracts (Deeb 2007, p. 3). Iraq was isolated

---

[16] For a full timeline of the invasion of Kuwait, see Colin Warbrick (1991a, 1991b) and Parasiliti (2003).

from the global economy from this point on; any new external debt would be illegal. As the sanctions did not deter Saddam, a US-led military coalition authorised by the UN began Operation Desert Storm in January 1991. The coalition swiftly won a military victory, and Iraq signed a permanent cease-fire in April. Kuwait, however, was left with extensive damage. The UN Security Council therefore established the United Nations Compensation Commission (UNCC) to oversee reparations payments. Reparations could be awarded to individuals, businesses, or governments for damages stemming from the illegal invasion of Kuwait. Annual claims could not exceed 30 per cent of oil exports, although this was reduced to 5 per cent after the American-led invasion in 2003 (UN Resolution 705 1991; UN Resolution 1483 2003b).

War reparations are compensation for war damages and are a mainly monetary restitution; they should, however, also represent broader justice for the victims (Sandoval and Puttick 2017, pp. 7–16). Reparations constitute liabilities but are not technically debt, at least according to the Paris Club definition.[17] For Iraq, the UN Compensation Fund automatically received revenue from Iraqi oil exports to fund the payments. In total, 2.7 million claims totalling 353 billion US dollars had been made as of December 2022. A total of 52.4 billion US dollars has been paid out to 1.5 million claimants. In December 2022, the Governing Council was terminated, after the President of the body stated that all claims had been paid in full. The termination happened in the UN Security Council which adopted UN Resolution 2621 (2022).[18] Estimates for Iraqi liabilities in the early 1990s were higher, at around 100 billion US dollars at 1990s prices. Enforcement of reparations payments were overseen by the UN, which had a legal framework for ensuring payments were made, unlike unsecured government debt.[19] Reparations added substantially to the Iraqi debt burden and must be included in a fair summary of external liabilities. But given they were left out of the Paris Club definition of debt, reparations are sometimes excluded in the total. The amounts

---

[17] Paris Club is a group of (mostly) developed countries that negotiate restructurings collectively. For a history of the Paris Club, Cheng et al. (2018). The Paris Club is discussed in Chapter 3 and later in this chapter.

[18] See the UN Compensation Commission website: https://uncc.ch/home (accessed 31 December 2022).

[19] One issue not addressed by the UNCC was whether, if a claim was submitted and partially awarded, the claimant would forgo the rest. Were the UNCC to use an election of remedies, one would be debarred from suing in court. This would later cause headaches for the lawyers undertaking the restructuring.

TABLE 12.4 *Iraqi debt by creditor, 1991*

	Outstanding debt (US dollar billion)	Per cent of GDP
Paris Club	18	143
Gulf States	53	431
Soviet and allies	11	89
Reparations (non-debt)	52	423
Commercial debt	9	71
Foreign exchange reserves	–	–
Total debt (ex-reparations)	90	733
Total liabilities	142	1,156

Note: All debts (except Gulf States) are nominal amounts restructured in 2003; that is, minus accrued interest. Reparations are total reparations awarded as of December 2022. This table and Table 12.3 do not reconcile because both are best estimates at each time, based on available sources.

Sources: Paris Club; Chung and Fidler (2006); UNCC; Alnasrawi (1994, p. 109).

included in this analysis are actual payments awarded and paid by the UNCC on behalf of Iraq as of 2022, despite initial estimates being higher. Table 12.4 shows Iraqi debt by creditor in 1991, compared with output that had collapsed to 12.3 billion US dollars from over 50 billion US dollars before the war.[20]

A quick methodological note is required before continuing. After 6 August 1990, when Resolution 661 was passed, it became impossible for Iraq to get new external loans. Working backwards from the sovereign debt restructuring, I use nominal amounts from the Paris Club, the IMF, and the UNCC. This means there is also a potential incoherence between Tables 12.3 and 12.4, though both are the best estimates available for each year. For instance, the Gulf States debt, 53 billion US dollars, is drawn from Chung and Fidler (2004) and is the amount that the restructuring team mentioned in 2006. Other bilateral loans (i.e., Paris Club countries and the Soviet Union in 1991) include only amounts that were restructured; if a loan was secretly written off between 1991 and 2003, it is not included. Commercial loans outstanding in 1991 are similarly the principal amount claimed in the restructuring. Therefore, the changes in debt levels from 1988 to 1991 are difficult to trace, as there are few historical sources. Jiyad (2001) suggests Iraqi debt decreased after the

---

[20] Alnasrawi (1994, p. 159) cites some sources that estimate output declined by as much as 50 per cent after the invasion.

war, but the amounts are minor compared with overall debt levels.[21] The politically motivated lending and the blurred lines between bilateral and commercial lending makes a perfect reconciliation difficult. Nonetheless, Table 12.4 presents a reasonably accurate snapshot of Iraqi debt as sanctions were imposed and the country withdrew from the global economy.

12.4 SANCTIONS (1991–2003)

Following the Gulf War, UN Resolution 678 placed Iraq under sanctions (UN Resolution 678 1990). It was a terrible time for Iraqi living standards: output collapsed, society was uprooted, child mortality increased threefold (Ascherio et al. 1992), and personal freedoms were reduced (Sluglett 2010, pp. 13–33). Oil production had already been decimated during the war, and what limited oil exports that took place were hit by the low oil prices of the 1990s.[22] No bank, investor, business, or government would touch anything flowing through Iraq, as failure to comply with sanctions would lead to exclusion from international financial markets. Iraq went into arrears to the IMF in 1990, and one US dollar bought 1,000 Iraqi dinars in 1995 compared with the official exchange rates of 0.311 (IMF 1995, p. 3). The sanctions were meant to be short-lived and to force out the government, yet Saddam's grip on power only increased, at least in Southern Iraq (Brown 1999; Dodge 2010, pp. 259–75). A part of Northern Iraq became a separate de-facto Kurdish state. Sanctions that had been intended to destabilise the government instead enhanced state power, which increased in every facet of daily life, especially the rationing of goods (Mazaheri 2010, pp. 253–68). Saddam wanted sanctions lifted but had to settle for the Oil-for-Food programme, enacted in 1996, which allowed some oil sales and food imports. Consequently, Iraqi GDP – which had been falling for fifteen years – tripled from 1996 to 2003, though this barely enabled it to surpass 1988 levels (see Figure 12.4).

Various domestic debts and credits existed, but no new external debt was taken on. The sanctions period devastated Iraq. Crime increased – perhaps surprisingly given Saddam's tight grip on the country – and the economy was in ruins. This meant the nominal value of Iraq's external debt – most of which was in hard currency and mostly in US dollars – had

---

[21] Identified debt decreased by 300 million US dollars; however, the overall stated debt is far lower from the actual and some scepticism is required for the numbers given.

[22] No Iraqi oil sales were allowed but small exports were approved subsequently; see Brown (1999, pp. 56–104).

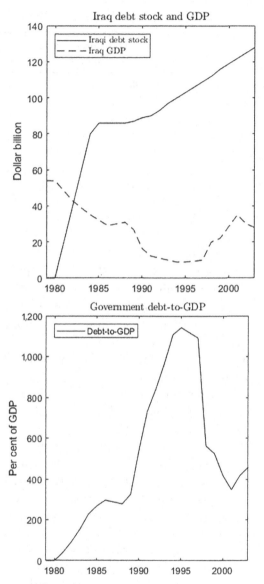

FIGURE 12.4 Iraqi debt and GDP.
Note: Iraq was isolated; little information flowed in or out. A healthy dose of scepticism around the numbers is therefore required, especially after the sanctions period.
Sources: Data for 1979–93 is from Alnasrawi (1994, p. 152); for 1993–2003 the source is the Central Intelligence Agency (2004, p. 208). Debt stock data is cited in previous tables and text.

TABLE 12.5 *Iraqi debt by creditor, 2003*

	Outstanding debt (US dollar billion)	Per cent of GDP
Paris Club	39	139
Gulf States	53	189
Non-Paris Club bilateral	17	60
Reparations (non-debt)	32	114
Commercial debt	20	70
Foreign exchange reserves	–	–
Total debt (ex-reparations)	128	458
Total liabilities	160	573

Sources: Paris Club, IMF, UNCC.

neither been eroded by inflation nor outgrown by a larger economy. Iraqi debt in 2003 can be seen in Table 12.5. This includes all debts that were restructured by the Paris Club; old debt from the Gulf States in their nominal amounts; non-Paris Club bilateral loans that were (to some extent) restructured, commercial debt; and war reparations. All amounts are before the sovereign debt restructuring.

Non-Paris Club bilateral outstanding debt represents IMF debt minus Gulf State debt (the IMF does not break down figures by country). Reparations are what remained to be paid in 2003. By that date, the Soviet debt had been absorbed into the Paris Club debt, while a separate non-Gulf, non-Paris line of debt appeared.

The economic stress that reparations were paid under was significant. Following the creation of the United Nations Compensation Commission to oversee reparations, Iraq was effectively shut out from the global economy. In the absence of any global relations, a two-currency system emerged (King 2004, pp. 11–16). In 1993, it was announced the 25-Iraqi dinar note would be exchanged with locally printed notes. In southern Iraq – where Saddam Hussein was in charge – the exchange went through. In the Kurdish areas in northern Iraq, meanwhile, the old 'Swiss dinar' kept being used.[23] From 1993, the Swiss dinar had a fixed money supply (it had gone out of circulation) and no government backing. The exchange rate between the new Saddam dinars and the old Swiss dinars is shown in Figure 12.5. Inflation eroded the purchasing power of Saddam

---

[23] The currency was called the 'Swiss dinar' because the plates used to produce it were from Switzerland.

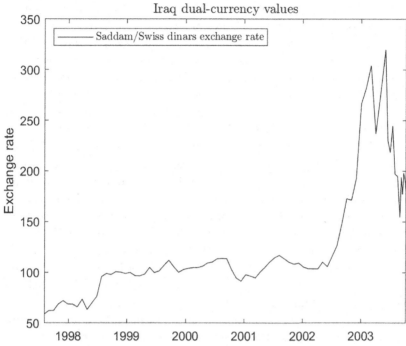

FIGURE 12.5 Iraqi dual-currency values (1998–2003).
Source: Data from King (2004) shared with the author. Replication file,
plot_iraqccy.m.

dinars. After the invasion in 2003, the Coalition Provisional Authority
(the temporary government set up by the US) announced that 1 Swiss
dinar would be exchanged for 150 Saddam dinars. In ten years, a fixed-
supply currency with no government backing had increased its value by
150 times compared to the official currency.

On the eve of the invasion in 2003, Iraq was the most indebted nation
in the world measured by its debt-to-GDP. It was the outcome of a phenomenal rise in debt to pay for wars in the 1980s combined with an
economic collapse.

12.5 TERMS OF IRAQI BORROWING

Geopolitics allowed Iraq to obtain financing on terms more favourable
than market terms. Iraq paid a total of 24.3 billion US dollars in debt service from 1980 to 1990, of which 6.7 billion US dollars was interest and
the rest amortisations (Jiyad 1994, pp. 20–21). The majority (96 per cent)

of known payments went to pay off Paris Club and commercial creditors, and the loans from the Gulf States appear to have had no identifiable interest rate. It suggests a prioritisation of debt service to Iraq's political backers in the war. The backers in turn offered generous terms of financing, even as negotiated reprofiling of debt occurred early, and defaults later, in the war.

The normal rationale for providing a loan is to receive an interest of return on the money lent. The interest rate is set to reflect the creditworthiness of the debtor and to compensate the creditor for the risk, balancing the supply and demand of credit. If a bank or an investor provides the credit, the main risk is to not be repaid (a default). The loans given to Iraq had a different purpose, and the actors involved were not primarily interested in a financial return. The lenders were a variety of financial institutions, corporates, and sovereigns, but in most cases they were not the ultimate underwriter. The end-creditor was a country. The US, the Soviet Union, and the Gulf States did not have a positive financial return as the primary, or even secondary, objective – their goal was political and military victory. In many ways, the loans look more like grants, despite being treated as debt by all parties. There was no public disclosure or transparent debt contracts that we know of, which makes it impossible to ascertain if the debt carried any specific conditions. The fact that much of the debt was given via complex and murky arrangements suggests that it was for arms purchases. Similar loans from the IMF or the World Bank would have required macroeconomic or fiscal adjustments, together with a DSA. As I have laid out here, Iraq was not able to borrow except from politically motivated lenders as its debt was unsustainable. Yet it managed to continue to borrow to finance its military expenditures throughout the war.

To understand just how generous Iraqi debt financing was, let us first compare it with US Treasuries, the safest asset in US dollars. Between 1985 and 1990, yields on Treasury bonds with a five-year maturity averaged 8.5 per cent. Because of inconsistent and missing data, it is impossible to construct a time series of Iraqi interest rates, so let us start by making a few conservative assumptions to calculate a risk premium on Iraqi loans. First, we know that the actual interest paid on loans was at least 6.7 billion US dollars. Second, let us assume that Iraqi debt service started in 1985, which is the year that most of its debt was reprofiled to. This is likely overly cautious because interest-bearing loans were given before 1985. Third, assume that only Paris Club and commercial debt carried interest, which was 35 billion US dollars, ignoring debt from the

TABLE 12.6 *Iraqi borrowing costs in US dollars and risk premium (1985–90)*

	Average interest rate	Risk premium
U.S. Treasuries	8.5	–
U.S. Investment grade	9.4	0.9
U.S. High yield	13.4	4.9
Iraqi borrowing costs	3.8	–4.6

Note: Average rates for the period are used. The US Treasury rate is the five-year constant maturity.
Sources: Jiyad (1994, pp. 21–31); Wilson and Fabozzi (1994, p. 184), and the Federal Reserve.

Soviet Union and the Gulf States. Solving for the interest rate under a five-year repayment (1985–90) equates to an interest rate of 3.8 per cent on average for Iraqi debt. A comparison to US Treasuries and risky corporate debt for the period is found in Table 12.6, with all interest rates in US dollars.

It is a crude comparison to make, but this suggests a negative risk premium for a country with a ballooning debt stock that negotiated moratoriums and extensions as early as 1982. There are several unknown factors, as there might have been non-public transfers of oil or direct payments. But debt service payments as a share of the total debt stock seem low regardless. High yield bonds, or junk bonds, had an average interest rate of 13.4 per cent during the same period, where the default rate was 6 per cent (Altman 1992, pp. 78–92). Iraq thus commanded a full 10 percentage points discount in its borrowing compared with highly risky companies issuing debt.

Another way to look at Iraq's debt is to compare it with other countries that required large external financing to fight a war. A similar picture emerges, which is one in which Iraq was unique in its ability to obtain debt financing, while still being required to repay the money. A clear risk to analyse is if the debt is legitimate or if it was at risk of being declared odious. The covert loans given to Iraq, as described in earlier sections, could easily fall under the definition of illegitimate debt that did not benefit the people (Jayachandran and Kremer 2006). The risk of having the debt declared odious should carry a risk premium, which should translate into a higher interest rate. There are scant episodes where the doctrine of odious debt has been used, but logic dictates that if the debt is at risk of being cancelled it should increase the risk, in the form of high interest rates or punitive conditionalities. One of the few historical episodes where 'odiousness risk' was present was when Cuban bonds were issued by the occupying Spanish force in the 1890s. The bonds demanded a premium of over 200 basis points as the bonds were ex-ante deemed unfair (Collet 2013). No such risk premium existed for Iraq.

Even if there was no risk of the debt being declared odious, Iraqi borrowing was cheap by historical standards. It is possible to see this by looking at historical precedents where countries borrowed to fight a war, while either being close to losing the war or having a financially powerful ally that could be borrowed from. The first example of a country at the risk of collapsing is Mexico. Mexico was able to keep borrowing as the state collapsed in 1912–13, with a long list of overseas banks offering credit. Although the country was able to borrow money, it did so at a material risk premium of over 4 per cent (Weller 2019). Other historical episodes of countries with a poor capital market reputation, such as the Confederate states during the US civil war, required an even higher risk premium (Weidenmier 2005). If we look at countries borrowing from a powerful financial ally, good examples are the two world wars. In World War I, UK interest rates were high and volatile to avoid capital flight (Hughes 1958). During World War II, the United States offered interest-rate free loans via the Lend-Lease Act, but it was to be repaid with an effective interest of 1.6 per cent after the war. The United States issued debt itself at a nominal interest rate between 0.4 and 2.5 per cent during World War II, so the loans were given with no distinct risk premium attached. The financing provided to its allies therefore never saw similar negative risk premium on its loans (Polk and Patterson 1946; Ohanian 1997). Looking at more recent history, the lowest risk premium for emerging market external debt (the EMBI index) was 1.8 per cent during 2006, at the height of capital inflows into emerging market debt securities. Even in all these exceptionally accommodating historical circumstances, it is difficult to find comparable episodes of negative risk premium, with almost no stated conditionality but still a demand for repayment of the loans.

Financial repression often happens to finance wars, but it is only possible for debt in a country's own currency. Iraqi borrowing costs on its external debt, meanwhile, were lower than those of the US government. What made Iraqi war financing special was, I would argue, the desire to avoid a regional hegemony in the Middle East. The geopolitical importance of Iraq as a proxy in its war against Iran meant it had many deep-pocketed international friends. Many countries were happy to provide loans early in the war, with few strings – or in some cases, no interest rates – attached. The military motivations for extending credit were clear: to avoid an Iranian regional hegemony. The hard-line approach that was imposed on many other sovereign debtors during the 1980s was noticeably absent from Iraq. But so was debt relief in the late 1980s. The military dominance of Iraq was not followed up by economic dominance. The geopolitical importance of avoiding an Iranian victory meant creditors were willing to extend loans to Iraq extremely cheaply. But it also meant that, to avoid Iraq emerging from the war as a new regional hegemon, its creditors were unwilling to restructure its debt burden in the aftermath of the war, to maintain a degree of economic and political control.

If there is one thing to take from Iraq's path to indebtedness, it is that it brought no good things for the citizens. Transparent debt agreements and public disclosure of debt should be a minimum requirement. The money Iraq borrowed went to fight a war, not to invest in infrastructure or build a durable welfare state. The money went to buy weapons that are still causing havoc in the region to this day. The political consequences are similarly long-lasting, both domestically and internationally. As great powers use proxies to fight in wars, it is important to remember that loans come with strings attached, even if they do not carry any fiscal conditionalities. The conditions in this case were that Iraq kept fighting a war it did not have the money to continue. The way Iraq's so-called allies used the country while it was becoming indebted should be a warning to everyone in future conflicts. The covert financing arrangements prolonged the conflict, even as the stated goal was a negotiated peace.

12.6 THE IRAQ SOVEREIGN DEBT RESTRUCTURING

Iraq was the most indebted nation in the world when the United States and its Coalition partners invaded on 19 March 2003.[24] In early 2003, the US government backed one of the largest sovereign debt restructurings in history to help reintegrate Iraq into the global economy. Getting rid of the debt burden was required to facilitate trade and avoid attachment of assets by creditors. The restructuring was a political process, setting it apart from most restructurings in the 1990s and 2000s, which were creditor-friendly affairs. The remaining part of this chapter details

---

[24] According to the IMF's online database on sovereign debt, the most indebted nation in 2003 was Liberia, with a debt-to-GDP of 515 per cent. The IMF does not include Iraq for 2003. Table 12.5 shows Iraq's total government liabilities were 573 per cent of GDP.

and analyses the Iraq sovereign debt restructuring, and shows how it managed to inflict harsh terms on its creditors while leaving war reparations intact.

Enforcement of sovereign debt repayments became easier with the rise of globalisation and interconnected capital markets. During the 1990s, holdout creditors increasingly sued wayward debtors, and won by cutting off countries from the global financial system (Buchheit and Gulati 2017; Fang et al. 2021). Iraq had no cash in 2003 and received all its foreign currency from the sale of oil, which made it vulnerable to aggressive creditors if the debt burden was not dealt with (IMF 2004, p. 29). If creditors could attach judgments to oil-related assets, the restructuring could prove tricky – to say the least.

The Iraq debt restructuring was able to circumvent aggressive creditors. Political pressure and a worldwide immunisation of foreign assets forced through one of the most complex debt restructurings to date.[25] The United States spent significant political capital and used close-to-unprecedented tools to force creditors to exchange debt claims. However, it stopped short of enshrining a doctrine of odious debt in international law, despite initial overtures in that direction. Political expediency was preferred to a new sovereign debt restructuring regime.

Earlier studies of the Iraqi sovereign debt restructuring focus mainly on the outcome of the negotiations and rely on secondary sources (Momani and Garrib 2010, pp. 155–74; Weiss 2011). The Iraq debt burden on the eve of the invasion was 160 billion US dollars, or more than 570 per cent of GDP, as shown in Table 12.5. The main creditors were Paris Club members, countries not part of the Paris Club (mainly Gulf States), and commercial creditors. The line between each was blurred because commercial lending was often given at the behest of governments, while bilateral loan documentation was missing. The money Iraq owed was not spent on the Iraqi people; it was provided in the name of geopolitics, leaving the Iraqi people saddled with debt while an oppressive regime was personally enriched (Blau 2003). But the debt burden still had to be dealt with.

In addition to the primary sources used so far, I have conducted interviews with people involved in the restructuring. When information from an interview is used, I use standard citation to show where

---

[25] The Iraqi debt stock included all types of debt (external bonds, commercial loans, bank deposits, trade credits, export grants) owed to different creditors (government, commercial, and private creditors).

the information has been sourced. The potential for bias is present: as memories fade, some might have a positive spin on their own actions. In addition, several involved parties have been involved in the sovereign debt literature. It is nonetheless the only way to gather certain information and all details provided have been checked against other interviewees as well as primary documentation.[26] The story is therefore this author's best attempt at reconstructing what happened between 2003 and 2006. The interviews include the lawyers for the Iraqi government, Lee Buchheit (2019) and Jeremiah Pam (2019); advisors for the commercial restructuring, Nazareth Festekjian (2019) from Citigroup and Daniel Zelikow (2020) from J.P. Morgan; officials for the US government, Anthony Marcus (2019), Clay Lowery (2019), and Olin Wethington (2019); and the UK negotiator for the Paris Club, Andrew Kilpatrick (2019). I also rely on primary sources – documents from the restructuring, press releases, annual reports – as well as some secondary literature.

12.6.1 Iraqi Debts

A debtor country usually knows how much money it owes, but not to whom, as this depends on the type of debt. External bonds are publicly traded and can be held by anyone, while bilateral government loans are easier to identify.[27] Iraq's creditors included all types of claims and creditors, with commercial creditors ranging from government contractors and suppliers to hedge funds, asset managers, banks, trade creditors, and state-owned entities. This affected the strategy of the restructuring because a loan from a bank that is given illegally might be considered odious, but trade credits for goods and services are probably not.

After the UN imposed sanctions in 1990, Iraq stopped keeping track of who was owed what, and the IMF had not conducted an Article IV consultation since the early 1980s (Takagi et al. 2018, p. 56). The restructuring was thus an extremely complex endeavour. The Iraqi obligors (the debtor entities) were a diverse group, as the line between the Iraqi government and Iraqi commercial enterprises had been blurred. The obligor included not only the government itself, but also ministries, state-owned

---

[26] Interviews were recorded with consent and are on file with the author. Each interviewee had the opportunity to review statements attributed to them for comment before publication.

[27] In between external bonds (unknown) to bilateral sovereign loans (known) are commercial loans, syndicated loans, trade credits, and supplier credits, for example, which have known creditors to various degrees.

enterprises, and quasi-governmental institutions such as banks – especially Rafidain and Rasheed.[28] Coordinating between the different debtors was more complicated than in normal restructurings, as the entire public sector of Iraq was included as a debtor (Deeb 2007, p. 5).[29]

Reparations were quickly left out of the restructuring, mainly for international political reasons. The US Treasury put together some initial numbers, but looked for reasons not to include reparations in the restructuring (Lowery 2019). Reparations had been structured by UN resolutions to be paid directly out of oil revenues and a new resolution would be required to change the legal setup (UN Resolution 705 1991). Unlike sovereign debt, reparations were easy to enforce because the UNCC had been set up to take money directly from Iraqi oil revenues. The original Resolution 705 stipulated 30 per cent of Iraqi oil revenues should go towards paying reparations. This was lowered to 25 per cent in 2000 and to 5 per cent in 2003.[30] Just changing the legal status of reparations would require a political battle at the UN, which could be vetoed by any one of the five permanent Security Council members.

12.6.2 Immunising Iraqi Assets and Reconciling Debts

UN Resolution 1483 lifted sanctions, terminated the Oil-for-Food Program, structured the post-invasion government, called for a debt restructuring, set up the Development Fund for Iraq (DFI), and called on all members to immunise Iraqi oil sales from creditor attachment.

The Central Bank of Iraq formally held Iraqi assets, both domestically and in foreign accounts. The assets could be attached by creditors, as Iraq was in default and could be sued. The DFI was therefore set up by the Coalition Provisional Authority (CPA), the interim government, to receive assets from the Central Bank of Iraq. The assets included future petroleum revenues and it was considered immune under UN privileges.[31] Other Iraqi assets were to be immunised by countries individually, which

---

[28] Definitions of obligors available at www.eyidro.com (accessed 22 July 2019).

[29] Most institutions were located outside the relative safety of the Green Zone in Baghdad, an added security risk.

[30] By UN Security Council Resolution 1330 (2000) and UN Security Council Resolution 1483 (2003).

[31] Iraqi savings were initially parked at the DFI, which at its peak held around 12 billion US dollars (Zelikow 2019). The Central Bank of Iraq slowly replaced the DFI as the main holder of Iraqi public savings. The DFI was administered by the New York Federal Reserve.

in the United States implemented through Executive Order 13303.[32] The DFI paid wages, pensions, and was used for cash disbursements (Article 12 of Resolution 1483 and Wethington 2019). Cash to run the government was withdrawn from the DFI and flown to Iraq. Immunising Iraqi foreign assets from 'any form of attachment, garnishment, or execution' (article 22 of Resolution 1483) was, alongside the creation of the DFI, the most important features of UN Resolution 1483 for the debt restructuring.[33]

Resolution 1483 was hotly debated, with the international community divided between the United States and its allies, and countries that opposed the Iraq war. The United States and the UK had circulated drafts of the resolution, which essentially legitimised the invasion. The immunisation of Iraqi oil assets was included in early drafts, and there is little evidence that it was a major point of contention.[34] It would protect Iraqi assets, but also enabled global oil companies, mostly American and British, to get involved without the risk of creditor judgments. From the US government's point of view, reconstruction depended on getting rid of the debt overhang (Lowery 2019), and on 16 October 2003, Congress urged Paris Club creditors to get together to provide debt relief.[35] There was a political argument for debt relief too. The White House and the Treasury could not go to Congress and ask for appropriations, only to turn around and see the money flow to other creditors, such as Saudi Arabia or China, on already delinquent loans (Lowery 2019). The Treasury appointed Olin Wethington to oversee the economy directorate at the CPA in October 2003.[36]

The CPA started to explore, but not to formally start, the restructuring until sovereignty passed back to Iraq (Pam 2019). The Trade Bank of Iraq (TBI) was established as a stopgap measure to facilitate imports and exports until then. Because of Iraqi's weak economic situation, it was key to establish an institution that could facilitate trade finance. The

---

[32] The order was renewed by both Presidents Bush and Obama. It expired in 2014, see Buchheit and Gulati (2019). The executive order was marred by controversy, as some argued it immunised US oil companies; see, for example, Kelly (2004).

[33] The security and government related questions are left for others to explore.

[34] Paragraphs 12–21 in the draft resolution governing the Development Fund of Iraq, available at www.globalpolicy.org/component/content/article/168/36079.html (accessed 29 September 2020). In early drafts, it was called the Iraqi Assistance Fund.

[35] US House Resolution 198 [16 October 2003], US 108th Congress. See also Paris Club (24 April 2003), and Paris Club (10 July 2003).

[36] His role was effectively to be the interim central bank governor, with the title of Director of Economic Policy, reporting to Bremmer (Wethington 2019).

two main banks, Rafidain and Rasheed, were in no position to offer letters of credit (normal in trade finance) and judgment creditors would have
attached collateral if they could. The TBI was therefore made immune from
attachment as well (Zelikow 2020). The legal structure allowed some relief
on Iraqi supply-chains, but its scope was limited (Wethington 2019).[37]

James Baker was appointed Special Envoy in December 2003 to lobby
Iraqi creditors for debt relief in a political capacity and to lay the ground-
work for the restructuring. He targeted key creditors that would have to be
engaged later. A group that included the Iraqi Finance Minister and Central
Bank Governor travelled the world to obtain political buy-in for a restructuring (Lowery 2019; Wethington 2019). In late 2003, The Treasury (for
financial matters), the State Department (diplomacy), and the National
Security Council (to represent the executive) gathered in the United States
to agree on an approach.[38] Meanwhile, the Treasury oversaw an initial
inventory of debt, as nobody knew how much debt Iraq had.[39]

The procurement process to hire separate legal advisors for Iraq started
in early 2004, with Cleary Gottlieb appointed in June 2004 (Deeb 2007,
p. 4). Lee Buchheit led the Cleary team, his job being to run the restructuring for Iraq and manage other financial advisors (Buchheit 2019). At the
first meeting between the White House, Treasury, IMF, and Cleary, the
main subject of discussion was whether Iraqi debt could be declared odious.
Doing so would imply that the debt was illegitimate and would have led to a
cancellation of all debt. There was talk at the highest levels in the US administration about taking this route, even going so far as to have Secretary of
the Treasury Snow suggest it publicly (Momani and Garrib 2010). This
generated lots of support and debate in the think tank world (e.g., Adams
2004) and academia, as a series of articles in the following years show (e.g.,
Jayachandran and Kremer 2006; Damle 2007; Gelpern 2007).[40]

---

[37] The TBI was incorporated as a bank and capitalised with 100 million US dollars. A
decade later, the financial sector was underdeveloped: credit from banks to the private
sector account for less than 10 per cent of GDP compared with over 55 per cent on average for the region; see World Bank Group (2017, p. 76).

[38] Additionally, US Paris Club negotiators were jointly from the Treasury and State Department; see Pam (2019) and Lowery (2019).

[39] A difficult process, as explained earlier. It started by looking at records in ministries and
the central bank and asking other sovereigns how much they thought they were owed.
The IMF played a coordinating role, but had no data from the 1980s when it left Iraq;
see Takagi et al. (2018, p. 60).

[40] These are examples of refereed articles. For the current debate at the time, see, for
example, the June 2005 edition of *Finance and Development* 42 (2), where the 'Letters
to the Editor' include discussions between several of the cited authors.

The US government took the position in public to support the idea of declaring Iraqi debt odious, but in private among the institutions directly involved – the US Treasury and the IMF – the concept was not discussed much. The IMF publicly rejected the idea (Rajan 2004). The institutions normally involved in sovereign debt restructuring judged a standard approach would be more efficient (Wethington 2019). Support for the idea seemed to mostly originate outside the institutions normally engaged in debt restructurings, particularly at the Pentagon, think tanks, and interest groups in Iraq and the United States.

The legal advisors advocated against the doctrine of odious debts, with the IMF and the Treasury strongly supporting a standard restructuring instead (Marcus 2019). They were against not because the debt was not odious, but because it would unnecessarily complicate the restructuring (Buchheit 2019). There is no legal doctrine for odious debt, and it would have been a minefield of definitions as there would have been a need to set a precedent for what parts of the Iraqi debt stock were illegitimate. According to some participants, the discussion never went to the National Security Council at the White House (Wethington 2019). There are also somewhat differing accounts of how much support the idea of declaring Iraqi debt odious had. Creditors at risk likely wanted to avoid enshrining a doctrine of odious debt into international law, and as a result were ready to take a larger NPV haircut. Iraq did maintain the right to declare specific debt odious, which it did for several commercial claims, but the idea of a broad invocation did not move forward.

The political buy-in (at least among the Coalition) meant substantial debt relief was available without any invocation of odious debt. In October 2003, the United States organised a conference to raise financial support for Iraqi reconstruction. It gathered pledges to write off 27 per cent of Iraqi outstanding debt, with the majority from Paris Club members (Momani and Garrib 2010, p. 160).

Sovereignty officially passed back to Iraq on 28 June 2004. It was decided that the Paris Club would be the best place to start restructuring negotiations.[41] Restructurings have a process but no manual: the debtor starts wherever a deal might be reached. The tactical reason for going to

---

[41] Eighteen members participated in the Paris Club restructurings: Australia, Austria, Belgium, Canada, Denmark, Finland, France, Germany, Italy, Japan, Korea, Netherlands, Russia, Spain, Sweden, Switzerland, UK, and the United States. Norway, the World Bank, the UN Conference on Trade and Development, the European Commission, the IMF, and the Organisation for Economic Co-operation and Development were observers.

the Paris Club was that a deal comes with a comparability of treatment clause, in addition to the political buy-in.[42] A deal would be a floor beyond which no other creditors could get a better deal (Buchheit 2019; Wethington 2019). Paris Club members all had substantial claims on Iraq and the geopolitical alliances of the Coalition were well represented, following James Baker's initial diplomatic rounds (Pam 2019). Normally, countries undergoing restructurings do not have a lot of political friends, because they are creditors. Iraq was different. Paris Club negotiations opened with the United States willing to stand up for Iraq, with some in the National Security Council (which represented the White House) aiming for substantial, possibly even total, debt relief (Buchheit 2019). The United States was keen on achieving a consensus outcome and the Paris Club was judged to be the best place to achieve it (Wethington 2019).

12.6.3 Paris Club Negotiations

The Paris Club is a well-oiled machine for sovereign debt restructurings, having executed 434 deals with 90 countries since it was first established in 1956.[43] Iraq required two types of debt relief: flow treatment and reduction of the debt stock. The first was relatively easy, as Iraq was not paying its current debt. However, at the Paris Club, flow treatment usually comes before debt stock reduction. For Iraq, stock reduction came up front, which is unusual (Marcus 2019). Iraq was treated under the Evian Approach, offering 'comprehensive debt treatment', reduction with no standard terms.[44] The approach was only approved in October 2003 and did away with economic indicators in favour of a non-standard DSA from the IMF for highly indebted countries (Weiss 2011, p. 6). The IMF had been brought in early 2003 to put together a DSA for the rescheduling, and to prepare Iraq to be party to a stand-by agreement (Wethington 2019).

The Iraqi solvency and capacity to pay its debts would be based on the DSA, which largely depended on assumptions about oil prices and production. The Iraqi government generated all its revenue from oil sales: between 2005 and 2007, 94 per cent of revenues, 96 billion US dollars in total, came from the sale of crude oil (GAO 2008, p. 2). The accuracy of the

---

[42] www.clubdeparis.org/en/communications/page/the-six-principles (accessed 26 July 2019).

[43] www.clubdeparis.org/en (accessed 22 May 2020). The Club is housed at the French Treasury in Paris. For a history of the Paris Club, see Cheng et al. (2018).

[44] www.clubdeparis.org/en/communications/page/evian-approach (accessed 23 July 2019).

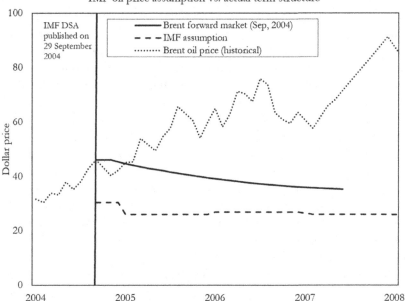

IMF oil price assumption vs. actual term structure

FIGURE 12.6 IMF oil price assumption and actual term structure.
Sources: The solid line is the forward oil market as of 29 September 2004, from
Bloomberg. The assumption for oil is from the IMF (2004, p. 25), DSA, dated
29 September 2004. The historical oil price is the spot price of Brent oil, as it
occurred over 2004–08.

assumptions was therefore essential for debt sustainability. Because of the
US desire for substantial debt relief, there was political pressure from the
negotiations team to reduce Iraq's capacity to service debt, according to a
report from the Independent Evaluation Office of the IMF issued in 2018
(Takagi et al. 2018, p. 57). The IMF assumed the price of oil would be
under 26 US dollars per barrel, forever (IMF 2004). Figure 12.6 shows the
futures market for Brent oil, as well as the oil price during negotiations. At
the time of the DSA's publication, the oil price was 46 US dollars and rose
throughout 2005 and 2006. The assumption did not change during the
negotiations, even as the price of oil rose to over 60 US dollars.

Initial staff meetings at the Paris Club started in July 2004, with bilateral meetings in the autumn. The deal was ultimately agreed in November
2004. Paris Club negotiations are generally completed within one day,
and usually no more than forty-eight hours (Buchheit 2019; Marcus
2019). The Iraqi negotiations went on for over a week, following months
of preparation.

At issue was a fundamental difference between the Coalition – led by the United States and the UK – and non-Coalition countries, mainly European countries and Russia. The Europeans considered the IMF's DSA a work of fiction because of how vastly its oil price assumptions differed from reality (Buchheit 2019). Iraq did not have enough cash on hand to do a cash-for-debt deal, so it would have to be debt-for-debt. The bid-offer on principal haircuts going into the negotiations was 95 per cent (US/UK) and 50 per cent (Europe/Russia).[45] However, an 80 per cent write-down was the likely outcome from the beginning. The US delegation and the head of the Paris Club had agreed on the number beforehand as a realistic compromise (Wethington 2019). The US delegation would negotiate with everyone who wanted a complete write-off, mainly the Iraqis and parts of the US government. The Paris Club secretariat would try to get the Europeans and Russians up from their 50 per cent principal haircut, while the United States would negotiate everyone else down to 80 per cent (Weiss 2011, p. 6).[46]

The last creditor holding out was Russia. The general sense was always that a reasonable compromise could be reached through diplomacy (Buchheit 2019). At the Asia-Pacific Co-operation summit in Chile (November 2004), President Bush personally got involved to close the deal with Putin. Three bilateral meetings at the summit's margins were required before Putin agreed to the 80 per cent principal haircut (Khalaf et al. 2004; Pam 2019).[47] In fact, the actual last party to agree was Iraq, which attempted to get 100 per cent debt relief (Wethington 2019). All creditors met on 21 November 2004, a Sunday, in Paris, expecting an agreement, but Iraq continued to hold out and only agreed a few hours after the deadline had passed.[48] The deal was struck, with the following terms outlined in the Agreed Minutes:[49]

- Debt reduction of 80 per cent in three tranches.
  - 30 per cent immediate debt cancellation, as of January 1, 2005.

---

[45] Paul Wolfowitz pushed for 100 per cent initially, then lowered the opening offer to 95 per cent alongside the UK, according to both Buchheit (2019) and Momani and Garrib (2010, p. 162). The White House deferred the final decision to the Treasury.

[46] The United States helped bring up several of the holdouts too (Wethington 2019).

[47] The Russian Finance Minister had been unresponsive until then, for reasons unknown.

[48] The Iraqi negotiators were the Finance Minister (Adel Mahdi), the Central Bank Governor (Sinan Al Shabibi), and Iraq's legal advisors, Cleary Gottlieb (Lee Buchheit and Jeremiah Pam).

[49] Paris Club, 'The Paris Club and the Republic of Iraq agree on debt relief' (11 November 2004), *Press release.*

- o 30 per cent additional debt rescheduling for twenty-three years, with a six-year grace period, conditional on approval of a standard IMF programme.
- o 20 per cent of initial debt stock debt rescheduled after three years on similar terms, conditional on review of the IMF programme (but no means testing).
- A six-year grace period for principal repayments, and a three-year grace period for (full and partial) interest rate payments.
- An interest rate of 6 per cent.
- Voluntary debt-for-debt swaps.
- Comparable treatment of other external creditors.
- NPV debt reduction of 89.75 per cent.

The deal was harsher on creditors than other restructurings during the same period: NPV haircuts on debt restructured between 1998 and 2005 ranged from 13 per cent (Uruguay, 2003) to 73 per cent (Argentina, 2005).[50] The restructuring spread out the principal haircuts, rather than taking them up front, mostly for accounting and budgetary reasons. All countries have different accounting rules, which means each country treats debt relief differently (Lowery 2019). It meant losses could be booked over many years (Festekjian 2019). Several countries – Germany prominent among them – had not marked down their loans. Any write-offs would hit the budget up front if they were front-loaded.[51]

Lazard Frères was brought in as financial advisors to execute the deal. In December 2004, the United States forgave 100 per cent of its 4.1 billion US dollars claim, while all other Paris Club members restructured according to the initial terms (Weiss 2011, p. 6).[52] Next, the focus turned to the remaining creditors. With an almost 90 per cent net-present value reduction of debt, Iraq had the terms to offer its other creditors.

12.6.4 Non-Paris Club Bilateral Debt Negotiations

Other bilateral creditors comprised two categories: Gulf States and countries not in the Paris Club, such as China. The Gulf States were

---

[50] According to data from Sturzenegger and Zettelmeyer (2008).

[51] Even though the loans had been on the books for many years and were clearly worthless; a principal haircut would be treated as a revenue hit; see Martin Kelleners (2012) and Lowery (2019).

[52] In 2011, Iraq settled with some US citizens for damages during the Gulf War; see State Department, 'Settlement of Claims of US Victims of the Sad-dam Hussein Regime with the Government of Iraq' (2011), https://2009-2017.state.gov/r/pa/prs/ps/2011/06/166691.htm (accessed 29 September 2020).

the largest creditor overall with 53 billion US dollars of debt. Iraq hired Houlihan Lokey Howard & Zukin as financial advisors, and Houlihan oversaw explaining to these countries what the Paris Club deal entailed (Pam 2019). The IMF DSA had assumed comparable treatment to the rest of the creditor universe. All countries were IMF members, and this helped obtain agreements in principle from bilateral creditors, but only in principle. Even if they did not restructure, then they would not obstruct the restructuring moving forward. A key point was the evidence of indebtedness clause. It meant each new loan superseded and replaced any old contracts (Deeb 2007, p. 7). Old debt would be foregone, and Iraq would have a new known stock of external debt.

The largest Gulf State creditors were Saudi Arabia (39 billion US dollars), Kuwait (8 billion US dollars), Qatar (1.5 billion US dollars), and Jordan (1.3 billion US dollars); as of this writing (2023) none has restructured. The Gulf States were opposed to debt relief in late 2003, having all been on the receiving end of Saddam's wars (Momani and Garrib 2010, pp. 167–68). Several soft pledges to restructure on Paris Club terms were made at the height of the restructuring talks in late 2004, but nothing came of them. In fact, Iraq and Saudi Arabia could not even agree on how much debt was outstanding.[53] As of 2020, Saudi Arabia still considers it is owed money, with the Foreign Minister, Adel Al-Jubeir, denying it has written off anything.[54] The second largest creditor, Kuwait, refused to budge as well, as did Qatar. Kuwait has tied repayment of debt to national recognition and is still owed reparations. There is no evidence that either Kuwait or Qatar has officially restructured any debt, despite significant international pressure early on. Jordan has a large claim – having been a long-term trading partner of Iraq – but has not provided any documentation (Marcus 2019). The claim is still outstanding, likely because of ineligibility.[55]

Most of the smaller creditors settled over the following few years. The Czech Republic, Hungary, Indonesia, Malaysia, Romania, and South Africa all settled on Paris Club terms, while Bulgaria, Bosnia, Serbia, and Slovenia settled on Paris Club-like terms for debt owed to former Yugoslavia.[56] Slovakia, Cyprus, and Malta wrote off all debt

---

[53] The Gulf States had political incentives not to restructure, as they wanted leverage over Iraq.

[54] Middle East Monitor, 'Saudi Arabia Denies Writing off Iraq's Debt' (31 March 2017). www.middleeastmonitor.com/20170331-saudi-arabia-denies-writing-off-iraqs-debt (accessed 29 September 2020).

[55] It could be that loans violated UN sanctions.

[56] They were essentially the same; some took a larger write-off for some cash up front.

(SIGIR 2008, p. 138). Others took a bit longer: China restructured its bilateral loans in 2007 (amounts unknown) and subsequently restructured 8.5 billion US dollars in claims in 2010, having originally pledged to do so as early as 2007. The claims were held by China's development banks and had to go through a budgetary process before a restructuring could be done (Acker et al. 2020). The UAE indicated it would write off its 4.2 billion US dollar debt in 2012, although there is no evidence it did (Dajani 2012). Egypt was difficult and did not settle until 2015, and even then, it only did so in exchange for oil shares (Aman 2015). The outstanding issue for Egypt was a tie-up of worker remittances from Iraq. The remittances had been delivered to Iraqi banks, but had been stolen before they were sent to Egypt (Lowery 2019). It was unclear if the remittances could be defined as debt, which stalled negotiations. The countries that took the longest time to settle all had similar outstanding issues.

By 2008, the last phase for the Paris Club write-down was complete. The Iraqi debt overhang was no longer a priority, with an implicit understanding that the Gulf States would not push for repayment (Lowery 2019; Marcus 2019). By 2019, sixty-five out of seventy-three sovereign creditors had restructured, with the remainder mostly consisting of Gulf State uncollected debt.[57] By 2019, the immunisation of Iraqi oil had lapsed, but sovereigns rarely pursue other sovereigns. Because the Gulf States were never brought on board as part of the early restructuring, they never restructured their claims. In addition to having been on the receiving end of Iraqi aggression, another reason is possibly the geopolitical and religious context. It is likely that creditors with Sunni majorities (all of them) had concerns about increased Iranian influence in Iraq and therefore hesitated in settling the claims.

12.6.5 Commercial Debt Claims and Restructuring

Dealing with the Paris Club and other governments was high politics, while the commercial restructuring was more operational in nature. The commercial restructuring deal-offer was made in 2005 and was fixed at Paris Club terms, with J.P. Morgan and Citi brought in as financial advisors to deal with the so-called London Club of large commercial

---

[57] Paris Club, 'The Paris Club delivers the 3rd phase of debt reduction for Iraq' (22 December 2008), *Press release*. I have been unable to find evidence that Brazil, Greece, Jordan, Kuwait, Pakistan, Poland, Qatar, Saudi Arabia, or Turkey have restructured.

creditors.[58] The US government was barely involved in the commercial restructuring, having achieved the Paris Club deal (Zelikow 2020). The structure of the deal was decided by the Iraqi government, following advice from J.P. Morgan, Citi, and Cleary Gottlieb (Pam 2019). The key things to decide for the structure were past due interest, that is, how much each claim had in accrued interest; whether to offer a cash-for-debt or a debt-for-debt swap; and how to reconcile claims.

The government decided each claim would receive 10.25 per cent of its accrued value. All loans would accrue at a fixed interest rate from the date of default, Libor + 75bps, according to the Reconciliation Methodology which was developed by the financial advisors.[59] It did not matter if the debt had a contract that accounted for past due interest; all claims were treated equally. The larger creditors, mostly European banks, held letters of credit or outright loans. The accrual rate was thus a good deal for all trade credit claims.[60] The French banks pushed hard for adhering to contracts when calculating the spread over Libor. This would have benefited the banks and larger claimants at the expense of smaller ones, and was dropped in favour of treating everyone equally (Buchheit 2019). Most small commercial claims were trade credits, with no interest rate specified in the contract (Festekjian 2019).

The deal was a debt-for-debt swap because Iraq did not have enough cash to pay all its creditors. There were hundreds of attachment orders outstanding against Iraq, which meant any deal had to resolve as many claims as possible (Zelikow 2020). Bonds were issued in return for restructured debt, but only for the largest creditors. Everyone owed more than 35 million US dollars in principal was offered a debt-for-debt deal, while smaller creditors – legally unable to hold external bonds – received cash. Issuing bonds had been preferred by J.P. Morgan and Citi (who make a living trading bonds), but had some backing in Iraq too – at least officially (Chung and Fidler 2006). The lawyers advised against a debt-for-debt swap, because all bond prospectuses included risk assessment disclosures, which would not align with the propaganda coming out of the White

---

[58] Iraq is unlike most Paris Club deals where the debtor leaves wanting to escape comparability of treatment terms; Iraq used it to argue for commercial creditors to accept a similar deal (Buchheit 2019).

[59] Reconciliation Methodology (ex. C) is available at: www.eyidro.com/recon-method.pdf (accessed 23 July 2019).

[60] The claims came in different currencies – mainly US dollars, yen, and European currencies – but given claims predated the euro's existence, a formula for converting old currencies was worked out, per Festekjian (2019).

House in 2005. For political purposes, Cleary Gottlieb suggested an all-cash offer on comparable terms to the Paris Club (Buchheit 2019).

The lawyers also wanted aggregate CACs, even though only one bond was being swapped into a 5.8 per cent coupon bond, maturing in 2028. The reason behind this was to make it easier for Iraq to re-open this bond or issue more bonds should it need to in the future. It ended with a compromise, as J.P. Morgan and Citi would only agree to single-issue CACs, which was the market-standard at the time, rather than second-generation CACs.[61] The lawyers did not consider using first-generation CACs a deal breaker at the time and did not push (Buchheit 2019).

The main issue for settling commercial claims was reconciling outstanding debt.[62] Ernst and Young (E&Y) was appointed as reconciliation manager, working out of Jordan. Debt had to meet the following definitions to be eligible:[63]

1 Evidence of written agreement.
2 Entered before the sanctions (dated 6 August 1990).[64]
3 Fit the definition of credit.
4 Be external debt (defined as debt in all currencies except Iraqi dinars).

If the claim had not been sold and E&Y could reconcile it to available documents, it would be settled. Because the debts were so varied, they were all treated equally in terms of eligibility, regardless of governing law and currency. From the moment a claim was submitted, the panel's decision became final, with about half of claims awarded to claimants (Buchheit 2019). In normal restructurings, creditors have Euroclear or Depository Trust & Clearing Corporation numbers to certify their claim,

---

[61] Also called first-generation CACs, working within one bond issue rather than the whole range.

[62] Cleary Gottlieb knew of several precedents of how not to do it. In 1975, Nigeria ordered 16 million tons of cement to arrive within a year to plug a shortage, far exceeding port capacity; see Marwah (2020). The result was a run-up in trade debt that needed to be settled. The government took out a newspaper ad, asking anyone it owed money, to contact them. A lot of people did, and Nigeria was inundated with claims, entangling it in a debt reconciliation nightmare. It settled only one-third of the claims (Buchheit 2019).

[63] Adopted from the Iraqi Ministry of Finance's *Memorandum for Potential Holders of Claims* (30 January 2008).

[64] The statute of claims according to both New York and English law is six years, so claims had expired. As claims were made under a plethora of different legal standards, however, the offering document specified that by submitting a claim, claimants agreed to forgo the right to sue. It was important that no agencies or ministries inside Iraq talked to the external debt holders, as acknowledgement of debt would have reactivated the claim. All talks had to go through lawyers.

which are mostly external bonds. Here, creditors turned up in Dubai and Jordan with boxes of paper (Festekjian 2019).

Iraq did not assert odious debt for all the claims, but it reserved the right to do so on specific claims (Zelikow 2020). One man from India showed up to a creditor meeting in Dubai with an old fax, showing a claim and wanting to be paid. He was kindly asked to submit his claim to E&Y (Festekjian 2019). Another gentleman had delivered 10,000 US dollars' worth of frozen chicken to the docks in Basra the morning the sanctions took effect (Buchheit 2019). He was not paid. An Irish meat exporter and a Swiss jeweller were told that documentation for the underlying goods would be required after they complained, and they withdrew their complaint. Sovereign debt restructurings do not normally include such unusual claims. In total, 817 claims (out of 11,776) could not be reconciled, and a special arbitration panel was convened (the rest were settled).[65]

Once the parameters were set, Iraq published the commercial debt offer on 25 July (Zelikow 2020). J.P. Morgan and Citi arranged meetings with individual creditors in Dubai to market the settlement. It was a take it or leave it offer, with no creditor committee negotiations. Five creditor committees were created nonetheless, none representing all creditors. The largest, the London Club Coordinating Group, represented European and Middle East banks, while the others were the Washington Club, the Iraq Creditors Club, the Korean Creditors Coordinating Committee, and the North African Trade Creditors Committee (Buchheit 2009). Advisors took the view that negotiating individually would be fatal, as it would negate the Paris Club deal if terms were improved. The argument for equal treatment was made by the Iraqi Central Bank Governor in 2005, in a letter to one of the creditor committees. The problem raised by him was not that the creditor committees made invalid points, rather that all had valid points. It was thus impossible to accommodate one group over another.[66]

A way to evaluate the fairness of the offer is to compare it with what the larger creditors had marked loans at in their books. The largest commercial creditor was the Italian bank BNL. The loan was marred in controversy. It originated in the late 1980s at the bank's Atlanta Branch and was underwritten by the US Department of Agriculture. The money was designated for agricultural imports but was used to buy weapons

---

[65] Iraqi Ministry of Finance, 'Iraq announces conclusion of commercial debt settlement' (18 July 2006), *Press release.*
[66] The full letter can be found in the appendix to this book.

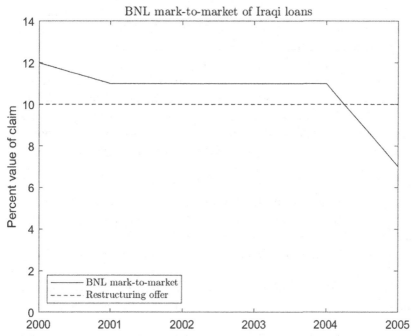

FIGURE 12.7 BNL mark-to-market of Iraq loans (per cent of nominal and accrued).
Sources: The mark-to-market is from the audited Banca Nazionale del Lavoro, *Annual Report, Consolidated Financial Statements* (2000, 2001, 2002, 2003, 2004, 2005). The restructuring offer is the NPV of the Paris Club offer.

illegally instead (see earlier in this chapter for the story). It is a prime example of odious debt. BNL held 3.4 billion US dollars' worth of loans (in notional and accrued interest) to Iraq and its state-owned banks, classified as non-performing loans. The loans figure in BNL annual reports from 2000 and were marked to fair value. They are listed explicitly in terms of accrued value and can be compared directly with the settlement offer. From 2000 to 2004, BNL valued the loans at between 10 and 12 per cent of accrued value (BNL 2000, 2001, 2002, 2003, 2004, 2005). In 2005, when the exchange happened, they received 683 million US dollars' worth of the 2028 bonds, valuing them at 239 million US dollars in their annual report, with the loans moving from 'non-performing' to 'performing' (BNL 2005, p. 64). Figure 12.7 shows the restructuring offer and the BNL marks in the years leading up to the restructuring. BNL's accounting valuation would suggest the offer of 10.25 per cent of accrued value was fair.

This is not to say that commercial creditors did not complain about being strong-armed; they did (Chung 2005). They also accepted the offer. The commercial debt settlement offer was made on 26 July 2005. By December, all large creditors had accepted (14 billion US dollars), triggering the second phase of the Paris Club, the IMF stand-by agreement of January 2006, and a 30 per cent further debt reduction (Chung and Balls 2005). The deadline for large commercial creditors to submit claims was fixed, and creditors who had earlier proclaimed they would not participate showed up with boxes of claims in hand, on the day (Festekjian 2019). A year later, on 18 July 2006, the restructuring was essentially complete.[67] In total, 11,776 individual Saddam-era claims were tendered (817 went through arbitration). Of 491 commercial claims, 96 per cent of eligible claims (as considered by E&Y) accepted the deal, for a total of 19.7 billion US dollars, according to the Ministry of Finance.

Two facts made the commercial restructuring a lot easier than that of the Paris Club. First, the immunisation of Iraqi oil assets was helpful in marketing the commercial offer (Festekjian 2019). It meant potential holdouts would have to wait a long time to collect, versus up-front payment on delinquent loans now. It took away the legal options for any vulture funds, who broadly speaking did not engage (Buchheit 2019). Second, commercial creditors – as opposed to governments in the Paris Club – must mark non-performing loans down, and as shown earlier the offer was about fair value, or better. It did not hit anyone's profit-and-loss statement.

12.7 Haircuts and Odious Debts

The Iraqi debt explosion was awesome in size when compared with any country or period in history. Few historical precedents exist in the intersection of post-conflict reconstruction and debt relief, amid such international political scrutiny.[68] Figure 12.8 shows NPV haircuts for all

---

[67] Press releases announcing settlements and participation rates are available at the Debt Reconciliation Office, run by Ernst & Young: www.eyidro.com (accessed 12 July 2019) and the Paris Club website: www.clubdeparis.org/en/traitements/iraq-21-11-2004/en (accessed 15 July 2019).

[68] A few were mentioned by participants in the restructuring. The closest was perhaps the German debt relief of 1953, when the London Debt Agreement cut external German debt in half, contributing to a successful reconstruction after World War II; see Galofré-Vilà et al. (2019). Another is Polish debt relief in the early 1990s. Poland got a Paris Club deal that cut its debt stock in half, received IMF help from 1990 to 1995, and turned things around in its re-entrance to the Western world; see Boughton (2012).

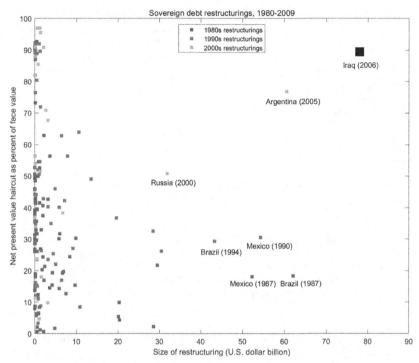

FIGURE 12.8 Comparison of NPV haircuts in debt restructurings (1980–2009). Sources: The data for Iraq's restructuring is the amount of debt from Table 12.5 that was restructured, as outlined in this chapter. The haircut for Iraq is the NPV from the Paris Club. All other NPV haircuts and sizes of restructuring are from the online appendix in Cruces and Trebesch (2013).

sovereign debt restructurings from 1980 to 2009, measured by the size of the restructuring. Iraq stands out as being particularly severe for creditors in the upper right corner.

The NPV haircut for Iraq was much larger than other restructurings. Only Argentina's 2005 restructuring comes close, and it came with a low participation rate of 76 per cent and years of litigation as shown earlier. Immunising Iraqi foreign assets was and is largely unprecedented (Buchheit and Gulati 2019).

The restructuring was thus a success, insofar as it removed the debt overhang and allowed Iraqi output to outgrow the debt stock.[69] Government debt-to-GDP in 2019 was 50 per cent, mostly thanks to

---

[69] The restructuring only. Iraq cannot be considered an economic or security success.

TABLE 12.7 *Iraqi debt by creditor, 2019*

	Outstanding debt (US dollar billion)	Per cent of GDP
Paris Club	6	3
Gulf States	49	22
Non-Paris Club official	18	8
Reparations (non-debt)	4	2
Commercial debt	–	–
External $ bonds	5	2
Local debt	36	16
Foreign exchange reserves	–65	–29
Total debt (ex-reparations)	113	50
Total net liabilities	53	23

Sources: the overall debt stock and GDP data is from the IMF's online database. Paris Club levels are based on term loans outstanding, sourced from Bloomberg; see text for Gulf States. Non-Paris Club debt is the residual and includes IMF and World Bank loans. Reparations outstanding as of December 2019 are for damages to oil-assets in Kuwait. External and local debt, as well as (positive) foreign exchange reserves are from the Central Bank of Iraq.

output growth rather than an outright fall in debt. The composition of the debt stock changed. External debt has fallen to 34 per cent of GDP, much of it loans to the Gulf States that have been de facto cancelled.[70] Iraq has increased its stock of local debt (in dinars) since the restructuring, although it has also increased its foreign exchange reserves. Table 12.7 shows outstanding Iraqi debt; almost half of gross debt is legacy debt owed to the Gulf States.

The Iraqi debt restructuring was therefore also a case of missed opportunities. The build-up of debt in the 1980s was political in nature, originating from the United States and its allies in support for Iraq during the Iran–Iraq War. If a doctrine of odious debt has any place in international law, a good place to start could have been Iraq's commercial and bilateral debt. There is no doubt that going to the Paris Club instead of declaring Iraqi debt odious was politically expedient, but it left unanswered the question of who was at fault.[71] It allowed the creditors to

[70] But not cancelled. It has political ramifications as collection can be attempted in some future point.

[71] It is possible the debate over odious debt meant it was easier to get creditors to agree, simply to avoid invoking the doctrine of odious debt. Another option, also not favoured by the United States, would have been the Sovereign Debt Restructuring Mechanism proposed by the IMF (2003).

settle debts owed without answering any uncomfortable questions about why loans were extended in the first place. Instead, the Paris Club deal, and the subsequent commercial restructuring, swept under the rug any debate about the morality of paying creditors at all. Through the whole story, reparations were repaid, and including them in the restructuring was never discussed. They were, as has often been the case, de facto senior sovereign debt.

13

When Nations Can't Default

The reparations studied in this book were all paid under very different circumstances. But they were repaid. The core thesis here is that the forced repayment of a sovereign liability can be economically costly, but that the capacity to repay is much higher than standard sovereign debt models would suggest. Reparations are in essence sovereign debt that you cannot default on. This means countries often issue more costly sovereign debt to pay reparations, which can lead to large stocks of sovereign debt. Financial crises or anaemic growth has sometimes followed. High capacity to pay sovereign debt does not imply that countries should prioritise debt payments to investors over investments in critical infrastructure or climate research. But that is exactly what reparations do.

Most models of sovereign defaults, such as the one presented in this book, concern themselves with willingness to pay. They offer a way to judge if it is in the country's interest to pay its debt. Willingness to pay sovereign debt has been the norm since 1907 when the Drago Doctrine agreed that countries would not enforce sovereign debts by military force.[1] The invasion of the Ruhr in 1923 was a reversal to the time before the Drago Doctrine, and it showed what a terrible norm the pre-Drago Doctrine was.[2] The idea of reparations is that they are involuntary, but

---

[1] Convention II, which was signed and ratified by all countries in this study (Germany, Finland, France, Russia, the UK, and the United States) by 1910. There are certain exceptions in Article I, which states that the convention does not apply if states refuse or neglect to accept an offer of arbitration.

[2] Without discussing the legality of the invasion (see, e.g., Allemés and Schuster 1924 for the case for and against), it was a break with the idea that creditors should not enforce debt contracts militarily.

they stand out as uniquely enforceable within sovereign liabilities. The reason is that they are political by nature. Both German and Finnish reparations were, to varying extents, a break with the Drago Doctrine.[3] The argument in this book, especially that of Chapters 6, 8, and 10, is that enforcement of reparations and reparations-related debt created a suboptimal economic outcome. In Germany's case, it prolonged repayment and ensured default came only after the Nazi takeover and years of austerity. In Finland's case, it forced three devaluations and years of economically costly repayment before it managed to grow its way out of debt. The cases of France (Chapter 4), Haiti (Chapter 5), Greece and China (Chapter 7), and Iraq (Chapter 12) show that reparations can be enforced over many years at high economic costs, no matter what international doctrine the world supposedly adheres to.

The World War II reparations stand out as the least reparations-like debt of it all, and the most successful reintegration of a country into the global trading system. West Germany was reintroduced into the Western alliance, which could happen because of debt forgiveness. The Iraqi case is another successful repayment, but only because reparations were directly linked to a revenue stream that kept coming – but most countries are not oil rich. The strict enforcement of legal contracts almost always create problems. It is the sovereign equivalent of debtors' prison – and it is a terrible idea. If debt is unsustainable, it should be restructured, and sovereign debt is never a goal in and of itself: peace and prosperity is.

---

[3] Germany more so than Finland, as there was arguably no military intervention to enforce Finnish debt, but it was there implicitly in the political intimidation.

Appendix: Letter to Creditor Committees

Letter from: Sinan Al Shabibi, Governor of the Central Bank of Iraq, 2005.

To: The London Club Coordinating Group; The Washington Club; The Iraq Creditors Club; The Korean Creditors Coordinating Committee; and The North African Trade Creditors Committee.

Over the past year, Iraq has consulted, individually and in groups, with many of [its] creditors. We have heard a common theme in these discussions. Claimants falling into each category (bilaterals, banks, contractors, suppliers, individuals, etc) have advanced plausible arguments for the proposition that – whatever Iraq's final settlement offer may be – their group should receive preferential treatment vis-a-vis other types of claimants. To give you just a flavour of these arguments:

- The bilaterals say they lent at below-market rates while commercial creditors advanced money at full market rates and took the corresponding full credit risk.
- The commercial claimants say that the bilaterals were lending to further their geopolitical or export development objectives and should therefore be subordinate to normal commercial counterparties.
- The commercial banks say that their support will be crucial in Iraq's reconstruction program and therefore they, above all others, must be treated gently in the restructuring.
- The trade suppliers say that the weight of sovereign debt restructuring precedents confirms that trade creditors should be exempted from, or treated more leniently in, any sovereign debt rearrangement program.
- The commercial companies say that they are not, like many other claimants, in the business of lending money or assessing (and bearing) sovereign credit risk.

- Construction companies ... note that they have worked on facilities that still provide critical services to the people of Iraq during this very difficult period.
- Individuals say they are individuals.
- The problem is not that these are illegitimate arguments; the problem is that they all have some element of legitimacy. But faced with this wide and contradictory array of positions, the Government of Iraq has concluded that the only fair and practicable course of action is to accord an even-handed treatment to all of the country's Saddam-era claimants.

Source: Buchheit (2009, p. 211).

References

PRIMARY SOURCES

BL, United States Bureau of Labor. 1898. 'Wages in the United States and Europe, 1870–1898'. *Economic Bulletin* 18, volume III. Washington, DC.

BNL, Banca Nazionale del Lavoro. 2000. *Annual report, Consolidated Financial Statements*.

2001. *Annual report, Consolidated Financial Statements*.

2002. *Annual report, Consolidated Financial Statements*.

2003. *Annual report, Consolidated Financial Statements*.

2004. *Annual report, Consolidated Financial Statements*.

2005. *Annual report, Consolidated Financial Statements*.

Buchheit, Lee C. 2019. *The Iraqi debt restructuring*. In-person interview on 1 May (New York). Recording on file with the author.

CIA, Central Intelligence Agency. 1982. 'Implications of Iraq's Victory over Iran'. *Special National Intelligence Estimate*, declassified in 2007.

1984. 'Iran–Iraq: Buying Weapons for War'. *An Intelligence Assessment*, declassified in 2011.

2004. 'Iraq Economic Data (1989–2003)'. *DCI Special Advisor Report on Iraq's WMD*, Volume 1.

Festekjian, Nazareth. 2019. *Restructuring Iraq's commercial claims*. In-person interview on 2 May (New York). Recording on file with the author.

GAO, Government Accountability Office. 2008. 'Stabilizing and Rebuilding Iraq: Iraqi Revenues, Expenditures, and Surplus'. *Report to Congressional Committees 08–1031*.

House Resolution 198, US. 2003. *United States 108th Congress*.

IACPC, Internal Auditing Commission for Public Credit. 2008. 'Final Report of the Integral Auditing of the Ecuadorian Debt'.

IMF, International Monetary Fund. 1983a. 'Iraq – Staff Report for the 1983 Article IV Consultation'. *IMF Staff Report 83/177*.

1983b. 'Iraq – Recent Economic Developments'. *Preliminary Article IV consultation memoranda 83/178*.

1995. 'Overdue Financial Obligations to the Fund – Development in Cases of Protracted Arrears to the Fund and Statistical Update'. *Prepared by the Treasurer's Department.*

2003. 'Proposed Features of a Sovereign Debt Restructuring Mechanism'. *Prepared by the Legal and Policy Development and Review Departments.*

2004. 'Iraq: Use of Fund Resources – Request for Emergency Post-Conflict Assistance'. *IMF Country Report 04/325.*

2006. 'Iraq: Request for Stand-By Arrangement – Staff Report'. *IMF Country Report 06/15.*

2013. *The IMF's Balance of Payments and International Investment Position Manual.* 6th ed. Washington, DC: IMF.

Iraqi Ministry of Finance. 2005a (26 July). *Iraq announces terms of commercial debt settlement offer.*

2005b (16 September). *Iraq announces the successful conclusion of first phase of commercial debt restructuring.*

2006 (18 July). *Iraq announces conclusion of commercial debt settlement.*

2008 (30 January). *Memorandum for potential holders of claims.*

Kerry, John, and Hank Brown. 1992. 'The BCCI Affair: A Report to the Committee on Foreign Relations'. 102–140. 102nd Congress.

Kilpatrick, Andrew. 2019. *Iraqi Paris Club negotiations.* In-person interview on 23 July (London). Follow-up by phone on 28 August 2019. Recording on file with the author.

Lowery, Clay. 2019. *The Iraqi debt restructuring.* In-person interview on 8 May (Washington, DC). Recording on file with the author.

Marcus, Anthony. 2019. *Restructuring Paris Club debt.* In-person interview on 6 May (Washington, DC). Recording on file with the author.

Pam, Jeremiah. 2019. *The Iraqi debt restructuring.* In-person interview on 7 May (Washington, DC). Recording on file with the author.

Paris Club. 2003a (24 April). Preliminary discussion on the situation of Iraq's Paris Club debt. *Press release.*

2003b (10 July). Paris Club creditors reviewed Iraq's situation towards them. *Press release.*

2004 (11 November). The Paris Club and the Republic of Iraq agree on debt relief. *Press release.*

2008 (22 December). The Paris Club delivers the 3rd phase of debt reduction for Iraq. *Press release.*

SIGIR, Special Inspector General for Iraq Reconstruction. 2008. *Quarterly Report and Semi-annual Report to the United States Congress.*

SSCI, Senate Select Committee on Intelligence. 1993. *The Intelligence Community's Involvement in the Banca Nazionale Del Lavoro (BNL) Affair.* 103–12. 103rd Congress.

State Department, US. 2011. 'Settlement of Claims of US Victims of the Sad-dam Hussein Regime with the Government of Iraq'. *Press release.* Washington, DC.

Udenrigsministeriet, Danmarks. 2007. 'Endelig besvarelse af spørgsmål nr. S 806'. Folketingets Lovsekretariat.

UN, Security Council Resolution. 1990a. *UN Doc S/RES/661.*

1990b. *UN Doc S/RES/678.*

1991. *UN Doc S/RES/705.*

2000. *UN Doc S/RES/1330.*

2003a. *US-UK Draft Resolution on Post-War Iraq*, published in *The New York Times*, 9 May 2003.

2003b. *UN Doc S/RES/1483.*

2022. *UN Doc S/RES/2621.*

WB, World Bank Group. 2017. 'Iraq: Systematic Country Diagnostic'. *World Bank Report* 112333-IQ.

Wethington, Olin. 2019. *The Iraqi debt restructuring.* In-person interview on 9 May (Washington, DC). Follow up by phone on 28 August. Recording on file with the author.

Zelikow, Daniel. 2020. *Restructuring Iraqi's debt.* Email correspondence on 10 March (Copenhagen). Records on file with the author.

TREATIES AND ACTS

Treaty of Lutatius of 241 BC
Treaty of Kalisz of 1813
Treaty of Chaumont of 1814
Treaty of Fontainebleau of 1814
Treaty of Paris of 1814
Second Treaty of Paris of 1815
Treaty of Guadalupe Hidalgo of 1848
Treaty of Frankfurt of 1871
Treaty of Shimonoseki of 1895
Hague Convention of 1907
Treaty of Brest-Litovsk of 1918
Treaty of Versailles of 1919
Paris Conference on Reparations of 1945
Paris Peace Treaties of 1947
Japanese Peace Treaty of 1951
US Civil Liberties Act of 1988

SECONDARY SOURCES

Abi-Habib, Maria. 2018. 'How China Got Sri Lanka to Cough Up a Port'. *The New York Times*, 25 June, sec. World. www.nytimes.com/2018/06/25/world/asia/china-sri-lanka-port.html.

Accominotti, Olivier, and Barry Eichengreen. 2016. 'The Mother of All Sudden Stops: Capital Flows and Reversals in Europe, 1919–32'. *The Economic History Review* 69 (2): 469–92. https://doi.org/10.1111/ehr.12128.

Acker, Kevin, Deborah Brautigam, and Yufan Huang. 2020. 'Debt Relief with Chinese Characteristics'. *Sais-Cari Working Paper Series* 39: 43.

Adams, Patricia. 2004. 'Iraq's Odious Debts'. *Policy Analysis* no. 526. Washington, DC: Cato. www.cato.org/sites/cato.org/files/pubs/pdf/pa526.pdf.

Aguiar, Mark, and Manuel Amador. 2014. 'Sovereign Debt'. In *Handbook of International Economics*, edited by Gita Gopinath, Elhanan Helpman, and Kenneth S. Rogoff, vol. 4. North Holland: Elsevier.

Aguiar, Mark, and Gita Gopinath. 2006. 'Defaultable Debt, Interest Rates and the Current Account'. *Journal of International Economics, Emerging Markets* 69 (1): 64–83. https://doi.org/10.1016/j.jinteco.2005.05.005.

Alazemi, Talal Z. A. 2013. 'Kuwaiti Foreign Policy in Light of the Iraqi Invasion, with Particular Reference to Kuwait's Policy towards Iraq, 1990–2010'. Doctoral thesis, University of Exeter. https://ore.exeter.ac.uk/repository/handle/10871/13803.

Alesina, Alberto, and A. Passalacqua. 2016. 'The Political Economy of Government Debt'. In *Handbook of Macroeconomics*, edited by John B. Taylor and Harald Uhlig, vol. 2: 2599–651. Amsterdam: Elsevier. https://doi.org/10.1016/bs.hesmac.2016.03.014.

Alesina, Alberto, and Guido Tabellini. 1990. 'A Positive Theory of Fiscal Deficits and Government Debt'. *The Review of Economic Studies* 57 (3): 403–14. https://doi.org/10.2307/2298021.

Alexander, Justin, and Colin Rowat. 2003. 'A Clean Slate in Iraq: From Debt to Development'. *Middle East Report*, no. 228: 32–36. https://doi.org/10.2307/1559378.

Allemés, M. Frederick, and Ernest Joseph Schuster. 1924. 'The Legality or Illegality of the Ruhr Occupation'. *Transactions of the Grotius Society* 10: 61–87.

Al-Marashi, Ibrahim. 2018. 'Iraq, Saudi Arabia, and the Counter-Shock'. In *Counter-Shock: The Oil Counter-Revolution of the 1980s*, edited by Duccio Basosi, Giuliano Garavini, and Massimiliano Trentin. London: I.B. Tauris.

Alnasrawi, Abbas. 1994. *The Economy of Iraq: Oil, Wars, Destruction of Development and Prospects, 1950–2010. II.* Westport, CT: Greenwood Press.

Altman, Edward I. 1992. 'Revisiting the High-Yield Bond Market'. *Financial Management* 21 (2): 78–92. https://doi.org/10.2307/3665667.

Aman, Ayah. 2015. 'Egypt Forgives Iraqi Debt in Exchange for Oil'. *Al-Monitor*, 23 January. www.al-monitor.com/pulse/originals/2015/01/egypt-iraq-talks-agreement-debt-oil-military.html.

Ams, Julianne, Reza Baqir, Anna Gelpern, and Christoph Trebesch. 2019. 'Sovereign Default'. In *Sovereign Debt: A Guide for Economists and Practitioners*, edited by S. Ali Abbas, Alex Pienkowski, and Kenneth Rogoff, 275–326. Oxford: Oxford University Press.

Andrade, Sandro C., and Vidhi Chhaochharia. 2018. 'The Costs of Sovereign Default: Evidence from the Stock Market'. *The Review of Financial Studies* 31 (5): 1707–51. https://doi.org/10.1093/rfs/hhx136.

Anil, Ari, Giancarlo Corsetti, and Luca Dedola. 2018. 'Debt Seniority and Sovereign Debt Crises'. IMF Working Paper 18/104. www.imf.org/en/Publications/WP/Issues/2018/05/09/Debt-Seniority-and-Sovereign-Debt-Crises-45840.

Antipa, Pamfili M., and Christophe Chamley. 2017. 'Monetary and Fiscal Policy in England during the French Wars (1793–1821)'. *Banque de France Working Paper* 627. https://doi.org/10.2139/ssrn.2983672.

Arellano, Cristina. 2008. 'Default Risk and Income Fluctuations in Emerging Economies'. *American Economic Review* 98 (3): 690–712.

Artz, Frederick B. 1934. *Reaction and Revolution 1814–1832*. New York: Harper & Row Publishers. https://archive.org/details/in.ernet.dli.2015.499217/page/n5.

Ascherio, Alberto, Robert Chase, Tim Coté, Godelieave Dehaes, Eric Hoskins, Jilali Laaouej, Megan Passey, et al. 1992. 'Effect of the Gulf War on Infant and Child Mortality in Iraq'. *New England Journal of Medicine* 327 (13): 931–36. https://doi.org/10.1056/NEJM199209243271306.

Asonuma, Tamon, and Christoph Trebesch. 2016. 'Sovereign Debt Restructurings: Preemptive or Post-Default'. *Journal of the European Economic Association* 14 (1): 175–214. https://doi.org/10.1111/jeea.12156.

Astore, Marianna, and Michele Fratianni. 2019. '"We Can't Pay": How Italy Dealt with War Debts after World War I'. *Financial History Review* 26 (2): 197–222. https://doi.org/10.1017/S0968565019000039.

Ayer, Jules. 1904. *A Century of Finance, 1804–1904*. London: The London House of Rothschild.

Balogh, Thomas, and Andrew Graham. 1979. 'The Transfer Problem Revisited: Analogies between the Reparations Payments of the 1920s and the Problems of the OPEC Surpluses'. *Oxford Bulletin of Economics and Statistics* 41 (3): 183–91.

Barro, Robert J. 1974. 'Are Government Bonds Net Wealth?'. *Journal of Political Economy* 82 (6): 1095–117. https://doi.org/10.1086/260266.

1979. 'On the Determination of the Public Debt'. *Journal of Political Economy* 87 (5): 940–71.

1987. 'Government Spending, Interest Rates, Prices, and Budget Deficits in the United Kingdom, 1701–1918'. *Journal of Monetary Economics* 20 (2): 221–47. https://doi.org/10.1016/0304-3932(87)90015-8.

Beers, David, and Jamshid Mavalwalla. 2018. 'The BoC-BoE Sovereign Default Database Revisited: What's New in 2018?' *Bank of England Staff Working Paper* 739. www.bankofengland.co.uk/working-paper/2018/the-boc-boe-sovereign-default-database-revisited-whats-new-in-2018.

Bernanke, Ben S. 2005. 'The Global Saving Glut and the U.S. Current Account Deficit'. In Remarks by Governor Ben S. Bernanke. Richmond, Virginia. www.federalreserve.gov/boarddocs/speeches/2005/200503102/.

2017. 'Monetary Policy in a New Era'. Speech at the Peterson Institute, Washington, DC. www.brookings.edu/research/monetary-policy-in-a-new-era/.

Bianchi, Javier, Pablo Ottonello, and Ignacio Presno. 2019. 'Fiscal Stimulus under Sovereign Risk'. International Finance Discussion Paper 1257 (September). https://doi.org/10.21034/wp.762.

Blackburn, Robin. 2006. 'Haiti, Slavery, and the Age of the Democratic Revolution'. *The William and Mary Quarterly* 63 (4): 643–74.

Blanchard, Olivier J., and Daniel Leigh. 2013. 'Growth Forecast Errors and Fiscal Multipliers'. *American Economic Review* 103 (3): 117–20. https://doi.org/10.1257/aer.103.3.117.

Blau, Justine. 2003. 'Where Are Saddam's Billions?' *CBS News*, 11 April, sec. Online. www.cbsnews.com/news/where-are-saddams-billions/.

Bolt, Jutta, Robert Inklaar, Herman de Jong, and Jan Luiten van Zanden. 2018. 'Rebasing "Maddison": New Income Comparison and the Shape of Long-Run Economic Development'. Maddison Project Database, Version 2018, Maddison Project Working Paper 10. www.rug.nl/ggdc/html_publications/memorandum/gd174.pdf.

Borchardt, Knut. 1990. 'A Decade of Debate about Bruening's Economic Policy'. In *Economic Crisis and Political Collapse: The Weimar Republic, 1924–1933*, edited by Jürgen B. V. Kruedener, 99–151. Oxford: Berg.

Bordo, Michael D., and Harold James. 2000. 'The International Monetary Fund: Its Present Role in Historical Perspective'. NBER Working Paper 7724 (June). https://doi.org/10.3386/w7724.

Bordo, Michael D., and Eugene N. White. 1991. 'A Tale of Two Currencies: British and French Finance during the Napoleonic Wars'. *Journal of Economic History* 51 (2): 303–16. https://doi.org/10.1017/S002205070003895X.

Borenztein, Eduardo, and Ugo Panizza. 2008. 'The Costs of Sovereign Default'. IMF Working Paper 08/238. www.imf.org/en/Publications/WP/Issues/2016/12/31/The-Costs-of-Sovereign-Default-22346.

Boughton, James M. 2004. 'The IMF and the Force of History: Ten Events and Ten Ideas That Have Shaped the Institution'. IMF Working Paper, no. 04/75. www.imf.org/en/Publications/WP/Issues/2016/12/30/The-IMF-and-the-force-of-History-Ten-Events-and-Ten-Ideas-that-Have-Shaped-the-Institution-17199.

——— 2012. *Tearing Down Walls, the International Monetary Fund 1990–1999*. Washington, DC: International Monetary Fund. www.imf.org/external/pubs/ft/history/2012/.

Bowley, A. L. 1898. 'Comparison of the Changes in Wages in France, the United States, and the United Kingdom, from 1840 to 1891'. *The Economic Journal* 8 (32): 474. https://doi.org/10.2307/2957090.

Brakman, Steven, and Charles van Marrewijk. 1998. *The Economics of International Transfers*. New York: Cambridge University Press.

Brock, Philip L. 1996. 'International Transfers, the Relative Price of Non-Traded Goods, and the Current Account'. *The Canadian Journal of Economics/Revue Canadienne d'Economique* 29 (1): 163–80. https://doi.org/10.2307/136157.

Brown, Sarah Graham. 1999. *Sanctioning Saddam: The Politics of Intervention in Iraq*. London: I.B. Tauris.

Bruffaerts, Jean-Claude, Marcel Dorigny, Gusti-Klara Gaillard, and Jean-Marie Theodat. 2021. Haïti-France, Les Chaînes de La Dette. November. Online. www.hemisphereseditions.com/haiti-france-la-chaine-de-la-dette.

Buchanan, James M. 1976. 'Barro on the Ricardian Equivalence Theorem'. *Journal of Political Economy* 84 (2): 337–42. https://doi.org/10.1086/260436.

Buchheit, Lee C. 2009. 'Use of Creditor Committees in Sovereign Debt Workouts'. *Business Law International* 10: 205.

——— 2013. 'Sovereign Debt Restructurings: The Legal Context'. BIS Papers chapters. Bank for International Settlements. https://econpapers.repec.org/bookchap/bisbisbpc/72-21.htm.

Buchheit, Lee, Guillaume Chabert, Chanda DeLong, and Jeromin Zettelmeyer. 2019. 'The Sovereign Debt Restructuring Process'. In *Sovereign Debt:*

A Guide for Economists and Practitioners, edited by S. Ali Abbas, Alex Pienkowski, and Kenneth S. Rogoff. Oxford: Oxford University Press. www .imf.org/~/media/Files/News/Seminars/2018/091318SovDebt-conference/ chapter-8-the-debt-restructuring-process.ashx?la=en.

Buchheit, Lee, and G. Mitu Gulati. 2002. 'Sovereign Bonds and the Collective Will'. *Emory Law Journal* 51 (4): 1317–63.

2017. 'Restructuring Sovereign Debt after NML v. Argentina'. *Capital Markets Law Journal*, January, 224–38.

2019. 'Sovereign Debt Restructuring and US Executive Power'. *Capital Markets Law Journal* 14 (1): 114–30. https://doi.org/10.1093/cmlj/kmy030.

Bullard, Nicola, Walden Bello, and Kamal Mallhotra. 1998. 'Taming the Tigers: The IMF and the Asian Crisis'. *Third World Quarterly* 19 (3): 505–55.

Bulow, Jeremy, and Kenneth Rogoff. 1989a. 'A Constant Recontracting Model of Sovereign Debt'. *Journal of Political Economy* 97 (1): 155–78.

1989b. 'Sovereign Debt: Is to Forgive to Forget?' *American Economic Review* 79 (1): 43–50.

Burnside, Craig, Martin Eichenbaum, and Sergio Rebelo. 2004. 'Government Guarantees and Self-Fulfilling Speculative Attacks'. *Journal of Economic Theory, Macroeconomics of Global Capital Market Imperfections* 119 (1): 31–63.

Calmon, Marc Antoine. 1870. *Histoire Parlementaire Des Finances de La Restauration*. Paris: Michel Lévy Frères. https://gallica.bnf.fr/ark:/12148/ bpt6k922225.

Calvo, Guillermo A. 1988. 'Servicing the Public Debt: The Role of Expectations'. *The American Economic Review* 78 (4): 647–61.

Caron, David. 2004. 'The Reconstruction of Iraq: Dealing with Debt'. *U.C. Davis Journal of International Law & Policy* (January): 123–43.

Carstens, Agustín, and Moisés J. Schwartz. 1998. 'Capital Flows and the Financial Crisis in Mexico'. *Journal of Asian Economics, Special Issue: Symposium on Money and Financial Markets in Asia: A Challenge to Asian Industrialization*, 9 (2): 207–26. https://doi.org/10.1016/S1049-0078(99)80081-5.

Carter, Zachery D. 2020. *The Price of Peace: Money, Democracy and the Life of John Meynard Keynes*. New York: Random House.

Chaney, Eric. 2008. 'Assessing Pacification Policy in Iraq: Evidence from Iraqi Financial Markets'. *Journal of Comparative Economics* 36 (1): 1–16. https:// doi.org/10.1016/j.jce.2007.11.003.

Chapman, Tim. 1998. *The Congress of Vienna: Origins, Processes, and Results*. London: Routledge.

Charles, Loïc, and Guillaume Daudin. 2015. 'Eighteenth-Century International Trade Statistics'. *Revue de l'OFCE N° 140* (4): 7–36. https://doi.org/10.3917/ reof.140.0007.

Chatterjee, Satyajit, and Burcu Eyigungor. 2012. 'Maturity, Indebtedness, and Default Risk'. *American Economic Review* 102 (6): 2674–99. https://doi .org/10.1257/aer.102.6.2674.

Cheng, Gong, Javier Díaz-Cassou, and Aitor Erce. 2018. 'Official Debt Restructurings and Development'. *World Development* 111 (November): 181–95. https://doi.org/10.1016/j.worlddev.2018.07.003.

Chiţu, Livia, Barry Eichengreen, and Arnaud Mehl. 2014. 'When Did the Dollar Overtake Sterling as the Leading International Currency? Evidence from the Bond Markets'. *Journal of Development Economics, Special Issue: Imbalances in Economic Development*, 111 (November): 225–45. https:// doi.org/10.1016/j.jdeveco.2013.09.008.

Choi, Stephen J., and Mitu Gulati. 2016. 'Customary International Law: How Do Courts Do It?' In *Custom's Future: International Law in a Changing World*, edited by Curtis A. Bradley, 117–47. Cambridge: Cambridge University Press. https://doi.org/10.1017/CBO9781316014264.006.

Christopher, Warren, and Richard M. Mosk. 2007. 'The Iranian Hostage Crisis and the Iran–U.S. Claims Tribunal: Implications for International Dispute Resolution and Diplomacy'. *Pepperdine Dispute Resolution Law Journal* 7 (2): 165–75.

Chung, Joanna. 2005. 'Iraqi Debt Restructuring Draws Complaints'. *Financial Times*, 20 December. www.ft.com/content/f2e6917c-7193-11da-836e-0000779e2340.

Chung, Joanna, and Andrew Balls. 2005. 'Crucial Phase in Iraq Debt Restructuring Completed'. *Financial Times*, 23 December. www.ft.com/ content/f23f8f60-73f2-11da-ab91-0000779e2340.

Chung, Joanna, and Stephen Fidler. 2006. 'Why Iraqi Debt Is No Longer a Write-Off'. *Financial Times*, 16 July. www.ft.com/content/ b94bccb4-14e7-11db-b391-0000779e2340.

Cirillo, Pasquale, and Nassim Nicholas Taleb. 2016. 'On the Statistical Properties and Tail Risk of Violent Conflicts'. *Physica A: Statistical Mechanics and Its Applications* 452 (June): 29–45. https://doi.org/10.1016/j .physa.2016.01.050.

Clement, Piet. 2004. '"The Touchstone of German Credit": Nazi Germany and the Service of the Dawes and Young Loans'. *Financial History Review* 11 (1): 33–50. https://doi.org/10.1017/S0968565004000034.

Cloyne, James, Nicholas Dimsdale, and Natacha Postel-Vinay. 2021. 'Taxes and Growth: New Narrative Evidence from Interwar Britain'. *Review of Economic Studies* (forthcoming). https://doi.org/10.3386/w24659.

Cohen, Benjamin J. 1967. 'Reparations in the Postwar Period: A Survey'. *Banca Nazionale Del Lavoro Quarterly Review* 20 (82): 268–88.

Collet, Stephanie. 2013. 'The Financial Penalty for "Unfair" Debt: The Case of Cuban Bonds at the Time of Independence'. *European Review of Economic History* 17 (3): 364–87. https://doi.org/10.1093/ereh/het007.

Corsetti, Giancarlo, and Luca Dedola. 2016. 'The Mystery of the Printing Press: Monetary Policy and Self-Fulfilling Debt Crises'. *Journal of the European Economic Association* 14 (6): 1329–71.

Corsetti, Giancarlo, Philippe Martin, and Paolo Pesenti. 2013. 'Varieties and the Transfer Problem'. *Journal of International Economics* 89 (1): 1–12. https:// doi.org/10.1016/j.jinteco.2012.05.011.

Corsetti, Giancarlo, Paolo Pesenti, and Nouriel Roubini. 1999a. 'What Caused the Asian Currency and Financial Crisis?' *Japan and the World Economy* 11 (3): 305–73.

    1999b. 'Paper Tigers?: A Model of the Asian Crisis'. *European Economic Review* 43 (7): 1211–36. https://doi.org/10.1016/S0014-2921(99)00017-3.

Costigliola, Frank. 1976. 'The United States and the Reconstruction of Germany in the 1920s'. *The Business History Review* 50 (4): 477–502. https://doi .org/10.2307/3113137.

Cotterill, Joseph. 2012. 'Ghana Shall Forthwith and Unconditionally Release the Frigate ARA Libertad'. *Financial Times*. http://ftalphaville.ft.com/2012/12/ 15/1309492/ghana-shall-forthwith-and-unconditionally-release-the-frigate-ara-libertad/.

Cremers, Emily T., and Partha Sen. 2009. 'Transfers, the Terms of Trade, and Capital Accumulation'. *The Canadian Journal of Economics / Revue Canadienne d'Economique* 42 (4): 1599–616. https://doi.org/10.1111/ j.1540-5982.2009.01560.x.

Crouzet, François. 1964. 'Wars, Blockade, and Economic Change in Europe, 1792–1815'. *Journal of Economic History* 24 (4): 567–88.

Cruces, Juan J., and Christoph Trebesch. 2013. 'Sovereign Defaults: The Price of Haircuts'. *American Economic Journal: Macroeconomics* 5 (3): 85–117.

Dajani, Haneen. 2012. 'UAE Cancels Dh21bn of Debt Owed by Iraq'. *The National*, 17 January. www.thenational.ae/uae/uae-cancels-dh21bn-of-debt-owed-by-iraq-1.357148.

Damle, Jai. 2007. 'The Odious Debt Doctrine after Iraq'. *Law and Contemporary Problems* 70 (4): 139–56.

Da-Rocha, José-María, Eduardo-Luis Giménez, and Francisco-Xavier Lores. 2013. 'Self-Fulfilling Crises with Default and Devaluation'. *Economic Theory* 53 (3): 499–535.

Das, Udaibir, Michael Papaioannou, and Christoph Trebesch. 2012. 'Sovereign Debt Restructurings 1950–2010: Literature Survey, Data, and Stylized Facts'. *IMF Working Papers* 12 (January). https://doi .org/10.5089/9781475505535.001.

Davis, Lance E., and Stanley L. Engerman. 2006. *Naval Blockades in Peace and War: An Economic History since 1750*. Cambridge: Cambridge University Press. https://doi.org/10.1017/CBO9780511511974.

De Paoli, Bianca, Glenn Hoggarth, and Victoria Saporta. 2009. 'Output Costs of Sovereign Crises: Some Empirical Estimates'. Bank of England Working Paper Series 362 (February). https://ideas.repec.org/p/boe/boeewp/0362.html.

Deeb, Hadi N. 2007. 'Project 688: The Restructuring of Iraq's Saddam-Era Debt'. *Restructuring Newsletter, Cleary Gottlieb*.

DeLong, J. Bradford, and B. Eichengreen. 1993. 'The Marshall Plan: History's Most Successful Structural Adjustment Program'. In *Post-War Economic Reconstruction and Lessons for the East Today*, 190–230. Cambridge, MA: MIT Press. www-nber-org.gate3.library.lse.ac.uk/papers/w3899.pdf.

DeLong, J. Bradford, and Lawrence H. Summers. 2012. 'Fiscal Policy in a Depressed Economy [with Comments and Discussion]'. Brookings Papers on Economic Activity (spring): 233–97.

Devereux, Michael B., and Gregor W. Smith. 2007. 'Transfer Problem Dynamics: Macroeconomics of the Franco-Prussian War Indemnity'. *Journal of Monetary Economics* 54 (8): 2375–98. https://doi.org/10.1016/j.jmoneco.2007.06.027.

Devereux, Michael B., Eric R. Young, and Changhua Yu. 2019. 'Capital Controls and Monetary Policy in Sudden-Stop Economies'. *Journal of Monetary Economics* 103 (May): 52–74. https://doi.org/10.1016/j.jmoneco.2018.07.016.

Dimitrova, Kalina, and Martin Ivanov. 2014. 'Bulgaria: From 1879 to 1947'. In *South-Eastern European Monetary and Economic Statistics from the Nineteenth Century to World War II*, 199–242. Athens: Bank of Greece.

Djajic, Slobodan, Sajal Lahiri, and Pascalis Raimondos-Moller. 1998. 'The Transfer Problem and the Intertemporal Terms of Trade'. *The Canadian Journal of Economics* 31 (2): 427–36.

Dodge, Toby. 2010. 'The Failure of Sanctions and the Evolution of International Policy towards Iraq, 1990–2003'. *Contemporary Arab Affairs* 3 (1): 83–91. https://doi.org/10.1080/17550910903525952.

Dong, Baomin, and Yibei Guo. 2018. 'The Impact of the First Sino-Japanese War Indemnity: Transfer Problem Reexamined'. *International Review of Economics & Finance* 56 (July): 15–26. https://doi.org/10.1016/j.iref.2018.03.013.

Dupuy, Alex. 2020. *Rethinking the Haitian Revolution: Slavery, Independence, and the Struggle for Recognition*. Lanham, MD: Rowman & Littlefield Publishers.

Dvorkin, Maximiliano, Juan M. Sánchez, Horacio Sapriza, and Emircan Yurdagul. 2021. 'Sovereign Debt Restructurings'. *American Economic Journal: Macroeconomics* 13 (2): 26–77. https://doi.org/10.1257/mac.20190220.

Eaton, Jonathan, and Mark Gersovitz. 1981. 'Debt with Potential Repudiation: Theoretical and Empirical Analysis'. *The Review of Economic Studies* 48 (2): 289–309.

Eaton, Jonathan, Mark Gersovitz, and Joseph E. Stiglitz. 1986. 'The Pure Theory of Country Risk'. *European Economic Review* 30 (3): 481–513.

Eichengreen, Barry. 1990. 'The Capital Levy in Theory and Practice'. In *Public Debt Management: Theory and History*, edited by Mario Draghi and Rudiger Dornbusch, 191–220. Cambridge: Cambridge University Press. https://doi.org/10.1017/CBO9780511628528.014.

———. 2008. *Globalizing Capital: A History of the International Monetary System*. Second edition. Princeton, NJ: Princeton University Press.

Eichengreen, Barry, Asmaa El-Ganainy, Rui Pedro Esteves, and Kris James Mitchener. 2019. 'Public Debt through the Ages'. In *Sovereign Debt: A Guide for Economists and Practitioners*, edited by S. Ali Abbas, Alex Pienkowski, and Kenneth Rogoff, 7–55. Oxford: Oxford University Press.

Epifani, Paolo, and Gino Gancia. 2017. 'Global Imbalances Revisited: The Transfer Problem and Transport Costs in Monopolistic Competition'. *Journal of International Economics* 108 (September): 99–116. https://doi.org/10.1016/j.jinteco.2017.05.010.

Esteban, Javier C. 1987. 'Fundamentos Para Una Interpretacion de Las Estadisticas Comerciales Francesas de 1787–1821 Con Referencia Espacial al Comercia Franco-Espanol'. *Hacienda Publica Espanol* 108–9: 221–51.

Esteves, Rui Pedro, Jason Lennard, and Sean Kenny. 2021. 'The Aftermath of Sovereign Debt Crises: A Narrative Approach'. CEPR Discussion Paper. www.parisschoolofeconomics.eu/IMG/pdf/the-aftermath-of-sovereign-debt-crises-a-narrative-approach.pdf.

Fang, Chuck, Julian Schumacher, and Christoph Trebesch. 2021. 'Restructuring Sovereign Bonds: Holdouts, Haircuts and the Effectiveness of CACs'. *IMF Economic Review* 69: 155–96.

Farquet, Christophe. 2019. 'Quantification and Revolution: An Investigation of German Capital Flight after the First World War'. EHES Working Paper, no. 149. www.ehes.org/EHES_149.pdf.

Fatum, Rasmus, and James Yetman. 2020. 'Accumulation of Foreign Currency Reserves and Risk-Taking'. *Journal of International Money and Finance* 102 (April). https://doi.org/10.1016/j.jimonfin.2019.102097.

Feibelman, Adam. 2010. 'Ecuador's Sovereign Default: A Pyhrric Victory for Odious Debt?' *Journal of International Banking Law and Regulation* 25 (7): 357–62.

Fisch, J. 1992. *Reparationen Nach Dem Zweiten Weltkrieg*. Munich: Verlag C. H. Beck.

Flandreau, Marc. 1996. 'The French Crime of 1873: An Essay on the Emergence of the International Gold Standard, 1870–1880'. *The Journal of Economic History* 56 (4): 862–97.

Flandreau, Marc, and Juan H. Flores. 2012. 'Bondholders versus Bond-Sellers? Investment Banks and Conditionality Lending in the London Market for Foreign Government Debt, 1815–1913'. *European Review of Economic History* 16 (4): 356–83.

Flandreau, Marc, Juan H. Flores, Norbert Gaillard, and Sebastián Nieto-Parra. 2009. 'The End of Gatekeeping: Underwriters and the Quality of Sovereign Bond Markets, 1815–2007'. *NBER International Seminar on Macroeconomics* 6 (1): 53–92. https://doi.org/10.1086/648696.

Fleisig, Heywood. 1976. 'War-Related Debts and the Great Depression'. *American Economic Review* 66 (2): 52–58.

Foote, Christopher, William Block, Keith Crane, and Simon Gray. 2004. 'Economic Policy and Prospects in Iraq'. *Journal of Economic Perspectives* 18 (3): 47–70. https://doi.org/10.1257/0895330042162395.

Frantz, Douglas, and Murray Waas. 1992. 'Bush Tied to '86 Bid to Give Iraq Military Advice'. *Los Angeles Times*, 7 May. www.latimes.com/archives/la-xpm-1992-05-07-mn-2518-story.html.

Furceri, Davide, and Aleksandra Zdzienicka. 2012. 'How Costly Are Debt Crises?' *Journal of International Money and Finance* 31 (4): 726–42. https://doi.org/10.1016/j.jimonfin.2012.01.012.

Galofré-Vilà, Gregori, Christopher M. Meissner, Martin McKee, and David Stuckler. 2019. 'The Economic Consequences of the 1953 London Debt Agreement'. *European Review of Economic History* 23 (1): 1–29. https://doi.org/10.1093/ereh/hey010.

GAO, Government Accountability Office, United States Government. 2008. 'Stabilizing and Rebuilding Iraq: Iraqi Revenues, Expenditures, and Surplus'. Report to Congressional Committees 08-1031. www.gao.gov/products/GAO-08-1031.

Gavin, Michael. 1992. 'Intertemporal Dimensions of International Economic Adjustment: Evidence from the Franco-Prussian War Indemnity'. *The American Economic Review* 82 (2): 174–79.

Gelpern, Anna. 2005. 'What Iraq and Argentina Might Learn from Each Other'. *Chicago Journal of International Law* 6 (1): 391–414.

2007. 'Odious, Not Debt'. *Law and Contemporary Problems* 70 (3): 81–114.

2010. 'Debt and the People, Part II: The Hot ... and Concluding Disquietudes'. *Credit Slips* (blog). 2010. www.creditslips.org/creditslips/2010/03/debt-and-the-people-part-ii-the-hot-disquietude.html.

2016. 'Sovereign Debt: Now What?' *The Yale Journal of International Law* 41: 45–95.

Gelpern, Anna, and Jeromin Zettelmeyer. 2020. 'CACs and Doorknobs'. *Capital Markets Law Journal* 15 (1): 98–114. https://doi.org/10.1093/cmlj/kmz024.

Ghulam, Yaseen, and Julian Derber. 2018. 'Determinants of Sovereign Defaults'. *The Quarterly Review of Economics and Finance* 69 (August): 43–55. https://doi.org/10.1016/j.qref.2017.12.003.

Gimbel, J. 1990. *Science, Technology, and Reparations: Exploration and Plunder in Postwar Germany*. Stanford, CA: Stanford University Press.

Gordon, Robert J., and Robert Krenn. 2010. 'The End of the Great Depression 1939–41: Policy Contributions and Fiscal Multipliers'. NBER Working Paper, no. 16380 (September). https://doi.org/10.3386/w16380.

Greenfield, Jerome. 2016. 'Financing a New Order: The Payment of Reparations by Restoration France, 1817–18'. *French History* 30 (3): 376–400. https://doi.org/10.1093/fh/crw038.

Grossman, Herschel I., and John B. Van Huyck. 1988. 'Sovereign Debt as a Contingent Claim: Excusable Default, Repudiation, and Reputation'. *The American Economic Review* 78 (5): 1088–97.

Gu, Grace Weishi. 2019. 'Sovereign Default, Trade, and Terms of Trade'. *Macroeconomic Dynamics* 25(6): 1346–80. https://doi.org/10.1017/S1365100519000701.

Hatchondo, Juan Carlos, and Leonardo Martinez. 2009. 'Long-Duration Bonds and Sovereign Defaults'. *Journal of International Economics* 79 (1): 117–25. https://doi.org/10.1016/j.jinteco.2009.07.002.

Hébert, Benjamin, and Jesse Schreger. 2017. 'The Costs of Sovereign Default: Evidence from Argentina'. *American Economic Review* 107 (10): 3119–45. https://doi.org/10.1257/aer.20151667.

Herrera, Helios, Guillermo Ordoñez, and Christoph Trebesch. 2020. 'Political Booms, Financial Crises'. *Journal of Political Economy* 128 (2): 507–43. https://doi.org/10.1086/704544.

Hersh, Seymour M. 1992. 'U.S. Secretly Gave Aid to Iraq Early in Its War Against Iran'. *The New York Times*, 26 January, sec. World. www.nytimes.com/1992/01/26/world/us-secretly-gave-aid-to-iraq-early-in-its-war-against-iran.html.

Hicks, J. R. 1937. 'Mr. Keynes and the "Classics"; A Suggested Interpretation'. *Econometrica* 5 (2): 147–59. https://doi.org/10.2307/1907242.

Hinrichsen, Simon. 2021. 'The Iraq Sovereign Debt Restructuring'. *Capital Markets Law Journal* 16 (1): 95–114. https://doi.org/10.1093/cmlj/kmaa031.

2022a. 'The Rise of Iraqi Indebtedness, 1979–2003'. *Middle Eastern Studies* 58 (5): 782–96. https://doi.org/10.1080/00263206.2022.2081553.

2022b. 'How to Restructure Sovereign Debt'. *Financial Times*, 16 September 2022. www.ft.com/content/1f46e9ac-a930-4ec0-b399-0c042c9d147c.

2023. 'Keynes, the Transfer Problem, and Reparations'. In *Keynes' Economic Consequences of the Peace after 100 Years: Polemics and Policy*, edited by

Giancarlo Corsetti, Maurice Obstfeld, Adam Tooze, and Patricia Clavin, 179–201. Cambridge: Cambridge University Press.

Ho, Tai-kuang, and Kuo-chun Yeh. 2019. 'Were Capital Flows the Culprit in the Weimar Economic Crisis?' *Explorations in Economic History* 74 (October): 101278. https://doi.org/10.1016/j.eeh.2019.06.003.

Holtfrerich, Carl-Ludwig. 1990. 'Was the Policy of Deflation in Germany Unavoidable?' In *Economic Crisis and Political Collapse: The Weimar Republic, 1924–1933*, edited by Jürgen Baron von Kruedener, 63–80. Oxford: Oxford University Press.

Homer, Sydney, and Richard Sylla. 2005. *A History of Interest Rates*. Fourth edition. Hoboken, NJ: John Wiley & Sons.

Hsu, Immanuel Chung-Yueh. 2000. *The Rise of Modern China*. Oxford: Oxford University Press.

Hughes, J. R. T. 1958. 'Financing the British War Effort'. *Journal of Economic History* 18 (2): 193–99.

Ikeda, Daisuke, and Toan Phan. 2019. 'Asset Bubbles and Global Imbalances'. *American Economic Journal: Macroeconomics* 11 (3): 209–51. https://doi.org/10.1257/mac.20140286.

IMF, International Monetary Fund. 2013. *The IMF's Balance of Payments and International Investment Position Manual*. Sixth edition. Washington, DC: IMF. www.imf.org/external/pubs/ft/bop/2007/bopman6.htm.

James, Cyril L. R. 1938. *The Black Jacobins*. London: Secker & Warburg Ltd.

James, Harold. 1986. *The German Slump: Politics and Economics 1924–1936*. Oxford: Oxford University Press.

Jayachandran, Seema, and Michael Kremer. 2006. 'Odious Debt'. *The American Economic Review* 96 (1): 82–92.

Jiyad, Ahmed M. 2001. 'An Economy in a Debt Trap: Iraqi Debt 1980–2020'. *Arab Studies Quarterly* 23 (4): 15–58.

Johnson, Harry G. 1955. 'The Transfer Problem: A Note on Criteria for Changes in the Terms of Trade'. *Economica* 22 (86): 113–21.

1956. 'The Transfer Problem and Exchange Stability'. *Journal of Political Economy* 64 (3): 212–25.

Jones, Matthew T., and Maurice Obstfeld. 2001. 'Saving, Investment, and Gold: A Reassessment of Historical Current Account Data'. In *Money, Capital Mobility, and Trade: Essays in Honor of Robert Mundell*, edited by Guillermo A. Calvo, Rudi Dornbusch, and Maurice Obstfeld. Cambridge, MA: MIT Press. https://eml.berkeley.edu/~obstfeld/ftp/account_data/copyright.html.

Juhász, Réka. 2018. 'Temporary Protection and Technology Adoption: Evidence from the Napoleonic Blockade'. *American Economic Review* 108 (11): 3339–76. https://doi.org/10.1257/aer.20151730.

Kaminsky, Graciela L., and Carmen M. Reinhart. 1999. 'The Twin Crises: The Causes of Banking and Balance-of-Payments Problems'. *American Economic Review* 89 (3): 473–500. https://doi.org/10.1257/aer.89.3.473.

Kelleners, Martin. 2012. 'Performance and Budget Modernization – the German Experience'. Finance Ministry Presentation at the 5th Annual Meeting of Middle East and North Africa Senior Budget Officials (MENA-SBO), Tunis.

www.oecd.org/gov/budgeting/D2-AM%20-%20Roundtable%20-%20 M.%20KELLENERS%20-%20Germany%20(English).pdf.

Kelly, Claire. 2004. 'The War on Jurisdiction: Troubling Questions about Executive Order 13303'. *Arizona Law Review* 46 (June): 483–517.

Kennington, Devin, Joyce Battle, and Malcolm Byrne. 2004. 'The Origins, Conduct, and Impact of the Iran–Iraq War, 1980–1988'. Timeline. Washington, DC: Wilson Center. www.wilsoncenter.org/publication/ the-origins-conduct-and-impact-the-iran-iraq-war-1980-1988.

Keynes, J. M. 1919. *The Economic Consequences of the Peace.* New York: Harcourt, Brace, and Hove.

　　1929a. 'Mr. Keynes' Views on the Transfer Problem'. *The Economic Journal* 39 (155): 388–408. https://doi.org/10.2307/2224179.

　　1929b. 'The Reparation Problem: A Discussion'. *The Economic Journal* 39 (154): 172–82. https://doi.org/10.2307/2224537.

　　1929c. 'The German Transfer Problem'. *The Economic Journal* 39: 1–7. https:// doi.org/10.2307/2224211.

　　1936. *The General Theory of Employment, Interest and Money.* Houndmills: Palgrave Macmillan.

　　1937. 'The General Theory of Employment'. *The Quarterly Journal of Economics* 51 (2): 209–23. https://doi.org/10.2307/1882087.

Khalaf, Roula, William Wallis, and James Harding. 2004. 'Iraq Debt Accord Ends US-Europe Stand-Off'. *Financial Times*, 22 November, US print edition, sec. Front page.

Kindleberger, C. P. 1993. *A Financial History of Western Europe.* Second edition. New York: Oxford University Press.

King, Jeff. 2016. *The Doctrine of Odious Debt in International Law: A Restatement.* Cambridge: Cambridge University Press. https://doi .org/10.1017/CBO9781316422809.

King, Mervyn. 2004. 'The Institutions of Monetary Policy'. *The Ely Lecture 2004,* The American Economic Association Annual Meeting, San Diego. www .bankofengland.co.uk/-/media/boe/files/speech/2004/the-institutions-of-monetary-policy.

King, Robert G., Charles I. Plosser, and Sergio T. Rebelo. 1988. 'Production, Growth and Business Cycles: I. The Basic Neoclassical Model'. *Journal of Monetary Economics* 21 (2): 195–232. https://doi .org/10.1016/0304-3932(88)90030-X.

Klug, A. 1993. 'The German Buybacks, 1932–1939: A Cure for Overhang?' *Princeton Studies in International Finance* 75: 1–62. www.princeton .edu/~ies/IES_Studies/S75.pdf.

Kollmann, Robert. 2002. 'Monetary Policy Rules in the Open Economy: Effects on Welfare and Business Cycles'. *Journal of Monetary Economics* 49 (5): 989–1015. https://doi.org/10.1016/S0304-3932(02)00132-0.

Kramer, Mark. 2009. 'The Soviet Bloc and the Cold War in Europe'. In *A Companion to Europe since 1945, Europe and the Cold War World,* edited by Klaus Larres, 67–94. Oxford: Wiley-Blackwell.

Krugman, Paul. 1979. 'A Model of Balance-of-Payments Crises'. *Journal of Money, Credit and Banking* 11 (3): 311–25.

1988. 'Financing vs. Forgiving a Debt Overhang'. *Journal of Development Economics* 29 (3): 253–68. https://doi.org/10.1016/0304-3878(88)90044-2.

1998. 'It's Baaack: Japan's Slump and the Return of the Liquidity Trap'. *Brookings Papers on Economic Activity* 1998 (2): 137. https://doi.org/10.2307/2534694.

Kuvshinov, Dmitry, and Kaspar Zimmermann. 2019. 'Sovereigns Going Bust: Estimating the Cost of Default'. *European Economic Review* 119 (October): 1–21. https://doi.org/10.1016/j.euroecorev.2019.04.009.

Lane, Philip R., and Gian Milesi-Ferretti. 2001. 'Long-Term Capital Movements'. *NBER Macroeconomics Annual* 16: 73–116. https://doi.org/10.3386/w8366.

2004. 'The Transfer Problem Revisited: Net Foreign Assets and Real Exchange Rates'. *The Review of Economics and Statistics* 86 (4): 841–57. https://doi.org/10.1162/0034653043125185.

Laskaridis, Christina, Nathan Legrand, and Eric Toussaint. 2020. 'Historical Perspectives on Current Struggles Against Illegitimate Debt'. In *The Routledge International Handbook of Financialization*, edited by Philip Mader, Daniel Mertens, and Natacha van der Zwan. London: Routledge.

Lee, Sang Seok, and Paul Luk. 2018. 'The Asian Financial Crisis and International Reserve Accumulation: A Robust Control Approach'. *Journal of Economic Dynamics and Control* 90 (May): 284–309. https://doi.org/10.1016/j.jedc.2018.03.010.

Levy-Leboyer, Maurice, and François Bourguignon. 1990. *The French Economy in the Nineteenth Century: An Essay in Econometric Analysis*. Cambridge: Cambridge University Press.

Lienau, Odette. 2014. *Rethinking Sovereign Debt: Politics, Reputation, and Legitimacy in Modern Finance*. Cambridge, MA: Harvard University Press.

Ljungberg, Jonas. 2019. 'Nominal and Real Effective Exchange Rates for Europe, 1870–2016. Some Methodological Issues'. *Lund Papers in Economic History* 200: 1–60. https://ekh.lu.se/en/research/economic-history-data/Exchange_Rates_1870-2016.

Lutz, H. L. 1930. 'Inter-Allied Debts, Reparations, and National Policy'. *Journal of Political Economy* 38 (1): 29–61.

Machlup, Fritz. 1964. *International Payments, Debts and Gold*. New York: Charles Scribner Sons.

Maddison, Angus. 2007. *Contours of the World Economy, 1–2030 AD: Essays in Macro-Economic History*. Oxford: Oxford University Press.

Mallez, P. 1927. *La Restauration Des Finances Françaises Après 1814*. Paris: Jouve & Cie.

Mantoux, Étienne. 1946. *The Carthaginian Peace; or the Economic Consequences of Mr Keynes*. London: Oxford University Press.

Markevich, Andrei, and Mark Harrison. 2011. 'Great War, Civil War, and Recovery: Russia's National Income, 1913 to 1928'. *The Journal of Economic History* 71 (3): 672–703.

Marks, Sally. 2013. 'Mistakes and Myths: The Allies, Germany, and the Versailles Treaty, 1918–1921'. *The Journal of Modern History* 85 (3): 632–59. https://doi.org/10.1086/670825.

Martinez, Jose Vicente, and Guido Sandleris. 2011. 'Is It Punishment? Sovereign Defaults and the Decline in Trade'. *Journal of International Money and Finance* 30 (6): 909–30.

Marwah, Hanaan. 2020. 'Untangling Government, Market, and Investment Failure during the Nigerian Oil Boom: The Cement Armada Scandal 1974–1980'. *Business History* 62 (4): 566–87. https://doi.org/10.1080/00076791.2018.1458839.

Mazaheri, Nimah. 2010. 'Iraq and the Domestic Political Effects of Economic Sanctions'. *Middle East Journal* 64 (2): 253–68.

Mehdi, Ahmen. 2018. 'Iraqi Oil: Industry Evolution and Short and Medium-Term Prospects'. *The Oxford Institute for Energy Studies Paper* 79. www.oxfordenergy.org/publications/iraqi-oil-industry-evolution-short-medium-term-prospects/.

Mendoza, Enrique G., and Vivian Z. Yue. 2012. 'A General Equilibrium Model of Sovereign Default and Business Cycles'. *The Quarterly Journal of Economics* 127 (2): 889–946.

Meyer, Josefin, Carmen M. Reinhart, and Christoph Trebesch. 2022. 'Sovereign Bonds since Waterloo'. *The Quarterly Journal of Economics* 137 (3): 1615–80. https://doi.org/10.1093/qje/qjac007.

Metz, Helen Chapin. 1990. *Iraq: A Country Study*. Washington, DC: Federal Research Division, Library of Congress. www.loc.gov/item/89013940/.

Metzler, Lloyd A. 1942. 'The Transfer Problem Reconsidered'. *Journal of Political Economy* 50 (3): 397–414.

Mill, J. S. 1844. *Essays on Some Unsettled Questions of Political Economy*. Second edition. London: Longmans, Green, Reader, and Dyer.

Mitchener, Kris James, and Marc D. Weidenmier. 2010. 'Supersanctions and Sovereign Debt Repayment'. *Journal of International Money and Finance* 29 (1): 19–36. https://doi.org/10.1016/j.jimonfin.2008.12.011.

Momani, Bessma, and Aidan Garrib. 2010. 'Iraq's Tangled Web of Debt Restructuring'. In *From Desolation to Reconstruction: Iraq's Troubled Journey*, edited by Mokhtar Lamani and Bessma Momani. Canada: Wilfrid Laurier University Press.

Monroe, Arthur E. 1919. 'The French Indemnity of 1871 and Its Effects'. *The Review of Economics and Statistics* 1 (4): 269–81.

Morrison, Rodney J. 1992. 'Gulf War Reparations: Iraq, OPEC, and the Transfer Problem'. *The American Journal of Economics and Sociology* 51 (4): 385–99.

Munro, Dana G. 1969. 'The American Withdrawal from Haiti, 1929–1934'. *The Hispanic American Historical Review* 49 (1): 1–26. https://doi.org/10.2307/2511314.

Na, Seunghoon, Stephanie Schmitt-Grohé, Martín Uribe, and Vivian Yue. 2018. 'The Twin Ds: Optimal Default and Devaluation'. *American Economic Review* 108 (7): 1773–819. https://doi.org/10.1257/aer.20141558.

Neto, Arminio Fraga. 1986. 'German Reparations and the Brazilian Debt Crisis: A Comparative Study of International Lending and Adjustment'. *Essays in International Finance* 163 (July): 1–46. https://econpapers.repec.org/paper/riotexdis/92.htm.

Nevakivi, Jukka. 1996. 'The Soviet Union and Finland after the War, 1944–53'. In *The Soviet Union and Europe in the Cold War, 1943–53*, edited by Francesca Gori and Silvio Pons, First edition. London: Palgrave Macmillan.

Nicolle, André. 1929. *Comment La France a Payé Après Waterloo*. Paris: E. de Boccard.

Obstfeld, Maurice. 1982. 'Aggregate Spending and the Terms of Trade: Is There a Laursen-Metzler Effect?' *The Quarterly Journal of Economics* 97 (2): 251–70. https://doi.org/10.2307/1880757.

Obstfeld, Maurice, and Kenneth Rogoff. 1995. 'The Intertemporal Approach to the Current Account'. In *Handbook of International Economics* 3: 1731–99. https://ideas.repec.org/h/eee/intchp/3-34.html.

1996. *Foundations of International Macroeconomics*. Cambridge, MA: MIT Press. https://mitpress.mit.edu/books/foundations-international-macroeconomics.

Ohanian, Lee E. 1997. 'The Macroeconomic Effects of War Finance in the United States: World War II and the Korean War'. *The American Economic Review* 87 (1): 23–40.

Ohlin, Bertil. 1929a. 'Mr. Keynes' Views on the Transfer Problem. Sec. 2, A Rejoinder from Professor Ohlin'. *The Economic Journal* 39: 400–4.

1929b. 'The Reparations Problem: A Discussion, Transfer Difficulties Real and Imagined'. *The Economic Journal* 39: 172–83. https://doi.org/10.2307/2224537.

Oosterlinck, Kim, Ugo Panizza, W. Mark C. Weidemaier, and Mitu Gulati. 2021. 'The Odious Haitian Independence Debt'. IHEID Working Papers, July. https://ideas.repec.org/p/gii/giihei/heidwp16-2021.html.

2022. 'A Debt of Dishonor'. *Boston University Law Review* 102 (4): 1247–76.

Oosterlinck, Kim, Loredana Ureche-Rangau, and Jacques-Marie Vaslin. 2014. 'Baring, Wellington and the Resurrection of French Public Finances Following Waterloo'. *The Journal of Economic History* 74 (4): 1072–102. https://doi.org/10.1017/S0022050714000862.

Orastean, Ramona. 2014. 'The IMF Lending Activity – A Survey'. *Procedia Economics and Finance*, Special Issue: 21st International Economic Conference of Sibiu 2014, IECS 2014 Prospects of Economic Recovery in a Volatile International Context: Major Obstacles, Initiatives and Projects, 16 (January): 410–16. https://doi.org/10.1016/S2212-5671(14)00820-X.

O'Reagan, Douglas. 2019. *Taking Nazi Technology: Allied Exploitation of German Science after the Second World War*. Baltimore, MD: John's Hopkins University Press.

O'Rourke, Kevin H. 2006. 'The Worldwide Economic Impact of the French Revolutionary and Napoleonic Wars, 1793–1815'. *Journal of Global History* 1 (01): 123.

2007. 'War and Welfare: Britain, France, and the United States, 1807–14'. *Oxford Economic Papers* 59 (October): 8–30. https://doi.org/10.1093/oep/gpm028.

Ottonello, Pablo, and Diego J. Perez. 2019. 'The Currency Composition of Sovereign Debt'. *American Economic Journal: Macroeconomics* 11 (3): 174–208. https://doi.org/10.1257/mac.20180019.

Pahre, Robert. 1998. 'Reactions and Reciprocity: Tariffs and Trade Liberalization from 1815 to 1914'. *Journal of Conflict Resolution* 42 (4): 467–92. https://doi.org/10.1177/0022002798042004004.

Papadia, Andrea, and Claudio A. Schioppa. 2015. 'Foreign Debt and Secondary Markets: The Case of Interwar Germany'. Working Paper. https://editorialexpress.com/cgi-bin/conference/download.cgi?db_name=RESConf2016&paper_id=1196.

Parasiliti, Andrew T. 2003. 'The Causes and Timing of Iraq's Wars: A Power Cycle Assessment'. *International Political Science Review/Revue Internationale de Science Politique* 24 (1): 151–65.

Phan, Toan. 2017. 'Nominal Sovereign Debt'. *International Economic Review* 58 (4): 1303–16.

Pihkala, Erkki. 1999. 'The Political Economy of Post-War Finland, 1945–1952'. *Scandinavian Economic History Review* 47(3): 26–47. https://doi.org/10.1080/03585522.1999.10419817.

Piketty, Thomas. 2020. *Capital and Ideology*. Cambridge, MA: Harvard University Press.

Polk, Judd, and Gardner Patterson. 1946. 'The British Loan'. *Foreign Affairs* 24 (3): 429–40. https://doi.org/10.2307/20029980.

Porter, Catherine, Constant Meheut, Matt Apuzzo, and Selam Gebrekidan. 2022. 'The Root of Haiti's Misery: Reparations to Enslavers'. *The New York Times*, 20 May. www.nytimes.com/2022/05/20/world/americas/haiti-history-colonized-france.html.

Porzecanski, Arturo C. 2010. 'When Bad Things Happen to Good Sovereign Debt Contracts: The Case of Ecuador'. *Law and Contemporary Problems* 73 (4): 251–71.

Rajan, Raghuram. 2004. 'Straight Talk: Odious or Just Malodorous?' *Finance and Development* 41 (4): 54–55. www.imf.org/external/pubs/ft/fandd/2004/12/pdf/straight.pdf.

Rangwala, Glen. 2013. 'The Finance of War: Iraq, Credit and Conflict, September 1980 to August 1990'. In *The Iran–Iraq War: New International Perspectives*, edited by Nigel Ashton and Bryan Gibson, 92–105. New York: Routledge.

Reinhart, Carmen M., and Kenneth Rogoff. 2009. *This Time Is Different: Eight Centuries of Financial Folly*. Princeton, NJ: Princeton University Press.

2010. 'Growth in a Time of Debt'. *American Economic Review* 100 (2): 573–78.

2011a. 'The Forgotten History of Domestic Debt'. *The Economic Journal* 121 (552): 319–50.

2011b. 'From Financial Crash to Debt Crisis'. *American Economic Review* 101 (5): 1676–706. https://doi.org/10.1257/aer.101.5.1676.

2014. 'Recovery from Financial Crises: Evidence from 100 Episodes'. *American Economic Review* 104 (5): 50–55.

Reinhart, Carmen M., and Christoph Trebesch. 2016. 'The International Monetary Fund: 70 Years of Reinvention'. *Journal of Economic Perspectives* 30 (1): 3–28.

Ricardo, David. 1821. *The Principles of Political Economy and Taxation*. Third edition. Kitchener: Batoche Books. https://socialsciences.mcmaster.ca/econ/ugcm/3ll3/ricardo/Principles.pdf.

Rieffel, Alexis. 1985. *The Role of the Paris Club in Managing Debt Problems*. Essays in International Finance, no. 161 (December). Princeton, NJ: International Finance Section, Department of Economics, Princeton University.

2003. *Restructuring Sovereign Debt: The Case for Ad Hoc Machinery*. Washington, DC: Brookings Institution Press.

Ritschl, Albrecht. 1996a. 'Sustainability of High Public Debt: What the Historical Record Shows'. *Swedish Economic Policy Review* 3 (1996): 175–98.

1996b. 'Was Schacht Right? Reparations, the Young Plan, and the Great Depression in Germany'. Working Paper, no. 23.

2001. 'Nazi Economic Imperialism and the Exploitation of the Small: Evidence from Germany's Secret Foreign Exchange Balances, 1938–1940'. *The Economic History Review* 54 (2): 324–45. https://doi.org/10.1111/1468-0289.00194.

2002. Deutschlands Krise und Konjunktur 1924–1934, Binnenkonjunktur, Auslandsverschuldung und Reparationsproblem zwischen Dawes-Plan und Transfersperre. Reprint 2014. Berlin and Boston, MA: De Gruyter. www.degruyter.com/view/product/228231.

2012a. 'Reparations, Deficits, and Debt Default: The Great Depression in Germany'. *LSE Working Papers in Economic History* 163 (12): 1–40. http://eprints.lse.ac.uk/44335/1/WP163.pdf.

2012b. 'The German Transfer Problem, 1920–33: A Sovereign-Debt Perspective'. *European Review of History* 19 (6): 943–64. https://doi.org/10.1080/13507486.2012.739147.

2013. 'Reparations, Deficits, and Debt Default: The Great Depression in Germany'. In *The Great Depression of the 1930s*, edited by Nicholas Crafts and Peter Fearon. Oxford: Oxford University Press. https://doi.org/10.1093/acprof:oso/9780199663187.003.0004.

Romer, Christina, and David Romer. 2019. 'Fiscal Space and the Aftermath of Financial Crises: How It Matters and Why'. Brookings Papers on Economic Activity, April. https://doi.org/10.3386/w25768.

Roos, Jerome E. 2019. *Why Not Default? The Political Economy of Sovereign Debt*. Princeton, NJ: Princeton University Press.

Samuelson, Paul A. 1947. *Foundations of Economic Analysis*. Cambridge, MA: Harvard University Press.

1948. *Economics*. First edition. New York: McGraw-Hill.

1952. 'The Transfer Problem and Transport Costs: The Terms of Trade When Impediments Are Absent'. *The Economic Journal* 62 (246): 278–304.

1954. 'The Transfer Problem and Transport Costs, II: Analysis of Effects of Trade Impediments'. *The Economic Journal* 64 (254): 264–89.

Sandoval, Clara, and Miriam Puttick. 2017. Reparations for the Victims of Conflict in Iraq: Lessons Learned from Comparative Practice. *Online report*. Minority Rights Group International. www.refworld.org/docid/5a1812b44.html.

Schacht, Hjalmar. 1967. *The Magic of Money*; Translated from the German by Paul Erskine. First edition. London: Oldbourne. www.filosofiadeldebito.it/wordpress/wp-content/uploads/2018/05/schacht_the_magic_of_money.pdf.

Schlegl, Matthias, Christoph Trebesch, and Mark L. J. Wright. 2019. 'The Seniority Structure of Sovereign Debt'. NBER Working Paper. www.nber .org/papers/w25793.

Schmidt, Rachel. 1991. *Global Arms Exports to Iraq, 1960–1990*. Santa Monica, CA: RAND Corporation. www.rand.org/pubs/notes/N3248.html.

Schmitt-Grohé, Stephanie, and Martín Uribe. 2003. 'Closing Small Open Economy Models'. *Journal of International Economics* 61 (1): 163–85. https://doi.org/10.1016/S0022-1996(02)00056-9.

2016. 'Downward Nominal Wage Rigidity, Currency Pegs, and Involuntary Unemployment'. *Journal of Political Economy* 124 (5): 1466–514. https:// doi.org/10.1086/688175.

2018. 'How Important Are Terms of Trade Shocks?' *International Economic Review* 59 (1): 85–111. https://doi.org/10.1111/iere.12263.

Schroeder, Paul W. 1996. *The Transformation of European Politics, 1763–1848*. Oxford: Clarendon Press.

Schuker, Stephen A. 1988. *American 'Reparations' to Germany, 1919–33: Implications for the Third-World Debt Crisis*, No. 61. Princeton, NJ: Princeton University Press.

Schumacher, Julian, Christoph Trebesch, and Henrik Enderlein. 2021. 'Sovereign Defaults in Court'. *Journal of International Economics* 131 (July): 103388. https://doi.org/10.1016/j.jinteco.2020.103388.

Séguin, Armand. 1824. *Considérations sur les systèmes suivis en France dans l'administration des finances*. Paris: Guiraudet. https://reader.digitale-sammlungen.de/de/fs1/object/display/bsb10425723_00005.html.

Sgard, Jérôme. 2016. 'How the IMF Did It—Sovereign Debt Restructuring between 1970 and 1989'. *Capital Markets Law Journal* 11 (1): 103–25. https://doi.org/10.1093/cmlj/kmv042.

Shea, Patrick E., and Paul Poast. 2018. 'War and Default'. *Journal of Conflict Resolution* 62 (9): 1876–904. https://doi.org/10.1177/0022002717707239.

Sluglett, Peter. 2010. 'Iraq under Siege: Politics, Society and Economy, 1990–2002'. In *From Desolation to Reconstruction: Iraq's Troubled Journey*, edited by Mokhtar Lamani and Bessma Momani, 13–33. Waterloo: Wilfrid Laurier University Press.

Smele, J. D. 1994. 'White Gold: The Imperial Russian Gold Reserve in the Anti-Bolshevik East, 1918-? (An Unconcluded Chapter in the History of the Russian Civil War)'. *Europe-Asia Studies* 46 (8): 1317–47.

Sommers, Jeffrey. 2015. *Race, Reality, and Realpolitik: U.S.–Haiti Relations in the Lead Up to the 1915 Occupation*. Lanham, MD: Lexington Books.

Sosa-Padilla, César. 2018. 'Sovereign Defaults and Banking Crises'. *Journal of Monetary Economics* 99 (November): 88–105. https://doi.org/10.1016/j .jmoneco.2018.07.004.

Steen, Kathryn. 2001. 'Patents, Patriotism, and "Skilled in the Art" USA v. The Chemical Foundation, Inc., 1923–1926'. *Isis* 92 (1): 91–122.

Stevenson, Angus. 2010. *Oxford Dictionary of English*. Oxford: Oxford University Press.

Stich, Rodney. 2005. *Iraq, Lies, Cover-Ups, and Consequences*. Nevada: Silverpeak Enterprises.

Sturzenegger, Federico, and Jeromin Zettelmeyer. 2006. *Debt Defaults and Lessons from a Decade of Crises.* Cambridge, MA: MIT Press.

2008. 'Haircuts: Estimating Investor Losses in Sovereign Debt Restructurings, 1998–2005'. *Journal of International Money and Finance* 27 (5): 780–805. https://doi.org/10.1016/j.jimonfin.2007.04.014.

Svensson, Lars E. O., and Assaf Razin. 1983. 'The Terms of Trade and the Current Account: The Harberger-Laursen-Metzler Effect'. *Journal of Political Economy* 91 (1): 97–125.

Takagi, Shinji, Donal Donovan, Bessma Momani, Lorenzo L. Perez, Miguel de Las Casas, and Michael Pisa. 2018. 'The IMF and Fragile States: Eight Selected Country Cases'. Independent Evaluation Office of the International Monetary Fund BP/18-01/02. IEO Background Paper. Washington, DC: International Monetary Fund. https://ieo.imf.org/~/media/IEO/Files/evalua tions/completed/04-03-2018-the-imf-and-fragile-states/bp02-eight-selected-country-cases.ashx.

Taussig, F. W. 1927. *International Trade.* New York: Macmillan.

Thimme, Julian. 2017. 'Intertemporal Substitution in Consumption: A Literature Review'. *Journal of Economic Surveys* 31 (1): 226–57. https://doi .org/10.1111/joes.12142.

Timbie, James P. 2004. 'Energy from Bombs: Problems and Solutions in the Implementation of a High-Priority Nonproliferation Project'. *Science & Global Security* 12 (3): 165–89. https://doi.org/10.1080/08929880490518036.

Tomz, Michael, and Mark L. J. Wright. 2007. 'Do Countries Default in "Bad Times"?' *Journal of the European Economic Association* 5 (2–3): 352–60. https://doi.org/10.1162/jeea.2007.5.2-3.352.

Tooze, Adam. 2018. *Crashed: How a Decade of Financial Crises Changed the World.* New York: Viking.

Tooze, Adam, and Martin Ivanov. 2011. 'Disciplining the "Black Sheep of the Balkans": Financial Supervision and Sovereignty in Bulgaria, 1902–38'. *The Economic History Review* 64 (1): 30–51. https://doi .org/10.1111/j.1468-0289.2010.00544.x.

Toutain, Jean-Claude. 1997. 'Le produit intérieur brut de la France, 1789– 1990'. *Economies et sociétés : Histoire économique quantitative* 31 (11): 5–136.

Trebesch, Christoph, and Michael Zabel. 2017. 'The Output Costs of Hard and Soft Sovereign Default'. *European Economic Review* 92 (February): 416–32. https://doi.org/10.1016/j.euroecorev.2016.10.004.

Tunçer, Ali Coşkun. 2015. *Sovereign Debt and International Financial Control: The Middle East and the Balkans, 1870–1914.* Palgrave Studies in the History of Finance. New York: Palgrave Macmillan.

Ulff-Møller, Jens. 2001. *Hollywood's Film Wars with France: Film-Trade Diplomacy and the Emergence of the French Film Quota Policy.* New York: University of Rochester Press.

Uribe, Martin, and Stephanie Schmitt-Grohé. 2017. *Open Economy Macroeconomics.* Princeton, NJ: Princeton University Press.

Veve, Thomas D. 1989. 'Wellington and the Army of Occupation in France, 1815–1818'. *The International History Review* 11 (1): 98–108.

Vuhrer, A. 1886. *Histoire de La Dette Publique*. Paris: Berger-Levrault et Cie. https://gallica.bnf.fr/ark:/12148/bpt6k1170767x/f61.image.

Waibel, Michael. 2015. 'Echoes of History: The International Financial Commission in Greece'. SSRN Scholarly Paper ID 2631393. Rochester, NY: Social Science Research Network. https://papers.ssrn.com/abstract=2631393.

Warbrick, Colin. 1991a. 'The Invasion of Kuwait by Iraq'. *The International and Comparative Law Quarterly* 40 (2): 482–92.

1991b. 'The Invasion of Kuwait by Iraq: Part II'. *The International and Comparative Law Quarterly* 40 (4): 965–76.

WB, World Bank Group. 2017. 'Iraq: Systematic Country Diagnostic'. 112333-IQ. *World Bank Report*. http://documents.worldbank.org/curated/en/542811487277729890/pdf/IRAQ-SCD-FINAL-cleared-02132017.pdf.

Weidemaier, Mark C. 2014. 'Sovereign Immunity and Sovereign Debt'. *University of Illinois Law Review* 2014 (1): 67–114. https://doi.org/10.2139/ssrn.2180228.

Weidenmier, Marc D. 2005. 'Gunboats, Reputation, and Sovereign Repayment: Lessons from the Southern Confederacy'. *Journal of International Economics* 66 (2): 407–22. https://doi.org/10.1016/j.jinteco.2004.07.006.

Weiss, Martin A. 2011. 'Iraq's Debt Relief: Procedure and Potential Implications'. *CRS Report for Congress*, no. 15. https://sgp.fas.org/crs/mideast/RL33376.pdf.

Weller, Leonardo. 2019. 'Loans of the Revolution: How Mexico Borrowed as the State Collapsed in 1912–13'. *The Economic History Review* 72 (3): 1028–47. https://doi.org/10.1111/ehr.12742.

White, Eugene N. 2001. 'Making the French Pay: The Costs and Consequences of the Napoleonic Reparations'. *European Review of Economic History* 5 (3): 337–65. https://doi.org/10.1017/S1361491601000132.

Woodward, Bob. 1986. 'CIA Aiding Iraq in Gulf War'. *Washington Post*, 15 December. www.washingtonpost.com/archive/politics/1986/12/15/cia-aiding-iraq-in-gulf-war/edc02d8f-0b37-478b-9b4a-16ca5d7034a3/.

Yee, Robert. 2020. 'Reparations Revisited: The Role of Economic Advisers in Reforming German Central Banking and Public Finance'. *Financial History Review* 27: 45–72. https://doi.org/10.1017/S0968565019000258.

Yeyati, Eduardo Levy, and Ugo Panizza. 2011. 'The Elusive Costs of Sovereign Defaults'. *Journal of Development Economics* 94 (1): 95–105. https://doi.org/10.1016/j.jdeveco.2009.12.005.

Zimic, Srecko, and Romanos Priftis. 2021. 'Sources of Borrowing and Fiscal Multipliers'. *The Economic Journal* 131 (633): 498–519. https://doi.org/10.1093/ej/ueaa051.

Index

Algiers Accords, 146
Allied Control Commission, 134
annexation
  Alsace-Lorraine, 104, 111
  Kuwait, 157
asset bubbles, 24
asset forfeitures, 139
austerity, 124

balance of payments, 22–25, 105, 116
  crises, 55, 57
Banca Nazionale del Lavoro, 154, 182
banking crisis, 124
Barings Brothers, 92, 110
bimetallic standard, 109
Bismarck, Otto von, 104
Bolshevik, 49, 130
Boxer Rebellion, 113
Brüning government, 125
budget balance, 89, 97, 101, 123
Bulgaria, 130–32

capacity to pay. *See* sovereign debt
capital flows, 24
capital structure, 126
cash flow, 20
Central Bank of Iraq, 170
Central Intelligence Agency, 151–52, 154
China, 41, 112, 179
Citigroup, 102, 179
Coalition Provisional Authority, 163, 170
Collective Action Clauses, 45, 181
confiscation of foreign assets, 110, 116
Continental Blockade, 94–96

credit default swap, 52
credit rating, 89, 109
creditors, 50, 113, 151, 177
  committees, 182, 191
  holdouts, 56, 155
Cretan War, 113

Dawes Plan, 120–22, 124
debt levels, 116, 136, 149, 163
debt service, 122
debt sustainability analysis, 64, 99, 124,
  129, 174
default set, 83–85, 107, 121, 125
deflation, 125
Denmark, 142–43
devaluation, 48, 137
Development Fund for Iraq, 170
Dillon Read, 123
Drago Doctrine, 1, 9, 188

Eurozone crisis, 42
exchange rate, 55, 81, 128, 137, 160
  nominal, 66, 109, 162
  real, 26, 30
Executive Order 13303, 171
exports subsidies, 128

Finland, 42, 67, 134–38
First Punic War, 4
first World War. *See* World War I
foreign reserves, 25, 150
France, 67, 86–100, 104–11, 124
Franco-Prussian War, 104
  indemnity, 105–11

GDP growth, 28, 53, 88, 109
Germany, 67, 115
  banking crisis, 123
  debt standstill, 126
  default, 120, 126–29, 143
  World War II, 140
Great Depression, 43, 123
Greece, 112
Gulf States, 151
Gulf War, 144, 157–60
gunboat diplomacy, 9, 12, 101

Hague Convention, 1, 2, 133
Haiti, 112
  indemnity, 103
  National Bank of Haiti, 101
Hilferding Loan, 123
history of sovereign debt, 42–45
Hope & Company, 92
Hundred Days War, 87
Hussein, Saddam, 147
hyperinflation, 119

IMF. *See* International
    Monetary Fund
indemnities, 89
  definition, 3
inter-Allied war debts, 116
International Court of Justice, 150
International Monetary Fund, 50, 57, 63,
    138, 152, 175
international trade, 54
Iraq, 42
  Iran–Iraq War, 147–57
  sanctions, 163
  sovereign debt restructuring, 187
Italy, 132, 141, 151

Japan, 140
J.P. Morgan, 123, 179

Keynes, John M., 6, 26, 43, 139

Lausanne Conference, 126
loan underwriters, 110
London Club, 57, 59, 182
London Schedule of Payments, 115

macroeconomic costs, 20, 62, 89, 137
Marshall Plan, 139
Mexican–American War, 112

Napoleonic Wars, 36, 43, 86
  reparations, 86–94, 97, 104
  net foreign assets, 94, 105, 109, 144

occupation, 3, 53
  costs, 89
  of Denmark, 142
  of France, 87
  of the Ruhr, 119
odious debt, 51, 60–61, 102, 144, 154,
    165, 172, 184–87
oil exports, 151
Oil-for-Food programme. *See* Sovereign
    debt, sanctions
Ottoman Empire, 113

pari passu, 60, 65, 113
Paris Club, 57–59, 174–77
Paris Conference on Reparations, 139
Paris Peace Treaties, 134
Poland, 133

Rafidain Bank, 152, 172
real wages, 109, 137
Reconstruction, 139, 157
Reichsbank, The, 122
rentes, 87, 104
reparations, 170
  commission, 115, 134, 158
  definition, 3, 17, 158
  enforcement, 17, 101, 102, 142
  financing, 19
  legal basis, 3
  non-monetary transfers, 141
  patents, 116
  restructuring, 61–65, 178
Rothschilds, 101, 110
Russia, 41, 49, 51, 62, 130, 176

Sino-Japanese War, 113
sovereign debt, 6–10
  capacity to pay, 10, 41, 99, 113, 141,
    174, 188
  default, 48–56, 71, 131, 156
  enforcement, 8, 113, 126, 168
  excusable default, 47
  haircuts, 184
  issuance, 92, 105
  lawsuits, 146
  non-contingent, 10
  reputation, 46, 91

sanctions, 46, 150
sovereign debt models, 47–48, 65–73, 109
willingness to pay, 6, 10–11, 14, 22, 41, 99, 188
Soviet Union. *See* Russia
state succession, doctrine of, 51

terms of trade, 12, 22, 25–40, 96, 105
trade balance, 89, 134
Trade Bank of Iraq, 171
trade sanctions, 95, 111
transfer problem, 25–27
Treaty of Brest-Litovsk, 130
Treaty of Chaumont, 86
Treaty of Frankfurt, 104
Treaty of Paris, 86
Treaty of Paris, Second, 87
Treaty of Shimonoseki, 113
Treaty of Versailles, 115

UK, 113
Ukraine, 65

UN Resolution
  661, 157, 159
  678, 160
  1483, 146, 170, 171
  2621, 158
United Nations Compensation
  Commission. *See* Reparations

War reparations. *See* Reparations
Waterloo, Battle of, 87
willingness to pay. *See*
  Sovereign debt
World Bank, 50, 138
World War I, 56
  reparations, 116
  Reparations Commission. *See*
  reparations
World War II, 56, 133–34, 143

Young Plan, 122–24

Zambia, 65